MW00587328

My Own Darling Wife

My Own Darling Wife

Letters from a Confederate Volunteer

Letters written by 2nd Lieutenant
John Francis Calhoun of Company C,
7th Regiment South Carolina Volunteers
To His Wife
Rebecca Noble Calhoun

Edited and Introduced

by

Andrew P. Calhoun, Jr.

SHOTWELL PUBLISHING
Columbia, South Carolina

My Own Darling Wife: Letters From A Confederate Volunteer

Produced in the Republic of South Carolina by

Shotwell Publishing, LLC
Post Office Box 2592
Columbia, South Carolina 29202

www.ShotwellPublishing.com

Dust Jacket: John Francis and Rebecca Noble Calhoun.
Designed by Tal Willis (TalWillis.com)

Interior Design: Melinda Moseley Design

ISBN-13: 978-1-947660-01-4

ISBN-10: 1-947660-01-2

10 9 8 7 6 5 4 3 2 1

Acknowledgements

My sincere thanks and gratitude go out to the professional staff at Shotwell Publishing, LLC for their hard work, advice and counsel. I wish them much continued success. Thanks to Karen Stokes of the South Carolina Historical Society for talking me into this project. Thanks also to Tal Willis for his excellent artwork on the cover. In addition, my extreme appreciation goes out to those in the family who have passed on since the 1860s but managed to save and preserve these letters giving me the opportunity to make them part of our Southern history and heritage.

Most of all I would like to thank my wife, soulmate, and fellow genealogist Milree Calhoun for her encouragement, support, and remarkable help with transcribing these letters. We both endured many days and nights of headaches and squinty eyes during this process. She is as much a part of this as I am.

TABLE OF CONTENTS

Prologue

IN 1733 JAMES PATRICK CALHOUN, his wife Catherine, four sons, (James, William, Ezekiel, and Patrick) and a daughter (Mary Calhoun Noble) arrived in Pennsylvania from Ireland. They were four generations removed from the ancestral Colquhoun home in Scotland. At the age of 45, James Patrick and his family settled in the Chestnut Level area of Lancaster County. At the time of his death in 1741 he had acquired a plantation, growing crops, livestock, farm equipment, and household furniture. Nonetheless, five years later, his widow Catherine decided to move with her married children to an area in the Roanoke valley of Virginia now known as Wythe County. The family stayed in this location for about ten years and records reflect large parcels of land bought and sold by the heads of Calhoun households. Various public services were assigned to and performed by family members as well.

In 1755 British General Edward Braddock's forces were defeated by the French and Indians at Fort Duquesne leaving the entire Virginia frontier, that lay below, exposed to Indian invasion. The Calhouns soon abandoned their homes and farms, fled to the Carolinas, and settled in the Long Canes creek area near Abbeville in South Carolina. Their community became known as the "Calhoun settlement." This settlement generally grew and prospered over the coming years with one tragic exception.

In February of 1760, the Cherokee Indians went on the warpath over various boundary disputes with upcountry settlers and as a reprisal for SC Governor Lyttleton's seizure of over 20 tribal headmen in Charleston. Hoping to escape to the safety of Fort Moore near Augusta, GA, the settlers left the area and were attacked as they were set to cross Long Canes creek. Among those killed were family matriarch Catherine Calhoun and her son James. Son William had two daughters, Anne and Mary, that were captured and taken away by the Indians. Anne lived among the Cherokees for many years and once peace was restored, she was returned to her family. Mary, however, was never seen again. Son Ezekiel's daughter Rebecca escaped death by hiding in the cane brakes for days until found by her uncle Patrick, who had returned to the scene. While there, he erected two stones marking the site, which still stand today. In 1765 Rebecca would become the wife of South Carolina Revolutionary War hero General Andrew Pickens.

Only through courage and resilience did these Scotch-Irish settlers decide to return to the area in the fall of 1760. Patrick started a plantation on the land of his sister, Mary Calhoun Noble called Cane Hill and, under the protection of a friendly party of Chickasaw Indians, he constructed a permanent fort on the property for the safety of the settlement. This was known as Fort Boone, named for South Carolina Governor Thomas Boone. The fort also served as a schoolhouse, meetinghouse, and church. In 1762, Patrick's brother Ezekiel returned to his abandoned homestead in Virginia to settle the estate. He was shot dead by an Indian as he stood on the porch of his former home.

Patrick, was deeply involved in community affairs and served as deputy surveyor of the upstate. Engaging in early South Carolina politics, he went on to become a representative to the Commons House of Assembly, a member of the 1st Provincial Congress and the General Assembly. During the American Revolution, Patrick and his surviving brother William were members of a SC militia group known as the Long Cane Regulators. They generally wreaked havoc and "rendered themselves obnoxious" to the British troops and their Indian allies in the upcountry. William was said to have been captured by the British and sentenced to hang. To his great fortune, William escaped the noose after a group of local patriots came to his rescue.

Patrick and his wife Martha Caldwell Calhoun also had four sons and a daughter, the most well known was United States Senator and Vice President John Caldwell Calhoun. Daughter Catherine married the area's most prominent educator and minister, Moses Waddel. Catherine died from complications in childbirth in 1796. Her brother John Caldwell was one of Waddel's more famous students, although he had many. Waddel had also founded a church near the Calhoun settlement. It became known as the Willingtown church because both the Huguenot and Presbyterian families in the area were "willing" to worship there together. An agricultural and business center soon joined the church in the area and it became known as Willington Community. Patrick's other three sons, James, William, and Patrick (Jr.) stayed in the area becoming merchants and farmers. Patrick also died in 1796 and is buried with his wife in a small Calhoun family cemetery near their former settlement. His grave, and that of his wife Martha and daughter Catherine, is marked by a square based octagonal obelisk erected by his son John C. Calhoun in 1844. With the exception of John C., all of his children and their spouses are buried there as well. Three generations of my ancestors; Patrick, his son Patrick (Jr.), and grandson Edward, are buried in this family cemetery.

Edward was the fourth generation of this Calhoun family to live in Abbeville District and his wife Frances Middleton's family hailed from Edgefield District. It was Edward's son, John Francis Calhoun, who authored these letters. He was born August 29, 1831 in that same Calhoun Settlement in Abbeville District South Carolina. John Francis had nine siblings of which only four survived to maturity. Brother Edwin, who served in the same Confederate Regiment as John Francis, and sisters Ida and Rosa were the survivors. Another brother, Patrick Ludlow, lived only to the age of 20.

Edwin, eight years younger than John Francis, married Sarah (Sallie) Tilman in December of 1860 and they had 10 children of their own. He passed on many of his war time experiences in a book compiled by his daughter titled "Reminiscences of a Confederate Soldier." Ida married Charles Atwood Alexander, brother of Confederate General Edward Porter Alexander, in April of 1862. She died in childbirth in 1867 and Charles later went on to marry her younger sister Rosa in 1880. They lived in Washington, Georgia.

After being "prepared" for college by the Rev. Octavious Theodore Porcher in Willington, John Francis entered the Junior class of South Carolina College in 1851. He was a member of the Clariosophic Society (a debating society) and Delta Psi fraternity. John Francis left South Carolina College in 1852, possibly as a result of the "Great Biscuit Rebellion." At that time, students were required to eat all their meals in the campus dining facility, which frequently served "wormy biscuits and rancid meat." After years of complaints, most of the student body signed an honor bound pledge to quit school if the trustees did not remove the requirement to eat in the campus facility. The trustees refused to comply and a 109 of 199 students left school in the spring of 1852.

He returned to Willington and took up farming with his father. In 1859, John Francis married Rebecca Clark Noble, daughter of Andrew Alexander and Susan Houston Noble, and the 1860 census shows them living next to his father in Willington. John Francis was the grand-nephew of the Honorable John C. Calhoun and Rebecca was the great-granddaughter of General Andrew Pickens.

During 1860, John Francis entered an operating co-partnership with Dionycious Moragne' Rogers at Calhoun Mills near Willington. This Mill operation also included a tan yard utilizing a bark tanning method to produce quality leather for shoes, boots and other leather goods. After the April 12, 1861 action at Fort Sumter, John Francis answered the call from his state and on April 15 joined the militia in Company C of the 7th Regiment, South Carolina Volunteers to provide local defense and special services.

Company C was made up mostly of men from the Abbeville District which included Willington. The volunteers were quickly mustered into Confederate service and ordered to the frontline in Virginia. The Mill continued operating throughout the War Between the States primarily under the direction of D. M. Rogers.

John Francis Calhoun wrote these letters during his first 12 months of service as a volunteer from April of 1861 through March of 1862. They disclose a first hand account of his participation in historic military events, his desire to resist Northern economic and political tyranny, and his patriotic belief in preserving Liberty and Freedom through Southern Independence. At the same time, they confirm his unwavering love for, and dedication to, his family, his home, his farm and his business.

I.

Letters of April, May, and June of 1861

BY THE TIME THE RINGING of December 20, 1860 secession bells over Charleston, SC was replaced by exploding cannon balls over Fort Sumter on April 12, 1861, five other states had succeeded from the Union and joined the Southern Confederacy. In addition, a provisional Confederate Congress had been seated, a provisional constitution was adopted, and a Confederate President had been elected.

Also during that time, the 7th Regiment of the South Carolina Infantry was organized and a call for volunteers went out. The Confederate Congress had passed an Act on March 6, 1861 calling for volunteers to provide Local (Public) Defense and Special Services.

John Francis Calhoun joined with many of his family, friends, and fellow Abbevillians in answering that call. He volunteered in Company C of that 7th Regiment and was elected 2nd Lieutenant. The 7th had been previously organized and accepted into South Carolina State service in January. The volunteers were mustered into service on Monday April 15, 1861 and Company C, along with the other companies of the 7th were assembled in Charleston. Later that week, on the 18th, they began drills and training. According to brother Edwin's "Reminiscences" the train ride from Abbeville to Charleston was unpleasant as the people on the train were "drinking and cursing."

While in Charleston, the South Carolina volunteers received a visit from Governor Francis Pickens in April urging them to go and defend Virginia along the Potomac river. The Carolinians resisted stating they had volunteered for the defense of South Carolina, that Virginia had refused any help earlier and had only recently joined the Confederacy.

Bad water and sickness in the camp caused the Regiment to be moved from Charleston to Camp Butler near Aiken in Barnwell District on May 2, 1861 for the duration of training. The Regiment was taken into Confederate service on June 4th and the Carolinians were ordered to move up to Virginia. The 7th South Carolina arrived at (ironically) Camp Pickens in Richmond on Saturday June 8, 1861 via the Orange and Alexandria railroad after a brief stop in Petersburg. In Virginia, the month of June began with a number of skirmishes between forces as the Northern Government pressed their soldiers to quickly put down this "rebellion." The Union army began probing into sections of Virginia along the Potomac to size up the Confederate strength and the engagements at Fairfax Court House, Big Bethel, and Vienna were all previews of the forthcoming major battle at Manassas several weeks later.

After the skirmish at Vienna, VA on June 17, which involved the 1st South Carolina Infantry, the 7th, along with other SC Regiments, was ordered to Centerville, VA on June 19, 1861 and arrived the afternoon of the same day. A day later, the 7th received orders to move to Fairfax Court House on June 20, arriving June 22, 1861. There they took their place in the battle line as a part of the First Brigade, Army of the Potomac (later named the Army of Northern Virginia) under the command of Brigadier General Milledge L. Bonham.

Meanwhile, life in Abbeville County continued at Willington and Calhoun Mills. There was an overwhelming opinion that the volunteers would not be needed for very long, that they would be disbanded and sent back home. The war, it was believed, would not last more than several months, that the north hadn't the will to fight and would sue for peace. Trusting he would not be long on the battle line, John Francis called upon his wife Rebecca to manage the business of both the farm and the mills. He often wrote her instructions as to managing the farm planting, the livestock, and directing the operation of the mills as well as the care of the slaves.

Now that husbands, fathers, sons, and brothers were all in the Army and away from home, Confederate women performed extra, extra duty by not only raising their children, but caring for their elderly, managing the family farms and businesses and seeing to the health and welfare of their labor force.

April 1861

CAMP BACON
CHARLESTON, S. C. Apr 23

My dear wife:

I wrote to you only three days since and as you may be anxious to hear again this week I write now as I have time. We will be moved somewhere in a day or two. I never in my life heard of as much sickness. Dr. Hearst[1] seems to be broken down and says he regrets accepting the surgeon's post. The water where we are encamped seems to disagree with the men. Most of them complain of diarrhea. I am much better than I was when I first landed here. On yesterday evening Gov. Pickens[2] came into camp with a fine German Band and at dress parade he received the entire line in company with

1 Dr. John Wardlaw Hearst of Abbeville, SC. Served in the South Carolina Legislature from 1850-1855. Volunteered with the 7th Regiment South Carolina Volunteers and was elected Surgeon. Later resigned that position. *Kershaw's Brigade*, p. 38; *Find a Grave*.

2 South Carolina wartime Governor Francis W. Pickens (1805-1869) from Edgefield, S.C. and 1st cousin, once removed of Rebecca Noble Calhoun. *Calhoun Family Genealogy*.

Gen. McGowan[3] and other officers; then all the commissioned officers were called to the front which was immediately in front of our company which is the first company on the right of the second Battalion – centre of the regiment. The Gov. made an appeal to induce the volunteers to go to Virginia, and was followed by Col. Bacon[4] & Gen McG. Col. Bacon seems not to favor going. Neither does Col Fair[5] and Gen Bradley[6] is determined not to go. He says Virginia does not deserve our sympathy and those who go will regret it. He says the officers may win a few laurels but the privates will have a hard time perhaps and no thanks. He says many of the fathers of the volunteers mustered under him 20 years since and put their sons under his care, and look to him as an adviser, and he can't induce any under the present circumstance to go to Virginia. We will be moved some think to Morris' Jct. and I think we will be dismissed. Go down to the mills this week and see how everything is getting on. Tell Mr. McCrevan[7] to ask Mr. Rogers[8] to lend me the ox wagon and team to go to the village after corn and tell him to weigh and measure it but he must not send a sack back unless it holds out. Tell Mr. Mc to have me a large crop of peas planted & send around our wheat fields. Cothran[9] went to the city last evening and did not return to the review and on the field Gen Bradley took sick and left me at the head of the company without even a Lieut. Kiss my sweet darling little Fannie[10] and give my love to all. I have a poor chance for writing as yet.

Most Devotedly
Your Husband
JOHN F. CALHOUN

3 General Samuel McGowan (1819-1897) was a General in the South Carolina Militia for 13 years prior to the War. He served as an aide to Colonel Maxcy Gregg in 1861 and later commanded a Brigade through the end of the war. *ORWR*, Vol II, Chapter IX, pp. 128-130. *Find a Grave*.

4 Colonel Thomas G. Bacon (1813-1887), born in Edgefield, SC and served in the 7th S.C. Volunteers, under General Milledge L. Bonham. *Kershaw's Brigade*, pp. 37, 53, 101, 557.

5 Colonel Robert Anderson Fair (1820—1899), 7th Regiment of South Carolina Volunteers. A lawyer before the war, he was ordained a Presbyterian minister in 1871. "Abbeville County Cemetery Records," Genealogical Publishing Co., 1982.

6 Patrick Henry Bradley (1813-1887) was a General in the S.C. Militia prior to the War. Once in Confederate service, he became a Captain of Company C, 7th S.C. Volunteers. Mostly referred to as "General Bradley." *Kershaw's Brigade*, pp. 37, 559. *Find A Grave*.

7 Mr. James McCrevan was the overseer at Calhoun Mills and John F. Calhoun's farm.

8 Dionysious Moragne' Rogers of Abbeville County, SC. Well known merchant and farmer, he owned Calhoun Mills from 1838-1876. Partnered with John F. Calhoun at the Mills prior to and during the War years.

9 Captain Wade Elephare Cothran (1837-1899) of Company C, 7th S.C. Volunteers. Graduated from the South Carolina Military College (Citadel) in 1859 and studied medicine. Discontinued his medical training to join the Confederate Army. *Kershaw's Brigade*, pp. 113, 559. *Find a Grave*.

10 Frances Middleton Calhoun, daughter of John Francis and Rebecca Calhoun. Born August 24, 1860. *Calhoun Family Genealogy*.

CHARLESTON HOTEL
APRIL 28, 1861

My Dear Wife

I was feeling so unwell on yesterday that I determined to come to the city and take a good night's sleep and this morning, Sunday, I feel like a new man. When the mail came in to camp yesterday evening and letters were distributed to the different volunteers, how much disappointment did I feel from learning that there was none for me. Many rec'd replies to letters since they came down. The Rogers[11] rec'd several. John[12] replied to Ed's[13] letter to father and Tucker[14] says he started from home since Zeke[15] wrote ____ and why is it that my wife will not write to me? I will not feel hurt until I can hear from you for you have surely written at least twice and the letters have been miscarried. The 7th Reg't has received orders to move to Aiken this week so when you write again, that is if you don't write until the 2nd or 3rd of May, direct to me there. I will be able to meet you in Edgefield or Hamburg if you can come down next month. Becca, I have not for many years had much fancy for Gov. Pickens & now I dislike him more than ever. He is offended from what I can learn with our Reg't for not volunteering to go to Virginia at his request and then threats and even says we have no business on earth in Charleston but ought to be immediately disbanded. You have no idea how much it costs the State but his Excellency now tells us we may move to Aiken and there kept until thoroughly drilled and then he intends on ordering us to Maryland or Virginia. He is determined now to throw us into the field. We did not volunteer for many reasons. Many left their houses at a great sacrifice but did so cheerfully to defend their native state. Now she does not need our services and her Gov offers our services to a state that refused to meet us 18 months since in convention saying she could take care of herself. We again objected to serve 12 months for a state which at that time did not belong to the southern confederacy. We were willing to assist any of the confederate states since Virginia joined our confederacy. I am willing to volunteer but

11 Theophilus A. Rogers from Willington, SC, a Lieutenant in Company C, 7th S. C. Volunteers. Referred to as "The" Rogers throughout the letters. Was the half-brother of Dionysius M. Rogers. *Kershaw's Brigade*, p. 559. *Calhoun Family Genealogy.*

12 John A. Houston, brother of Rebecca's mother Susan Houston Noble.

13 Edwin Calhoun (1839-1917) was the younger brother of John F. Calhoun and also served in Company C, 7th S.C. Volunteers. *Calhoun Family Genealogy. Kershaw's Brigade*, p. 559.

14 Samuel Tucker, a slave or white assistant at Calhoun Mills and/or the Calhoun farm.

15 Ezekiel Noble was the son of William Pickens Noble and 1st cousin of Rebecca Noble Calhoun. According to his father's 1875 will, Ezekiel was, "lost sight of and supposed to be dead." *Calhoun Family Genealogy.*

Gov P says now I will make you. I can't be forced by a thousand governors. I will resign my commission if he attempts force and then tender my services to Virginia. I am determined that a mad Gov shall not force me into service. He may not call on any other regiment, if so in all probability only one or two, but ours first. Sure he must have satisfaction out of us. If he should approach us in a different manner, we may nearly all volunteer. Everyone of whom I have heard speaking of it says he has no power to order us out of this state volunteering as we did for a specific purpose.[16] I have no idea he can change the service. Give my love to all and tell John I read his letter to Ed. He is now at home. Many have been discharged and some off on furlough. A bed was so comfortable last night-being the first I have slept on since I left Abbeville. Sam Harris[17] is well and when we get to Aiken I hope all will enjoy better health. Kiss sweetness over and over for her father. I will send you my photograph if I can get a chance to have it taken tomorrow. Do write often this is five letters that I have written. Have I not done well! Good bye my own loved Rebecca,

Faithfully, your own devoted husband

J. F. C.

16 An Act of the Confederate Congress dated March 6, 1861 called for volunteers for local defense and special services in each of the Confederate states. *The Laws of the Confederate States.* Public Acts of the Provisional Congress of the Confederate States, Statute I, Chapter XXVI, pp. 45, 46.

17 Samuel Noble Harris was a 2nd cousin of Rebecca Noble Calhoun and a member of Company C, 7th S.C. Volunteers. *Calhoun Family Genealogy. Kershaw's Brigade*, p. 559.

May 1861

CAMP BUTLER, BARNWELL
MAY 24, 1861

My dear wife:

I reached Camp on Wednesday night 11 o'clock sound and safe. Zeke was very uneasy (sic) all they (sic) way. I showed him the situation he had placed himself in an awkward position & was liable to punishment he promised to follow my advice & seemed mortified and frightened. Gen Bradley wrote to him by order of Col Bacon, ordering him back to Camp. He did tell Capt Bradley to send and assist him, but he said for the respect for his father he would run the risk of disobeying the order to assist and order him back. I went around with him to see Col Bacon & I explained all things to the Col and he has done nothing, but he is broken from his rank he is now a private. I will write a long letter in a few days and give you all the news. I merely write now to let you know that I am well. Give my love to all, kiss Fannie. I am writing from the Guard House, being on Guard duty—I have two prisoners, four men with their muskets guarding them. I send this by The Rogers—Gib[18] has gone home on sick furlough. The Band is playing delightfully. Farewell

Your own husband
J F C

18 Gilbert C. Tennant, a 1st cousin of John F. Calhoun and member of Company C, 7th S.C. Volunteers. *Calhoun Family Genealogy. Kershaw's Brigade*, p. 559.

CAMP BUTLER, BARNWELL DISTRICT
May 26, 1861

My dear wife:

I wrote you a short letter from the "Guard house" a few days since which I sent by The Rogers. On yesterday evening, Gen McGowan and staff reviewed our Regiment and the call for volunteers for Virginia was made when all of the Regiment volunteered but about one hundred I am doubtful that there were that many. Then Gen McGowan made one of the most effective and eloquent speeches I ever heard from him. He said we acted nobly and that we would soon be marched to the frontier to join our comrades. He was proud of us and had urged us to it although he lost his commission by it. He said that he had come out to bid us a farewell, although he hoped to join us in the field, for when the heart was right a soldier could find a place to fight – three feet of soil was all he needed to defend his country. The general's voice trembled, his eyes filled frequently and I was sure he would burst into tears. He said that he was no longer a Brigadier General of S.C.V. we had passed from his command, but still he gloried to think we had so willingly offered to meet the foe. He thought from the Telegraphic-news this evening that there was a clash of arms upon the frontier, and that the other two SC Regiments had met the foe[19] and was holding in check and "he said" me thinks they are beckoning the 7th Regiment to join them in the fray. All of our company except two volunteered. 8 or 9 are off on furlough – including Gen B[20] & Dr. Hearst. We have let off near 40 from our company to go home and make their arrangements to leave. We will be mustered into the Confederate service day after tomorrow week[21] and we may start immediately for Virginia. I don't know though when we will start. It may be that I will not be able to come home at all, if not you can come to Abbeville C H, however I will see & write you all about our movements. I heard a soul stirring sermon to day from our Chaplain Mr. Carlisle.[22] He said it would be the last sermon that he would preach us here, as he had procured permission to leave on tomorrow to join our Regiments in Va for he said he intended be with them in every trial. He said we all had to serve, some had wives, children, mothers, fathers, &c he had a wife and 5 sons at that moment offering up their prayers in their Greenwood

19 Company A and Company F of the 2nd Regiment S.C. Volunteers were sent to Virginia between April 30, and May 2, 1861. *Kershaw's Brigade*, p. 35.

20 Patrick Henry Bradley. See note 6 above.

21 The 7th Regiment was mustered into service for twelve months on June 4, 1861. *Kershaw's Brigade*, p. 38.

22 J.M. Carlisle, Chaplain for the 7th Regiment S.C. Volunteers. He left for Virginia with the two Companies already dispatched. *Kershaw's Brigade*, p. 557.

home for him. He made many a stout soldier's eyes fill with tears, yes many shed tears abundantly. I am in charge of the company today and will have to take it out on Dress Parade Sunday as it is. Zeke & Sam are both with the former in standing sentinel today. Give my love to all and Kiss Fannie. Have our cow fed well and milked 3 times a day if Mr. McCrevan thinks proper. Tell him I will write to him soon. Write to me after you visit home and inquire all about the corn, &c. Call and see father[23] & Ida[24] and give my love to them I will write soon. Good bye my dear wife

Most Affectionately your husband
J. F. CALHOUN

23 Edward Calhoun (1809-1862) of Willington, SC. He was a farmer and planter and the father of John F. Calhoun. *Calhoun Family Genealogy.*

24 Ida Calhoun (1841-1867) sister of John F. Calhoun. Married Charles Atwood Alexander, brother of Confederate General E. Porter Alexander of Washington, GA. *Calhoun Family Genealogy.*

Direct to Woodward SC Barnwell Dist
CAMP BUTLER
May 29: 1861

My own dear wife,

I have written to you twice since I came here and I hope you have red'd both letters. Some think we may start to Virginia immediately after we are mustered into service. It is said that we will be paid off next Tuesday, and will receive pay as if in the Confederate Army, which is much more. Becca I don't know that there is any use in our meeting at Abbeville, as parting again will be painful. Many of the Officers do not intend going home. Capt Talbert[25] says he does intend going home. If this reaches before Zeke or any of the others leave send me any of my shirts, handke[rchief]s, or socks that are good - if you can find any good ones. The Camp looks lonely as so many of (sic) men are off. I see your uncle John[26] here occasionally. Sam Harris was put in the Guard-house the other day. He wanted to "play smart" & went to the Guard-house & told the officers of this Guard that Col. Bacon ordered him to be put under arrest for misconduct to a woman; the officer said go in there. Sam bowed and walked off and was opening the carriage door & was about helping out some ladies when a Corporal of the Guard & a file of men arrested him & put him in the G.H. Sam was astonished cried, said he was joking & promised not to try to play off any more such jests whereupon he was let off. I heard several say that Sam tried to be too familiar. Give my love to all. I will write again soon give my love to all. Tell your father[27] if he or your uncle William[28] will either sell their Revolvers, I will give several dollars more than they gave as the officers will be generally provided as the sword will not be very effective in case we should have a close engagement. I wrote to uncle Frank[29] to see if he would sell me his. Tell your father to see him if he can. Give my love to all. I must close as the mail is near ready.

Affectionately your husband

J. F. C.

---

25 Captain Bartley Martin Talbert (1819-1881) of Edgefield, SC. Captain of Company K, 7th S.C. Volunteers. Was married to Adelaine E. Middleton, younger sister of John F. Calhoun's mother Frances Middleton. *Calhoun Family Genealogy*.

26 John A. Houston, brother of Rebecca's mother Susan Houston Noble.

27 Andrew Alexander Noble (1810-1880) farmer and planter in Willington, SC and father of Rebecca Noble Calhoun. *Calhoun Family Genealogy*.

28 William Pickens Noble (1806-1876), well respected Lawyer known as "The Esquire" Was the older brother of Andrew Alexander Noble. *Calhoun Family Genealogy*.

29 Francis Augustus Calhoun (1820-1893), brother of John F. Calhoun's father Edward. *Calhoun Family Genealogy*.

Tucker sends word to the _____ that he is well & would be glad to hear from them as soon as possible. His wages now is he says $42.50 per month. He expects to go to Virginia.

CAMP BUTLER
May 29. 1861

My Dear Wife

I wrote to you this morning & sent it by Washington but for fear it may not reach you tomorrow. I will write another & send it by Columbia. Tell your father to see Uncle Frank and to try and get his revolver for me and if he will not dispose I wish he would see if your Uncle William will sell his. I am willing to pay more than they gave for them. Some of the officers think that we ought to have pistols as swords would less efficient in the event that we get into close quarters. The papers say that our troops killed 600 of the northern troops, only 50 of ours killed. Troops from the confederate states are still pouring into Virginia. Five SC regiments will move off next week or week after I expect. Send one good shirt if you can find one and one or two hand[kerchief]s if you can find them and they will do me until I get back from Va. Go down home & see how everything is getting on. Have the Durham cow milked three times per day if she gives much milk. She may be injured by allowing too much milk to collect. Tell Mr. McC to do his best & make her a "No 1" milk cow & not to spare the feed. I want him to feed Nettie high and try & raise me a fine colt. Another thing that interests you particularly, Bess will have pigs in two or three weeks & she ought to be fattened up some before hand and when she has pigs have them highly fed. Tell Mr. McC to cut enough wheat to feed on for two weeks at least. Still, I had just better leave everything to him as he knows best what ought to be done. How many chickens & turkeys have you? Let the negroes have at least one good mess of vegetables a week, more if they can get them. Tell Mr. McC to have an abundance of garden seed saved and save as much as he can for winter use for if I am not able to enjoy them this summer, I hope I will be spared to enjoy whatsoever you save in the winter. Love to all & a kiss to my little daughter. Give my love to John & father & tell them to write to me. Goodbye. Write me a long letter & send by Zeke as it may not reach me by mail. Most affectionately,

Your husband

J.F.C.

Your Uncle John is here now taking dinner with Col. Bacon about 20 steps from my tent.

June 1861

CAMP PICKENS
RICHMOND, VA
June 12, 1861

My Darling Wife:

I wrote to you from Petersburg and once since I have been here and this will be the third time in less than one week; that is constant is it not my darling? There is little or no news, although we hear of a small fight nearly every day, but let me tell you not to believe one-half you see in the papers. As near as we are we can't get the correct reports. The news reached camp this morning that a large body of federal troops had landed in So.Ca. but few believe the report. President Davis,[30] Toombs,[31] and Wigfall[32] came out to review Bacon and Jenkins[33] Regiments. The president was riding a grey horse, plain saddle, &c – was dressed in a plain grey suit, no one would ever have taken him for a president. He is slender, but erect and every inch a soldier, thin lips, keen dark grey eyes, and a striking man when speaking. He made but a short speech, somewhat like the one Wigfall made us the other night: told us what was expected of us &c. a short solid speech. I spoke to Mr. and Mrs. Toombs, the latter introduced me to Mrs. Davis, a lady about 30 or 35, fine looking, a Mrs. Brown, I suppose Senator Brown's[34] wife, and a sweet young lady. Some say Mrs. D is the second wife of the President. She is young and pretty. One of the Alabama regiments near us has just moved off. I suppose to the border, no one knows. Jeff Davis manages his own affairs and keeps his own secrets. In all his movements there is no fuss or parade. Col. Cash's[35] Regiments will next move, then ours, but we have no idea when that will be.

30 Hon. Jefferson Davis, President of the Confederate States of America.

31 Robert Augustus Toombs (1810-1885) of Georgia was a US Senator prior to the War. Resigned to become one of the Founding Fathers of the Confederacy and its first Secretary of State. He fled the country after the war, returning in 1867. Toombs never requested a pardon and never regained his U.S. citizenship. *New Georgia Encyclopedia.*

32 Louis Wigfall (1816-1874) born in Edgefield, SC but moved to Texas in 1848. Served in the Texas Legislature, U.S. Senate, and later in the Confederate Senate. *Biographical Directory of the U.S. Congress. Find a Grave.*

33 Colonel Micah Jenkins (1835-1864) of the 5th S.C. Infantry. Became a brigadier general and was accidentally killed by friendly fire at the Battle of the Wilderness May 6, 1864. *Kershaw's Brigade*, pp. 15, 349. *Find Grave.*

34 Senator Albert Gallatin Brown of Mississippi. *Biographical Directory of the U.S. Congress.*

35 Colonel Ellerbee B.B. Cash (1823-1888) of the 8th S.C. Infantry. Was a Major General in the S.C. Militia before the War. *Kershaw's Brigade*, p. 103. *Find A Grave.*

Ladies and gentlemen in great numbers crowd to witness our dress parades. One of the Ala volunteers was shot yesterday for drawing a pistol on a Lieut., and two from one of the Edgefield companies will be tried for their lives, one for threatening to shoot a Lieut. Blocker, the other for something of the same kind. They may both be shot. There is a company of 120 or so from the Pee Dee County coming on to join our reg. I never saw such fine cattle as they have around here, mostly Durhams. The clover grows finely around here, the oats is not headed out yet, the wheat just turning. The days are warm but the nights cool. I sleep under one blanket the first part of the night and two the latter and that is little enough at that. We get the finest beef here I ever saw. Uncle William and Ed and Bob Middleton[36] are all here. I wrote Father and requested him to furnish you in money, and I will return it when I return home. I wrote to Father the other day and told him to let you see it. When I write to you let him alwa[y]s hear all the news I write and it will save me the trouble of writing so often. When you write do give me all the news. You know every little thing that occurs about home will interest me. Give my love to your mother and father, & Sam and all of my own family. Kiss sweet little Fannie for me and write me every smart thing she does. Bless her dear heart she will not know me when I return. I am writing on a book in my lap and must close as it is near the hour for drilling. Direct your letters to me as you did before, Care of Public Ware House, Richmond, VA. I will alwa[y] s number my letters hereafter if I think of it. This is the third, I am still enjoying fine health. Do write soon twice a week, sometimes at least. Farewell my own precious wife.

Most devotedly your own husband
JOHN F.

36 Ed: William Edward Middleton (1826-1862) , I 7th South Carolina Volunteers. (Bob) Robert Henry Middleton (1829-1896) I 7th South Carolina Volunteers and brother of William. Both uncles of John F. Calhoun. *Calhoun Family Genealogy*.

MANASSAS JUNCTION
PRINCE WILLIAM COUNTY, VA
JUNE 14, 1861

My Dear Wife

I wrote to you on yesterday immediately after we landed here yesterday evening and would not write again but I found this letter which I wrote before leaving Richmond and as it is so much trouble to write I will send it anyway. We are well & quiet. No enemy yet - Gen Beauregard said yesterday evening to Col Bacon that he had a good whipping ready for the Lincolnites whenever they attack us. He said that he would have given a great deal if he could have had our troops here some time since then he would have had possession of Arlington Heights & Alexandria. Tell Mr. McCrevan to buy me some hogs & open the pasture as soon as possible. I will write again next week. Love to all. Direct here often to me at "Manassas Junction, Prince William County, VA. Write, write, write I have not received a word from home in ten days.

Devotedly your most loving husband,
JFC

[*Note: This letter was written on the back on another letter dated June 12, 1861 and written from Camp Pickens in Richmond, VA.*]

Tuesday Morning
June 17, 1861

I must close my letter so as to send it to Manassas to be mailed. I have no more news. We have now been in the service 2 months and two days. Senator Chestnut[37] is aide to Gen. B., Wm Porcher Miles[38] also. The Picket guards are scattered around for mile. They take up any man they meet. No one can pass from this camp to Kershaw's[39] without a permit signed by the Col. and countersigned by Gen. Beauregard.[40] Gen. Bonham & staff even were halted by them yesterday evening. I wrote to Mr. McCraven this morning. Read it if you wish and hand it to him as soon as you can. Let him know all the news I have written to you as I did not give him any. Do write twice a week as one letter may be miscarried. Remember the postage to Manassas Junction is only 5 cents. Tell your father to look at all of my stock, wheat, oats, corn &c and write me what he says about them. How much will the wheat &c turn out. If my buggy needs ____ or anything done to it get your father to have it attended to. Give my love to your father and mother, Sam, father and John, uncle Dock[41] and Frank. Kiss my darling little Fannie and tell me all of her smart & sweet tricks. How I long to see you both, but when will we meet! Howdy to all the negroes and tell them to be faithful and obedient. I will write you again the last of this week. I am very much improved in health. They told me yesterday that I was fattening. This morning is quite cool, enough so for fires. It feels like an October morning. Is it so in SC? Let me know when you write. The wheat in this section is not even sprung, the corn not more than ten inches high. It is a beautiful country between here and Richmond.

---

37 Senator James Chestnut, Jr. (1815-1885), signer of the Confederate Constitution and previously a U.S. Senator. Was an Aide to General Beauregard and later to President Davis. His wife was diarist and writer Mary Boykin Chestnut. *Biographical Directory of the U. .S Congress.*

38 William Porcher Miles (1822-1899), Mayor of Charleston, 1855-1857, member of the U. S. House, 1857-1860, and a member of the Confederate Congress 1861-1865. He was Aide de Camp to General Beauregard in Charleston and later in Manassas, VA. Miles was also the designer of the Confederate Battle Flag. *Kershaw's Brigade*, pp. 508-509. *Encyclopedia Virginia.*

39 Colonel Joseph B. Kershaw (1822-1894), born in Camden, SC and commanded the 2nd Brigade S.C. Volunteers. Was promoted to General in February of 1862. After the War he returned to South Carolina and served in the State Senate. *Kershaw's Brigade*, pp. 86-88.

40 Brigadier General P.G.T. Beauregard, commander of the Confederate Army of the Potomac. *Kershaw's Brigade*, pp. 21-23.

41 Hugh Graves Middleton, uncle of John Francis Calhoun. His wife Martha was the sister of "The" Rogers.

Such long green pastures, fat stock &c and the clover looks beautiful, fields of it over knee high. Many are cutting this down and curing it. You must write me a long letter. I have duties to be attended to and must close. Good bye my darling wife.

Most devotedly your husband,
J.F. CALHOUN

HEAD QUARTERS 7TH REGIMENT
SCV, NEAR MANASSAS
CAMP WALKER
June 18, 1861

General Beauregard

Dear Sir

We the undersigned Officers of the 7th Regiment of SCV hereby express the desire that we will remain under immediate command in any military arrangements which may hereafter be made. Hoping that our petition can be consistently complied with,

We are most respectfully
Your Obdt Sols

B.M. Talbert Capt comdg Com K
John F. Burris 1st Lieut
H.G. Seigler 2nd Lieut

Samuel J. Hester Capt Com D
Jown T. Owen 1st Lieut
E.F. Power 2nd Lieut
Hugh M. Prince 3rd Lieut

P. H. Bradley Capt CoC
Wade E. Cothran 1st Lieut CoC
John F. Calhoun 2nd
T.A. Rogers 3rd

Wm E. Clark 1st Lieut Co G
H. C. King 2nd Lieut

John T. Hard Capt. Com. F
Thomas A. Jennings 1st Lieut
J.B. Gregg 2nd
Cas E. Rorden 3rd Lieut.

D. Denny Capt Com E
Wm. A. Rutland 2nd Lieut.

W. Lud Hodges Capt. Co "B"
E.R. Clinkscales 1 Liet.
G.F. Hodges 2nd

B.A. Fair Lt. AC

CENTERVILLE, VA NO. 7
JUNE 20, 1861

My Darling Wife

We were ordered on yesterday to this place which is still nearer the enemy and a frightening march we had of it. After the first three or four miles the road side was strewn with soldiers from our regiment who "fell out" to rest and many a one came near failing on the way. They had to carry buckets on their shoulders was one reason why they tired so soon. I did not have scarcely a wet thread on me but my feet pained me very much as I had just put on a fine pair of high quartered English shoes of my friend Capt. Brooks[42] and being new they hurt my feet in marching so far. Brooks presented them to me this morning. Gen Bonham[43] and staff are here, McGowen too. What he is doing, I don't know. He intends fighting on his own hook it is said. We passed Col. Kershaw's regiment encamped about 3 miles from here. We rested under the large shady oaks on the creek which runs by his camp, the ground covered with grass. I stretched myself in the crowd and was sound asleep in five minutes and slept as soundly as I ever did in my life until some of our men waked me to let me know that the Regt. was ready to march. I little thought two or three months since that I could sleep in the midst of a thousand men talking, singing, laughing, etc. About eleven or twelve o'clock last night I heard a horse passing at a rapid speed and in fifteen minutes Col. Bacon came around and waked Capt. Bradley and told him that Gen. Beauregard had just sent one of his aides to him with orders to furnish 550 men and they must prepare 3 days rations and immediately the campfires were started and the men ready for the march. Col. B ordered 7 companies to get ready, ours among the number. Hester's[44] will remain with a cohat joined just before we started to VA. It is now 8 o'clock in the morning and the order to march has not been given. There is never any knowing one hour what we will do the next. Gen B is a cautious man. Col. Gregg[45] attacked a train near Alexandria with a Regt of Massachusetts troops on board, fired into them and killed eight or ten and he

42 Either Captain Warren D. Brooks of Company F or Captain J. Hampden Brooks of Company G, 7th S.C. Volunteers. *Kershaw's Brigade*, p. 560.

43 General Milledge Luke Bonham (1813-1890) commanded the 1st Brigade of the Army of the Potomac under General Beauregard. He resigned his commission in 1862 and became Governor of South Carolina from 1862-1864. *Kershaw's Brigade*, pp. 51-54. *Find a Grave*.

44 Captain S. J. Hester of Company D, 7th S.C. Volunteers. *Kershaw's Brigade*, p. 559.

45 Colonel Maxcy Gregg, organized the 1st Brigade S.C. Volunteers as Colonel. Gregg was on a scouting mission and came upon Union troops coming in on the railroad. He set up an ambush and this initiated the Battle of Vienna, VA on June 17, 1861. Gregg was later promoted to General and was killed at Fredericksburg December 15, 1862. *ORWR*, Vol II, Chapter IX, pp. 128-130.

has returned to Fairfax about 6 miles from here. The report is that 5000 of the enemy are in 5 miles of him. I know we are to go there. Col Cash is here with his Regt. He will furnish 5 or 600 & perhaps Kershaw the last named is strongly fortified and Gen B said a few days since that there would be the battleground. We may be sent forward to open the fight and retreat so as to draw the enemy to Kershaw's strong hold & then cut them in pieces – no one knows for a certainty as there is always danger of the Baggage being taken in war, and as we will leave only 200 men in camp. I read last night between 12 & 1 o'clock all of your letters to me. "Jewels" they were to me and some of mine to you before and during our engagement & then committed them to the flames, not wishing by any chance to have them fall into the hands of the enemy. Cothran took his wife's likeness out of his trunk and put it in his pocket. All this was doubtful unnecessary still there is no objection to being prudent. Mounted & foot pickets are moving in every direction and no one can move scarcely without being taken up. This is a fine county for grain, stock, etc. Rich golden butter sells for 12 ½ cents, eggs the same. We are in sight of the Blue Ridge Mountains & within 18 to 20 miles perhaps up of the border. During the war so far as I can learn not more than 6 or eight of our men have been killed, whilst hundreds of the enemy have been made to bite the earth. They can't shoot. We left 2,000 soldiers at our last camp. Seven SC Regts. are now in Va....Col Jenkins at Manassas, Cols Williams and Sloan[46] at Richmond. I am still hearty and am prudent with myself and intend remaining so. We slept on our arms last night. Cash's men have been doing so for 4 nights. I slept nearly all night with my revolver buckled around me & I am writing by a large rock with it by my side. Nearly every officer wears them all the time. The Rogers went to Richmond the day before we left camp and was to have returned last night, if he did he will be disappointed & if we are ordered to march today he may not get with us in several days. We are in the woods, a beautiful grove and two springs near us. The coolest water I ever tasted. Anyone would suppose it had ice in it judging from the taste. I have not received a line from you since I came to VA. Do write at least twice a week and write me the same in both as in all probability not more than half will reach me. They will come to hand sometime perhaps like those you wrote me to Charleston. Sam, Zeke, and Gib are all well. We have just heard that Gregg fired into some horseman around his camp last night—2 more Yankees taken last night. You will get this about next Wednesday or Friday—so my darling Friday, Saturday, and Sunday evening before sun down a few minutes-1/2 hour and during sun set think of your husband far away, he will be

46 Colonel James H. Williams , 3rd S.C. Volunteers. Colonel J.B. Sloan, 4th S.C. Volunteers. *Kershaw's Brigade*, pp. 15, 551.

thinking of you and Fannie at that time ____ between 8 & 10 o'clock. I will give my entire thoughts to you every evening & night at those hours. Now don't forget. Give my love to your father, mother, &c Sam and kiss sweetness & as soon as she can prattle teach her to lisp her father's name. Do write me often and long letters – direct as before. Love to father & Ida, always let him hear from me as soon as you can after getting a letter. God bless you my own dear wife.

Most Devotedly your own dear Husband
JOHN F.

CENTREVILLE, VIRGINIA
JUNE 22, 1861

My Own Precious Wife

I wrote to you this morning but as I will have an opportunity of sending this by John Owens,[47] I have concluded to write again. J.O. resigns by the advice of the surgeon. He has a ball in his foot, a wound from an accidental discharge of a pistol in Feb. He can't stand the marches so resigns. We are to move this evening to Fairfax C.H. and will then be therefore with the regiments of Col's Gregg, Kershaw, & Cash comprising the first Brigade commanded by Gen. Bonham. Gen Beauregard is near at hand and plans the entire campaign. Kershaw went by last night. Artillery has passed and from all appearances the "dogs of war" will soon be let loose. You have no idea of the bustle and excitement of a moving army… couriers riding "to and fro." Gen. Bonham came into camp this morning, dismounted at Bacon's but wrote hurriedly for a few minutes, orders I suppose, then rode off again. McGowan came in, remained only five or ten minutes without dismounting and off again. Aides too are dashing about, all forebodes war. Our men are bold and determined & are ready yea, eager for the attack. When we get to Fairfax CH we will be within a short distance of the enemy, only one days march in fact up of Washington City. My darling before this reaches you we have to face the bristling bayonets of the bold members of our enemies. Come what may, now in the face of the enemy I say in calmness that you will not be ashamed of your husbands conduct on the field of battle midst the roar of cannons and the rattle of musketry I will not forget "my name" and that I have a wife and child at home. For indeed, fear not that I will falter in the hour of trial. As this hour approaches I grow calmer but darling don't be apprehensive for as yet we lost not more than six or eight in all. The enemy begins to be discouraged; they dread us and may not yet meet us. I have strong reasons to think they will not. I wanted to prepare you for the worst. We may not have a battle for some time yet and not much of one then. No one knows. Some times we look for it every day. Six of Lincoln's men gave themselves up a few days since saying they were fed on rotten meat and got whipped in every battle and would in the end get whipped so they thought it best to give up now. They can't stand "the fire" & we are all very sanguine as to the result. I will write to you again from Fairfax. I have to command our company in battalion drill and in company drill too sometimes. Gen Bradley is often unwell. He can't stand fatigue and I think is tired of the service. He does not command one time in five or six, he says the Lieutenants must take a turn about in commanding. Cothran and I will have it all to do. Some one else can't do it for many reasons. Carie[48]

47 Lieutenant John T. Owen of Company D, 7th S.C. Volunteers. *Kershaw's Brigade*, p. 559.

48 Caroline E. Noble, sister of Rebecca Noble Calhoun. *Calhoun Family Genealogy.*

wrote me that Aleck Noble[49] was dead. This is the 9th letter & still not a line from you. Do, do write and tell me everything. Continue to direct to Manassas Junction 18. Four horse wagons are waiting to transport the baggage of our Reg. and they can't carry near all. The privates will have to leave some of their baggage. They will have their blankets & clothes to carry on their backs or at least most of them. Ours will be carried in the wagons. Our company numbers 105 and is the ranking company in the regiment. Capt Bradley is the senior Capt and I am Sr. 2nd Lieut. When I have leisure, I will "pass in review" all of the officers in the regiment from Col to 3rd Lieuts., their competence and popularity etc. I can write four pages a day that is enough transpires to write about. Give my love to all & my precious, write, write, write. I think very strange that I have not rec'd a line from in the two weeks or more. In haste we are packed and ready. I subscribed to the daily Richmond Dispatch and had it directed in my name to Mt. Carmel as you can get all of the news from it as to our movements. Good bye, Love darling

With eternal devotion,
Your own husband,
JFC

49 Alexander Noble, II (1827-1861) son of South Carolina Governor Patrick Noble. Died in Lavaca, Texas. Was1st cousin, once removed, of Rebecca Noble Calhoun. *Calhoun Family Genealogy.*

FAIRFAX C[OURT] H[OUSE] VA
June 26, 1861

My Dear Wife:

This will be the eleventh letter that I have written to you since leaving SC and only one has been received in reply. What in the world is the matter? Surely you don't write twice a week as I have requested. Do you wish me to write two or three times a week? You must certainly know how anxious I am to hear from my little family. Far, far away as I am anything from home will interest me and my own loved one, I hope you will write twice a week at least for a while until you get tired of hearing from me so often. Nothing of much interest has transpired since I last wrote although I will write everything that takes place which possibly interest. We are still as ignorant of our future movements as I was when I last wrote. I entertain the same opinion now about the prospect of war that I did and I find many of the officers begin to entertain the same opinion.. Gen Moragne[50] came over to our camp yesterday evening and said he did not think there would be any fighting until the 4th of July. The Lincoln congress meets then and although Lincoln will send a strong war message, still I think the peace propositions will be numerous and quiet things. If they would just meet us in open battle before the 4th then I am confident they would sue for peace. Greely[51] is for peace and a great mass at the north. The[y] dread our troops if we advance, they retreat. Gen Beauregard will out maneuver them, he will not make a head long rush upon any of their strongholds just merely for a victory, but counts the cost in the way of loss of life. He will not have his men killed up, but will maneuver and defeat them ultimately at every point. Our pickets took two more Yankees yesterday and one of them mistook Gen Bonham whilst he was reconnoitering a few miles from town, fired at him and came near his head. It was a young man in Perryman's[52] company by the name of McKeller[53] son of Peter McKeller, near Greenwood. They say he did not hail the Gen, but feeling sure he was an enemy just fired without a word. He ought to be punished and may be punished. We had orders read last evening at dress parade fixing the hour for Tattoo at 8 ½ o'clock & reveille at 3 ½ in the morning. Only one officer from a company is required to be present at roll call so we take it turn about getting up. Col Bacon seems to be worn out in fact he has everything to do. Col Fair[54] is a

50 Assistant Adjutant General W.C. Moragne', a member of General Bonham's staff. Held the actual rank of Colonel. *Kershaw's Brigade*, p. 45.

51 Horace Greeley, editor of the *New York Tribune*. Initially supported secession saying that "peaceful separation of the south is preferable to civil war." Later, banged the war drum for a Union attack.

52 Captain W.W. Perryman of Company F, 2nd S.C. Volunteers. *Kershaw's Brigade*, p. 548.

53 Either G.W. McKellar or J.R. McKellar of Company F, 2nd S.C. Volunteers. *Kershaw's Brigade*, p. 549.

54 Lieutenant Colonel Robert A. Fair, 7th S.C. Volunteers. *Kershaw's Brigade*, p. 557.

perfect specimen of laziness and I fear it will injure him with the regiment. He is sprawled out flat of his back in his tent nearly or moping about looking half dead. He does nothing nor does he seem to care about doing anything. I like him as he is an amiable man. When we came from Centerville here Gen Bradley broke completely down and asked Col Fair for one of his horses. He said if he could make any arrangements for his servant he could take the horse he was riding. The idea of a grownup hearty young fellow having to ride like a gentleman and hundreds of gentlemen were marching with guns and knapsacks on their backs. The Gen will not forget it. Aiken[55] has gained popularity very fast; he seems now to take all of our company. He gives up his horse to any of the privates who take sick on the way and takes it on foot like a man. Gen Bradley is complaining three fourths of the time and consequently seldom goes out with the company, in fact he seems to shrink from it and does not improve like the other Captains & sometimes I think that is the reason he gives the company up to Cothran & me. There is one man about whom my opinion has changed very much and I know your father can scarcely believe it. Dr. Hearst is one the most ill natured, fretful, cross men in the Reg.. He is nearly half of his time like a sore headed bear, some times he gets so that he can't make a kind reply about anything. He speaks to the men sometimes like they were negroes, insulting in tone. He speaks cross to Cothran, The and me and at last, I told him about it, he said he did not intend anything by it and remarked that his friends frequently tell him that he speaks in a manner calculated to offend. Gen. Bradley is a kind good old man and every one likes him. I told Cothran that I intended calling upon Dr. H about speaking so short. He said he would do it and remarked that the Dr. was an enigma to him, that he was a curiosity. He has been less cross since I had a talk with him. The crops are suffering from want of rain, but it looks very much like rain today. I will close until this evening or tomorrow morning hoping that I may get a letter from you by the mail today.

11 o'clock As I will have an opportunity of sending this direct to Richmond I will finish it and send it immediately. Give my love to your father and mother & Sam. I wrote to Mr. McCrevan yesterday & will write to father next week. Always let him hear all the news I write. Love to him & Ida. Zeke is well. Tell his mother not to fear about his not being attended to sick or well. Zeke looks to me for advice and that makes me take more interest. Tell Mrs. Noble[56] the last promise I made her was to advise and take care of Zeke and I will do it. He is getting on very well indeed. Sam also. I wrote to Mr. McCrevan to have your fowl & smoke house built & you must get your father or father to advise with you as to the locality &c. Willis owes me so he must

55 Colonel David Wyatt Aiken (1828-1887), 7th S.C. Volunteers. Was wounded at Antietam and later Gettysburg. He resigned in mid-1864 to enter politics. Served in the S.C. House 1864-1866 and the U.S. House 1877-1887. *Kershaw's Brigade*, pp. 164, 557. *Find a Grave.*

56 Mrs. William Pickens Noble (Louisa), aunt of Rebecca Noble Calhoun and mother of Ezekiel (Zeke) Noble. *Calhoun Family Genealogy.*

build them & Shed[57] had better be engaged to help him. Tell Mr. McC to send in time for the turnip seed & tell him to have an acre or 1-1/4 planted & highly manured. Have an abundance of every variety of garden seed saved. Have your peas & beans dried in tin pans two or three days in the sun, then they will be sure not to have worms. Save tomatoes and any other vegetables you can for winter use as we get none here & I hope to be spared to enjoy winter vegetables saved by my "darling." Have you recd the Richmond Dispatch which I subscribed to and had sent to my address Mt. Carmel? It is the daily. Make the arrangement with J.L. Covin[58] about the letters & I recommended it will save you trouble & tell him about the high charge of postage. The Rogers gets his letters from the Mills at 5 cts and everybody else & ours go to any part of SC for 5 cts. Keep an account of the number of letters you get from me. Kiss my darling little Fannie for me & tell her to write to her pa. Ask if she remembers her pa. Always let me know about the crops every time you write & the rains &c. Do write me often and a long letter, write as I have begged you over & over again twice a week. Don't mind the expense which will be swallowed up by the pleasure. Love to your aunty (&) uncle & all relations. Farewell my "own loved one."

Most Devotedly your
Husband
J.F. CALHOUN

57 Willis, Shed believed to be Negroes at Calhoun Mills.

58 James Louis Covin, resident and Postmaster of Mount Carmel, SC, near Calhoun Mills & Willington.

II.

Letters: July, August, September of 1861

THE 7TH REGIMENT, South Carolina Volunteers remained deployed on the front lines near Fairfax, Virginia as the summer months of 1861 began. Time was spent building fortifications, drilling, continuous picket duty and, of course, the occasional skirmish with the enemy.

The Union Army under the command of General Irwin McDowell continued probing Confederate held positions along the front and on July 18, 1861 a battle ensued at Blackburn's Ford. This proved to be the prelude to the war's first major conflict three days later at Bull Run Creek (Manassas) on July 21,1861. Professor Thaddeus Lowe, had been named the Union's first Chief Aeronaut by President Abraham Lincoln and he brought forth a new style of aerial reconnaissance to the battlefield. In spite of the use of his balloon to observe Confederate troop positions and movements, the Southern troops performed admirably. The Union Army was completely routed and retreated in great confusion. In so doing, they left behind arms, equipment, and wagonloads of supplies, including whiskey and champagne that they expected to consume at a picnic in celebration of their great victory over the Confederates. The northerners were shocked at their unexpected defeat and President Lincoln quickly signed a bill providing for the enlistment of an additional 500,000 men for up to three years of service. Although somewhat more quiet in their reaction, the Confederate Congress also sent out a call for additional troops.

The Rebels rousing defeat of the Union Army at Manassas boosted the South Carolinians' spirits and they believed the Yankees would never risk another fight. Hope was emerging that the war would now end soon, the troops disbanded, and all would be sent back home. That hope, however, was short lived as the Confederate forts at Cape Hatteras were captured in August by the Union Navy on the North Carolina coast. In late September a group of Confederate generals in Virginia appealed to the Davis Administration to reinforce and resupply them, allowing them to make an invasion into the northern territory of Washington. A bold move that could have possibly ended the war.

Sickness began to take its toll on the Regiment and the Brigade. Hundreds were reported unfit for duty resulting from measles, bad drinking water, and eating "green corn." Whether in camp, bivouacked along the front, or on extended picket duties, John Francis kept up his writing as promised. He always inquired about the farm, the mill, and tan yard, asking the opinions of both his father and Rebecca's father as to the state of his business. He still depended on Rebecca to follow through with his instructions regarding the management of foodstuffs for family, slaves, and livestock as well.

John had now been away from home for several months. As a 12 month volunteer, he had expected to receive a short furlough to return home, see his family, and personally attend to his business affairs. Although initially promised, none was granted and the continued denial of furloughs ignited talk of resignations throughout the camp.

July 1861

FAIRFAX C.H. VA
July 5: 1861
12th letter

My Dear Wife

I have written to you eleven times and this will be 12, three has been rec'd in reply, but I am expecting one today. When you write always let me know how many letters you have rec'd. We are still lying here drilling and fortifying, but in future I must be more particular what I write about our movements &c as orders were read before the Army cautioning the officers & men not to write anything respecting our position, forces, fortifications, movements &c as it is in violation of the Articles of War. Still we will not be very much restrained by this as our friends can judge of that which should be kept secret. Yesterday was the 4th and by daylight Old Abe's guns began in Washington in celebration of the day. Gen Beauregard ordered Col Kershaw's regiment with Col Munford's[1] reg't of cavalry to go to Cloud's Mills to capture the troops and stores including several hundred bbl's of flour at that place. Col M's cavalry was stationed in the rear then all of Col K's[2] reg't but two companies which he took forward with one or two cavalry companies to open the fight and decoy the enemy by retreating to the strong pass where our troops were lying in ambush. Capt Perryman's[3] rifle company was deployed, extended at intervals along the road on the extreme left nearest the enemy. Col K was about 1 or 1 ½ miles in advance when Col F[4] sent two men forward in a gallop to tell Col K that he saw some troops of the enemy skirmishing on his right. They passed the entire time and as they approached the extreme left of Perryman's company they halted, turned their horses, drew their pistols & said (before turning however) here are pickets, mistaking them for the enemy whereupon John Parks[5] 2nd Lieut of Capt P's Co drew his pistol & fired, the troopers dashed back at full speed and a rattling fire was given as they went

1 Colonel Thomas T. Munford (1831-1918) of Virginia. Graduated Virginia Military Institute in 1852. Mustered into Confederate service in May of 1861 and served with the 30th Virginia mounted Infantry at 1st Manassas. Later promoted to Brigadier General serving until the end of the war with Fitzhugh Lee's cavalry division. *Virginia Military Institute Civil War Generals*.

2 Colonel Joseph Brevard Kershaw (1822-1894) of Camden, SC. Commanded the 2nd Brigade of South Carolina Volunteers. Was promoted to Brigadier General in February 1862. Survived the war and returned to Camden serving in the State Senate and as a Circuit Court Judge (1877-1893) and then Postmaster until his death. *Kershaw's Brigade*, pp. 36, 86-88.

3 Captain W.W. Perryman of Company F, 7th South Carolina Volunteers. *Kershaw's Brigade*, p. 374.

4 Colonel Robert A. Fair of 7th South Carolina Volunteers. *Kershaw's Brigade*, pp. 38, 557.

5 Lieutenant J.T. Parks of Company F, 2nd South Carolina Volunteers. *Kershaw's Brigade*, p. 548.

from P's company then Capts Pickett & Wallace's[6] company in part fired and just as they passed horses and riders fell...a most unfortunate affair. It cast a gloom over the entire camp. One was a son Judge Tyler[7] of this circuit. This sad affair defeated the adventure. I expect a court of investigation will be held. Park is very much censured. Capt P told me last night he felt very much mortified, he said that he had cautioned his co and ordered them not to fire until he ordered, but they felt that Park's firing was equivalent to an order or at least a justification for them firing – one man had his arm twice broken, shot in the foot, his gun shot nearly in pieces, his clothes riddled, a half dozen balls through his hat, & eight or ten balls through his horse...a providential escape. Capt Brooks[8] (and I walked over to the C.H. last evening & just as we got in town Capt Todd[9] from Laurens and a Va trooper came in with a prisoner. Capt T made himself ridiculous by his conceit & pomposity, he was so proud of a low life yankee prisoner. He said his picket took him, the Va trooper said "and mine Capt" yes, yes said Todd. He wanted to claim all the honor. The prisoner said he had been 10 years in the Dragoon service of the U.S.A., had been in Texas etc looked like an independent fearless fellow, an Irishman I think & was drinking a little. He asked some of the bystanders for a cigar as soon as he halted. Mr. Aleck McCaslon has just come. He has a son[10] in our company. The northern congress met on yesterday. I expect Gen B is waiting to see what action they intend taking. I am perfectly hearty, in better health than I have been I think in two or three years. Some from our company, 40 worked day before yesterday at the fortifications. Sam Harris among them and 24 yesterday, Zeke in that party. Some of the men said that Sam was lazy. I could have told them all of the family were lazy. He is getting on very well indeed, Zeke too. In fact all of our men are doing very well at present. Dr H. seems to have grown much more amiable since I talked to him about being so cross. We have not been paid off yet, expecting it any day. The Rogers has been sick but is well again. He has not drank anything for some time, although we have whiskey in our mess. Have you written twice a week like an affectionate wife? Do write longer letters-write me all the neighborhood news & don't hurry through as you seem to. I wrote to Carie last week; tell her to write me a long letter. It was very cool here on the 2nd , 3rd, & 4th. On the 2nd nearly cool enough for frost. It is cool enough here every night for 2 blankets and fire is comfortable every morning. Make me some drawers &

6 Capt. William Wallace, Company C, 2nd South Carolina Volunteers. *Kershaw's Brigade*, p. 36.

7 Unidentified

8 Either Warren D. Brooks or J.Hampden Brooks, *Kershaw's Brigade*.

9 Captain R.P. Todd of Company G , 3rd South Carolina Volunteers. *Kershaw's Brigade*, p. 555.

10 Private G.D. McCaslon, Company C, 7th South Carolina Volunteers. *Kershaw's Brigade*, p. 559.

shirts during the summer. Give my love to all and present my compliments to miss Fannie Calhoun, your daughter, with numberless kisses. This is Friday, I will write again Monday. Good bye my own precious wife.

Devotedly your
own fond husband,
JOHN F.C.

PS

There is various rumors in circulation this evening in camp. Sam Hester[11] who was out with the picket guard said he saw three signals thrown up last night by the enemy. It is rumored the enemy advanced 1 ½ miles last evening & also that Gen Scott[12] said he was ready and his plans for the subjugation of the south matured and he would subdue the south at any and every hazard, again that 50,000 troops were moving this side of Washington, 10,000 passed through Baltimore all this is camp rumor, I don't believe one half of what I hear. That prisoner said we could have taken their forces at Falls Church yesterday as they were all "light." He said he was on a "fast" & with an orderly thought they would see how far they could get without being taken. The orderly halted & told him if he did not turn he would report him, he said report be d---d & he soon found himself in our hands. He said he was after a "buss." He said we would a ""devil" of a whipping in three days, but thought we only had 7 or 800 men here. Do write often my darling.

JOHN F.C

11 Captain Samuel J. Hester of Company D, 7th South Carolina Volunteers. *Kershaw's Brigade*, pp. 37, 559.

12 Union General Winfield Scott (1786-1866). Known as "Old Fuss and Feathers" because of his belief in the discipline offered by a regular army. Was originally commissioned in the U.S. Army in 1808 and served on the staff of General Wade Hampton I in the War of 1812. He had a storied military career through several U.S. conflicts and when the War Between the States began, he was made General-in-Chief of the Union Army. In early 1861, Scott developed the "Anaconda Plan" to split the South in half and enforce total subjugation on the Confederacy. By this time he was 74 years old, weighed 300 pounds and suffered from numerous health problems. He could not mount a horse or review his troops and, in a play on his old nickname, he was called "Old Fat and Feeble." Scott was replaced as General-in-Chief by General George B. McClellan in November of 1861. *Encyclopedia Virginia. Find a Grave.*

HEAD QUARTERS 7TH REG
S.C.V., FAIRFAX C H
VA. July 9: 1861

My dear wife:

I wrote you a long letter day before yesterday, but as it is a pleasure and not a task for me to write my wife I will write again although this time I have no news at all. The weather is quite warm here now but the nights are pleasant. We will finish our fortification today and then we will be prepared for the Lincolnites although I don't much look for them to attack us here. It is said General Beauregard will be here this evening to inspect the fortifications. We had orders to send all the sick who would not be able to do duty in two or three days back to Culpepper C. H. Champ Gillebeau & Peter[13] from our company, although not much sick were sent. One had measles, the other a sore foot. Some think this looks like a Battle is expected soon. I don't look for anything of the kind. I notice in the "Press"[14] that my name is incorrectly published. I wrote to Lee[15] to correct it. The Rogers rec'd a letter from home when I rec'd the one from you and today he got another. He generally gets two to my one but I trust it won't be so in the future. The prisoners taken on the Privateer Savannah have been condemned and Gen Beauregard sent Col Taylor[16] with 15 men and a white flag to Washington yesterday to say to Lincoln that if he hung the prisoners, he would hang the Federal prisoners which he had taken. We have I expect near 200 in all. Col Taylor has not yet returned. Billy Harris[17] came into camp today, he is now with us and says he intends staying through the war. Bob Middleton rec'd a letter from uncle Docks wife & she sent love to The, begged to be remembered to Gib & Sam, but never sent a word to me. I don't know whether it was intentional or not. Give my love to uncle Dock and tell him of it for me. I expect you have had roasting ears & water melons before this but I will not get any this season. I have seen no corn higher than my shoulder around here. How are your

---

13 Champ and Peter Gillebeau were brothers from the Willington, SC area and members of Company C, 7th South Carolina Volunteers. *Kershaw's Brigade*, p. 559.

14 *The Abbeville Press* was a newspaper published from Abbeville, SC beginning in 1844. *Abbeville Press and Banner. Chronicling Historical American Newspapers.*

15 William Augustus Lee was the owner of the Abbeville Press at this time. In 1861 he turned over publishing duties to a former partner and enlisted in the Confederate Army. *Abbeville Press and Banner. Chronicling Historical American Newspapers.*

16 Lt. Colonel Thomas Taylor of Kentucky carried a letter from Confederate President Jefferson Davis to US President Abraham Lincoln. Lincoln had considered the captured crew of the Confederate Privateer "Savannah" pirates and had them indicted. If found guilty, they were to be hanged. Davis insisted they were not pirates but prisoners of war and, accordingly, should be illegible for a prisoner exchange. The trial resulted in a "hung" jury, and the crew were treated as prisoners of war. *The Papers of Jefferson Davis, 1861*, p. 223.

17 William Harris was a member of Company H, 7th South Carolina Volunteers. *Kershaw's Brigade*, p. 561.

water melons at the mills? Take them home whenever you go down. I hear that Wm Rogers' wife is quite ill & that Jim Porter's daughter was burned to death. When you write, direct to Fairfax C. H., Fairfax County. Some say there is another place by that name. Give my love to all & kiss Fannie for me. I will write again Friday if nothing prevents. This is Tuesday. Good bye and may God bless you my darling wife and my infant daughter too. Do do write oftener.

Most devotedly your husband
JOHN F. CALHOUN

HEAD QUARTERS 7TH REGIMENT
S.C.V., FAIRFAX C. H. VIRGINIA
JULY 12: 1861

My own darling wife:

This morning the mail came in to camp and I was seated in front of my tent when Capt Brooks came by and held up a letter and shook it at me. I asked him if he had a letter. I thought he was exulting over me as he had rec'd one from his wife but when he came near he said a letter for Lt J. F. Calhoun and it is needless to assure you that I seized it eagerly and devoured its contents with delight. My darling I am so thankful that you write to me twice a week and you must not think hard of my sometimes complaining of your not writing for it is only caused by my great anxiety to hear from you. I will not complain any more now that I know you write regularly twice a week but I did not know before that you wrote but once a week. I am now satisfied and if I don't get two a week I will know that it is not because you have not written. I am glad you sent me Fannie's sweet little scrawl. I could almost imagine that I could see her eyes sparkling all impatience as you and Carie were directing her hand in writing to "her pa." I am glad to hear that my wheat is turning out well. I will get 38 ½ bushels from Dr G's[18] and I ought to make 115 or 20 at home. Let Mr. Burt[19] know as soon as your father thinks Bess' pigs are (large) enough to take away. Two months old will be long enough, earlier perhaps. The money is yours my dear. I am in hopes Mr. McCraven can get me some peas. Have all the wheat straw saved. Is the wheat box made? What about my colt and calve? As Col Cash moved off yesterday evening at the head of his regiment I thought he was riding one of the prettiest and most dashing horses I ever saw. A slick coal black with one of the thickest – heaviest tails I ever saw. I have just returned from the old gentleman that sold the horse to Col Cash. He says he is only three years old & he got $250 for him. He is large now & will of course grow & is fine blood. In the night, Maj. Seibels[20] came around to all the officer's tents and told all the Captains to meet him at his tent. I suppose to consult & arrange everything in the event of an attack, but as I wrote you I don't believe the report yet although many did. Col. Fair came around and told us that the enemy were advancing. Gen Bonham believed it. Mr. Carlisle after prayer meeting last night urged upon the volunteers to be calm and not to allow themselves to be disturbed & excited by the rumors, but to be cool and determined and they will be the better

18 Dr. John Albert Gibert (1821-1892) of Willington, SC and grand-son of the SC Huguenot pioneer Pierre Gibert. Gibert owned several farms and plantations in the area.

19 Armistead Burt (1802-1883). Lawyer by education, but was engaged in politics and farming in the Abbeville, SC area. His wife, Martha, was a 1st cousin-once removed of John Francis Calhoun. *Calhoun Family Genealogy.*

20 Major Emmett Seibels of the 7th South Carolina Volunteers. He was once detailed with a group of about 30 soldiers to make soap for the Confederate troops. *Confederate Veteran Magazine*, Vol 22, p. 55.

prepared to meet the issue that we may have to meet. He is a noble fellow and when the fight comes off he will make his mark. He shoulders his musket whenever there is an alarm. I think yet that it will be two or three weeks before the enemy will attack us here if then. Mr. McCaslan[21] intends starting home this evening & I will give him this to mail on the way. I will send a little book "The Bow in the Clouds" which I read through one Sunday in the woods lying under a shade tree near where Mr. Carlisle preaches. My thoughts whilst reading it was continually of you my darling & my child. Read it Sunday evenings and think of me. I got it from Mr. Carlisle and marked many passages that struck me as beautiful. Hand it to Ida to read. I will send a few cherry seed[22] which Mr. McC will have sent to the mills as soon as he gets home. Plant them before they get dry. Divide them out with your friends, your aunties, father, Mat Gibert, aunt Lou. They are delightful cherries and the trees grow as large as the wild cherry trees in our county—spreads more and are loaded with fruit. I have rec'd 5 letters from you, the last two dated July 1st & 5. How many have you written? This is my 16th I think, 15 I know have all been rec'd. Zeke, Sam & Gib are well. Give my love to all & to Aunt Lu & family, uncle Dock, fathers, and your aunts and uncles. Nobles and Cowans. Love to Mat Gibert when you see her. Make up those grey pants and two pair of stout drawers and two or three shirts as I will need them if I have to stay here even until Oct. I don't look forward to it but still it is the best to be prepared and if you will have them made up in time you can find an opportunity of sending them on by some one. I will need some socks for winter. It will begin to turn cold the last of Sept I expect. The snow covers the fences nearly in the winter. I send a few of the cherries with their seeds they will keep moist and will be more apt to come up. I had some choice seed but I can't find them they were grafted cherries and would not do as well as the native in all probability. Tell Mr. McCraven to have as much hay, fodder, and pea vines saved as he can. Father may have more fodder than he can gather and if so tell Mr. McC to get father to let him pull the low grounds nearest to me. Now be sure and tell him. I am anxious to see an abundance of forage, &c. Write me long letters. Tell Carie to write to me at least once a week. Good bye my own precious love.

Most devotedly your husband
JOHN F. CALHOUN

---

21 Father of Private G.D. McCaslan Company C, 7th South Carolina Volunteers.

22 While on picket duty, part of the Company C of the 7th South Carolina Volunteers came upon a field filled with cherry trees. Many soldiers took the opportunity to relax, some took naps, and some climbed the cherry trees to pick the fruit. Suddenly a hail of bullets whizzed over their heads and all scrambled to arms and the cherry pickers jumped down from the trees. Seems a Union scout party spotted the pickets, fired at them and then fled for their lives. No one was injured. *Kershaw's Brigade*, pp. 48, 49.

P. S. Just as I opened this pocket in my trunk to get an envelope the note which I enclose fell out and to my great surprise I found it to be a note I wrote to you during our engagement. I was sure I had destroyed all. I have taken everything out several times, and I don't know yet how it was overlooked. A coincidence connected with the matter is this. The note was written 12th July 1859—just two years ago. This is the 2nd anniversary of the writing of the note. Read it and think how happy we were then. Lovingly your own.

P.S. Mr. McCaslan intends postponing his departure until Monday 15th. Gen. Bradley requested him to do so as by that time we would be paid off and some would want to send money home. Gen B said that many would have more than it would be safe to keep about them. I believe I will act upon his suggestion and send you about $100 and out of it you can pay your father what I borrowed.

BULLS RUN CREEK
JULY 22, 1861

My own darling Wife

I received two letters from you on yesterday and read them whilst all was confusion preparing for a battle.[23] We held the center with Col Williams[24] SC Regt & a NC Regt. At ½ past eight o'clock their Batteries began their fire upon us, and the rifle cannon balls fell around us thick shells bursting and the fragments strewed around. At the same hour heavy cannonading was heard to our left and such rattling of musketry scarcely ever was known. The fire seemed to get farther & farther & occasionally a loud shout was heard. The battle raged for six or seven hours. Many officers say the hardest fight ever known in America, but Gen Beauregard said before sun rise that morning that before the sun went down he would give the enemy a Waterloo defeat. We did not know when our time would come as the musketry began on o[u] r right, but they dreaded attacking the sabastapool of the line excepting with cannon. The famous New Orleans Flying Artillery[25] were sent down to our line and planted one of their guns at the breastwork of our company, they are brave fellows and were eager to fire but Gen B for some reason restrained them. The heavy firing on the left wing still continuing, at last about four or five o'clock pm. Gen Bonham read a dispatch to us that the enemy were badly whipped and were retreating in great confusion hotly pursued by our troops & that our time had now come and as we [*Unreadable line on a fold*] a shout was raised as all got ready. I thought it would be a deadly fight, one Regt after another dashed through the creek and whirled right to left to attack then on both sides. Bonham's Brigade on the right of them & Gen Longstreet's on the left on we dashed with deafening shouts[26] and when we got in a few hundred yards the hated Stars & Stripes that had just been fluttering in our sight were no longer to be seen, and when we reached their camp we found it just deserted, boxes, barrels, coffee, sugar, pork, blankets, uniforms, nice oil cloth coverings, &c. &c strewn on all sides for more than a mile,[27] we pursued them until sundown then moved back loaded with trophies. We loaded several wagons took a Major & other prisoners &c. Thousands must have been killed above, the ground was said to be covered with the dead. Four of our Regt

23 1st Battle of Manassas on July 21, 1861. It was the first major battle fought in the War Between the States. *ORWR*, Vol II, Chapter IX, pp. 484-504.

24 Colonel James H. Williams of the 3rd South Carolina Volunteers. *Kershaw's Brigade*, p. 551.

25 The well-known Washington Artillery of New Orleans.

26 Finding themselves about to be victorious in battle, the Confederates gave way to their emotions, and let out a loud, shrill yell which became known as the "Rebel Yell." *Kershaw's Brigade*, pp. 58, 59.

27 The Yankees were routed and began to retreat in wild confusion and the Carolinians continued to push them back further. When they reached the enemy camps, they found supplies, provisions, tents, and baggage of every kind abandoned and left behind. *Kershaw's Brigade*, p. 65. *ORWR*, Vol II, Chapter IX, pp. 528-530.

were reported to have been engaged Hampton's Legion, Kershaw's, Cash's, & Sloan's Regt's.[28] The deadly battery of Sherman was captured he killed it's said.[29] You will get a full account in the Dispatch, there are too many reports to attempt to give you an account it takes several days to get the truth. As you know yesterday was Sunday and I thought often and prayed often for my wife & child during the heavy firing upon us which we had to face. Gen Bradley said we were more exposed than our men were on the islands during the battle of Ft. Sumter. Billy Harris will ruin himself, he shouldered his musket at first but after the first day he has been lying among the wagons when we were expecting a fight every day & night and last evening when we raised the shout he came down but pretended that he was "broke down" before he got ½ mile and actually got in our ambulance in the rear, and stuck to it all the way – shameful. I don't know when we will advance upon the enemy – one of Kershaw's men who was taken & made his way back says Pres. Davis & Beauregard were both upon the field. Love to all & may God bless you my wife & child. I pray for you often.

Write to me at Manassas
Devotedly your Husband
J.F.C.

July 24, 1861

We never had over 15,000 in the fight at any time while the enemy had from their own account from 35 to 40,000 but from what we can learn they had had from 50 to 65,000. Our loss is estimated at from 6 to 900 killed & wounded. Four or 500 killed and perhaps 5 to 700 wounded may be nearer the number, but I am sure that is too high an estimate. The enemy loss is from 10 to 15,000 killed & wounded and from 1 to 2,000 prisoners taken. I did not go to the battlefield but those who did tell me it was an awful sight for near two miles the ground is covered with the dead and wounded many with arms & legs shot off, others mortally wounded calling for water and begging to be killed. This was the next day our wounded were carried to Manassas as fast as they were wounded. Some one told me a wagon load of arms & legs were taken to Manassas. Some time the next day our men attended to the enemy wounded and began to bury their dead. Aiken[30] rode over the field and said

28 All of these units combined to trounce the Yankees and force the aforementioned retreat. *Kershaw's Brigade*, p. 64.

29 Later Union General William T. Sherman. The rumor of his capture proved not to be true.

30 Colonel David Wyatt Aiken (1828-1887). Born in Winnsboro, SC and after second marriage settled in Abbeville. Enlisted in the Confederate Army in the 7th South Carolina Volunteers, becoming Colonel.

he thought there were 2 or 300 horses killed. He counted 12 or 15 in ten steps. An officer who was in the battle took him to see one place where they were thick and Aiken said he counted 32 or 3 of Ellsworth's Zouaves[31] laying in a perfect line together but the officer said there were over 100 the day before, they had been buried, this was on yesterday, Tuesday. Aiken told me that on his way to Centerville to meet us, not the road from our comp, but the road the enemy retreated, he saw 4 dead bodies on litters on the road side 2 miles from the Battlefield. Officers he thought. A man on the road begged him to stop and report that house to Gen Bonham. Aiken went in and found 30 or 40 men badly wounded some shot through the eyes, throwing themselves about with delirium, six or seven had died and had been dragged into the yard and were putrefying. All along the road dead men can be found some got to Centerville, 30 or 40. I can't tell you all the horrors of this Bloody Battle. We took from 40 to 60 pieces of cannon, one the great Armstrong Gun drawn by 10 horses, fine rifle cannons, ammunition. I hear that on the upper road by which some retreated, a great quantity was taken. In all near 200 horses from 1 to 150 wagons, 50 or 60 cannons, loads of baggage, provisions &c ammunition is lying in the road yet. I saw one pile of boxes piled as high as the fence, 2 wagon loads I expect, boxes of crackers & barrels of molasses are still lying in the road. I saw at one place 20 or 30 pots and I expect 2 or 300 spades & picks scattered, 3 wagons still left. The road for 10 miles was strewn with every description of articles. Aiken said about 2 miles this side of the Battlefield he saw a fine new carriage door smashed. There are wrecks of Buggies- no doubt it was old Scott's[32] carriage door as it is said he reviewed the field before the battle in his carriage. It is reported that Lincoln and Seward were in sight and many ladies from Washington on their way to Richmond. They had a wagon load of Champagne & liquor and it is said they expected to have a grand picnic on Bull Run the day after the battle. Gen Bonham I heard has some of the Champagne and whiskey. The prisoners say they were badly whipped and disappointed, they did not expect much resistance at Bull Run. One of the letters found written back to a friend said they would have a small fight at Manassas and a tighter brush at Richmond but they would be there soon. The prisoners were thunderstruck when they saw our position and I told them it would not compare with Manassas. Our heaviest Guns are there and Richmond must be reached through that place if at all. Gen Beauregard did not throw his reserves in the field until late and but a few then.[33] The

Aiken's description of the battlefield at Manassas is confirmed in General Beauregard's report in the *ORWR*. *Biographical Directory of the U.S, Congress*. *Find a Grave*. *Kershaw's Brigade*, pp. 164, 557.

31 Union Colonel Elmer Ellsworth (1837-1861) commanded the 11th New York Volunteers and trained and dressed them in the style of French Zouaves. Ellsworth was known as the first casualty of the war, killed after removing a Confederate flag from an Alexandria Hotel on May 24, 1861. His former command suffered heavy casualties in the Battle of Manassas. *Smithsonian Magazine*, April 2011. *Find a Grave*.

32 General Winfield Scott. It was reported that since he was unable to ride a horse, Scott had toured the field prior to the battle in his personal carriage.

33 During the battle, Company C and other 7th Regiment companies were held in reserve to observe

enemy lost nearly everything they had - such a complete rout has never been known. They went through the fields in such great confusion, throwing away their arms, leaving their cannons with the horses hitched to them. The old men at Centerville said Gen McDowell tried in every way possible to rally them but they dashed by as if they did not hear him and said they were not going to stop this side of the Potomac. They left or threw down 20 or 30000 stand of arms at Fairfax and never stoped (sic) even at Falls Church but are said to be at Alexandria. The(y) would have went across the Potomac but the boats were carried over on the other side and the long Bridge blown up to keep them from crossing - so it is reported. I think the war is nearly at an end. These troops will never risk another fight with us. Their officers deceived them, some of them said they had no idea of crossing the Potomac when they volunteered. They were told by their officers that we would not stand long, the S Carolinians would stand a while but they would soon give way. I hear today they were badly whipped near Norfolk and some other point on the same day. Sunday has always been a lucky day with old Scott, most of his battles or at least the important ones were fought on that day. They acknowledge in the papers that they were badly whipped, routed and disorganized. We are within two miles of Falls Church 4 or 5 miles nearer than we have ever been before. It is said Gen Beauregard is moving by different approaches 50 or 60,000 troops towards Alexandria. I don't know what comes next. I think the Northern Congress will soon come to terms. Gen Bradley says this one Battle he expects will cost the enemy 20 million. I am out with our entire company upon Picket duty; we marched from 11 last night until near seven this morning. I received two letters from you and one from Ed. All the morning we were being bombarded and read them under the fire of the enemy guns and destroyed them immediately. To-day is Fannies birthday 11 months old to-day.[34] Oh how anxious to see you all. It was two months this morning since I saw you. I have a poor chance to write now so if you fail to hear from me every week, don't be uneasy. I will write as often as possible

WEDNESDAY MORNING JULY 31ST 1861

I am up early this morning my love to finish my reply to your letter of Monday 22 the first rec'd since Sunday 21st so you must have written that one about the 15th or 16th the one between must have miscarried. I will keep

the movements of the enemy. The center of Bonham's Brigade (7th and others), although not closely engaged, were exposed to the fight for the entire day. *ORWR,* Vol II, Chapter IX, pp. 498, 528-530.

34 The date of this letter is believed to be July 24, 1861 because of its content and the reference to Fannie's 11 month birthday. She was born August 24, 1860. *Calhoun Family Genealogy.*

an account hereafter, and let you know the date of every letter I receive. Do the same by mine. I will set down the date of every one I write to you from this. I am glad the book, poetry & cherry seed have been rec'd. Let me know if you don't also think the book pretty. The poetry is one of the finest productions of the day. I am very glad you made Martha Middleton[35] know that we noticed her neglect. I will write to uncle Frank soon. I suppose cousin Martha Burt[36] is President of the Female clothing establishment. I dreamed last night that she was dead. By last night's mail I also received a long letter from Ida written Wednesday night-17th the night you were with her. It must have been detained a long time on the way. Ida says Fannie is the prettiest, smartest & sweetest being living and she said that you gave her several slaps that night –mind how you slap my little pet. I know she must be sweet. You don't write me enough about her sometimes you merely mention her. You must devote at least a ½ page of every letter to her. I see that Mr. L[37] publishes a few hastily written lines from me to him while we were at Fairfax. I wrote them very hurriedly but no one knows they are from me. I wrote him to send his paper to me. You did not say a word in your letter about the preaching at Willington and Mr. Lindsay's[38] prayer for us, there is a great deal that you omit that would be highly interesting to me. Nearly all, at least every one that I have heard express an opinion upon the subject say that in our great struggle the kind & merciful providence of God is plainly to be seen & in the abundant harvest & flattering prospect for a large crop. If any people on the globe have cause to praise & thank God we have & I hope to devote myself more to his service than I have ever done before. Ida writes me that father thinks my corn & pea crop very good, needing rain a little at that time, my swamp corn "splendid." He thinks I will make 5 or 600 bushels. What does your father think? Get him to look at it when you go the Mills again. Tell Mr. McCrevan to write to me and let me know how everything is getting on. Tell him to try and gentle Nettie[39] so as to get her to working in the buggy. Let Mr. Burt know two or three weeks before his pigs are large enough to be weaned which I want done as early as possible if they grow fast 6 weeks will be old enough. Zeke has been complaining for three or four days, but is doing very

35 Martha Middleton was the wife of Hugh Graves Middleton and aunt of John Francis Calhoun. She was also the sister of Theophilus A. Rogers and half-sister of Dionysius M. Rogers. *Calhoun Family Genealogy.*

36 Martha Calhoun Burt, wife of Armistead Burt and 1st cousin once removed of John Francis Calhoun. *Calhoun Family Genealogy.*

37 William Augustus Lee.

38 Reverend John Oliver Lindsay, minister of Willington Presbyterian Church and father-in-law of Gilbert C. Tennent. *Willington Church Historic Marker. Calhoun Family Genealogy.*

39 John Francis Calhoun's prized mare.

well now. I will write again in two or three days. Give my love to all and kiss Fannie. Has Ida gone to Pendleton & how long does she intend staying? Do write long letters to me.

Ever your Devoted Husband,
J. F. CALHOUN

August 1861

CAMP GREGG, VIENNA, VA
AUGUST 6, 1861
NO 3

My darling wife

The mail last night brought me another letter. No 4 from my darling. I am so glad that you write so often and that your letters are reaching me so regularly now. Yesterday was pay day and we were all paid of and in turn "paid off ourselves." It is expensive living now that is for the officers, as we furnish our selves and everything is so high. Coarse black sugar 16 cents per pound, everything in proportion butter 25, frying fowls 25 there are so many troops in the field all kinds of eatables are raised enormously high. I want to send you on some money by the first opportunity and what is left I believe I will send to father to appropriate to my debts so as to stop the interest, and as fast I get paid I will make the same use of it after furnishing you with an abundance and you must not stint yourself, but must have whatever you want. I will have 100 dollars to pay off any debts with and in 24 days the first of Sept. pay day will come again and I will have 125 or 30 again to spare after saving as much as I need. I was paid 200 yesterday and the first of Sept. will get 160 more. I want to pay your father what I borrowed from him when I left home. Zeke rec'd a letter from Lu yesterday containing one from William[40] to Gib. Wm writes that he and Dr Gibert wish to come on and join Capt. Bradley's Company and want to know if they can get in. If you see either of them tell them I asked the Capt and he said yes, they would be received. We will be glad to have the Dr & Wm. if they wish to come on soon, tell them to write to me at once and I will send their certificate of membership so that they will be passed over the Rail Roads free. We have a great deal of sickness mostly measles. Zeke is sitting up by me in his room writing. He is improving fast. Jimmie Calhoun[41] has never been lost it is a mistake. It will injure him I expect leaving at such a moment. Billy Harris has not returned from Culpepper or wherever he has gone. He is doing himself no credit, better if he had remained at home. I am sorry to hear that we are still needing rain but hope by this time will have had enough. I am glad to hear that your father's crop is so good. Next to my own I believe I want him to make a good crop, certainly just as soon as my own fathers, for so far as our interest goes it is the same. I do hope both may make a good crop. Will he make thirty 30 bales if the season continues favorable does he think? And how much corn?

---

40 William T. Tennent, brother of Gilbert Tennent. His wife Susan Rebecca Noble was 1st cousin of Rebecca Noble Calhoun. *Calhoun Family Genealogy.*

41 James Lawrence Calhoun, 1st cousin once removed of John Francis Calhoun. *Calhoun Family Genealogy.*

I will bet you can't get him to say. Does Fannie love water melons? I would like to see her eating them. I know how she would hold out her head "grub" at it with her hands and smack her mouth. I hope she is well by this time. Be particular with Fannie. I will enclose ten $10 dollars in this letter. I am afraid to enclose more as it may be lost. Be sure and let me know by return mail whether or not it reached you safely. I will send more if you need any. Don't hesitate, my darling if you do. Let no one know what I wrote you about Zeke in my last as I would not for any thing hurt the feelings of the family. He told Dr. Hearst that he never would be able to do much service again. I have been up here more than ½ an hour and I don't think he has coughed more than once. Give my love to all and kiss Fannie. I did intend writing to your father this time but it is a hard matter for me to write to anyone but you. I mean I always feel like writing to you when I take my seat to write to any one. I will write to him soon. Good by love, my own sweet darling wife. Most devotedly you own Husband.

JFC

I am not certain whether this letter is No 3 or 4. I will make it 3 and in future will note down every number written and received so as to not make any mistake. I would advise you to do the same. Has Ida gone to Pendleton and did father go? How did you hear that we were going to Washington? We are still here. We tease The about writing that tale about the Blackberries. It is new to me. We have some hardships it is true sometimes exposure but we do as well as we could expect far, far better provided in every respect than our Revolutionary fathers were. We are engaged in a similar cause and any who can't willingly put up with everything cheerfully & without a murmur, does not deserve the name or privileges of freemen. Capt B will send on the papers to Dr. G & Wm so they can come on any time. My darling when you write always read over my letters so as to answer every question. this the way I am doing yours. Did your aunty take on about Zeke when she heard of the Battle? You have never written me whether or not you receive the Dispatch regularly or not. Save all the papers that speak of the battles or anything relating to our Brigade. Congress has passed a very convenient law for the volunteers. viz. not requiring the postage prepaid, all that is required will be for the volunteer to endorse his name upon the envelope, company & Reg, also his rank. I don't know when it goes into effect. I will learn soon. So you will have it to pay. It is very inconvenient to get silver out here to prepay postage. You can get it more conveniently. I will furnish you the paper bills. My friends and relations ought to do all they can to assist me in the way of patronizing me and getting me custom. I am away fighting their battles as well as mine. Why doesn't Carie write! She doesn't even send me a message. Is she courting? How does she look as Miss Noble? Tell your father I am taking care of the Revolver. The Rogers sends regards.

Love again to all. Howdy to negros. Does Lou[42] behave? Write long and loving letters to me darling. You are all in all to me dearest.

Thine forever

J. F. C.

42 This Lou is believed to be one of the Calhoun Mills slaves.

CAMP GREGG, VIENNA
Virginia Aug 8, 1861
No 4

My Darling Wife

I wrote to you on yesterday enclosing ten dollars and I sent one hundred and fifty to Richmond by Dr. Hearst to buy a check drawn in your favor which I requested him to send on immediately. I hope both letters may reach you. The money and check were enclosed in different envelopes. We moved camp about a mile back to a grove and I am up before sunrise writing. We have a great deal of sickness in our Regt and the entire Brigade. There are between 3 and 400 reported unfit for duty in our Regt alone, some are very sick. Dr. Link[43] had the measles and he now has brain fever and is lying very low. Capt Bradley does not think he can live. Sam Link[44] says though, that Joe[45] and his father both become insensible from the least fever. Dr. Hearst intends telegraphing Dr. Link. Zeke is up going about but is trying to get a discharge. I persuade him out of it every time I hear of his speaking of it; he never speaks to me about the matter but tries to get Dr. Drennan to speak to the Capt & Dr. Dozier. Dr. Drennan[46] consulted me yesterday and said Zeke said he never would get well or at least would not be able to do any more duty. I asked Dr. D. his opinion he said he could give him no certificate to that effect and remarked Zeke was for home regardless of reputation. I talked to Zeke and told him he had promised to take my advice, that he had injured himself in SC the way he acted before and said he would stick to the Army in future if it killed him. I told him not to apply for any discharge but go to Charlotte or Culpepper and recruit if he wished. I told him he would ruin himself, mortify his parents &c. I found he had his heart fixed on home like a baby, refused to eat, tried to act and look sick. I asked him what was the matter, for I could not tell, he said he "felt bad." I had become tired of talking to a big grown up boy like a child when he was so head strong, takes no ones advice, so I told him to take his own course, that I was tired talking to him and advising and I was now done. He is in camp and doing just as well as he could expect. I dreamed of you and Fannie last night, heard her say "pa-pa" and make some queer faces and monkey motions that had been taught her. The entire Regt

---

43 Dr. William E. Link was a physician from Willington, SC and a member of Company C , 7th South Carolina Volunteers. Wife was Louisa Catherine Harris. *Calhoun Family Genealogy. Kershaw's Brigade*, p. 559.

44 Samuel Link, member of Company C, 7th South Carolina Volunteers. *Kershaw's Brigade*, p. 559.

45 Joseph Link, member of Company C, 7th South Carolina Volunteers. *Kershaw's Brigade*, p. 559. These three Links were brothers and sons of John Link from the Willington, SC area.

46 Doctor Dozier & Doctor Drennan were Surgeons and members of Company C, 7th South Carolina Volunteers. *Kershaw's Brigade*, pp. 557, 559.

I expect will have a winter uniform made. We had our company's measure taken by a tailor and sent on to James H. Wideman[47] who Capt B said would take an interest and attend faithfully to it. We intend getting "Austrian Grey" cloth if we can get it and Mr. Shelito I expect will cut the uniforms and the ladies societies will make them. The officers intend uniforming in the same. It will be a frock coat upon the "hunting shirt" order. I can't describe it but it will be very pretty and appropriate - Mr. Wideman will visit the factories and select thick suitable cloth. Can you make the coat do you think or shall I get Mrs. S to make it? You can make the pants as well as anyone. I don't know that we will get the uniform in six or eight weeks. Mr. Robert Hester[48] is with his brother Sam. Mr. R. has a son in Col Thomas' Regt near Manassas. The weather is just as warm here as it is in SC, this is said to be the warmest month I believe in the section of the world. Has it been very hot in SC? Be sure and write me if the letter containing the ten ($10) dollar bill and the check reached you safely! I just directed an envelope and gave it to Dr. Hearst to enclose the check in. Billy Harris returned yesterday. Very few of the men will have any money in a short time, they will soon eat it up and buy anything. Sam Harris is one. I will get a letter from you on Friday-tomorrow, none came last night. I may not get an opportunity to send this to Manassas today if not I will write a few lines in the morning. Give my love to all and many kisses to sweetness. Does Carie intend writing to me? We have been here in Va two months it seems like 6. Does it seem so you? Oh how I long to see my darling, precious wife and child. You are so very dear to me. Write loving letters my darling to your ever true and devoted Husband

J.F CALHOUN

---

47 James H. Wideman, farmer and merchant in the Willington, SC area. He was also a member of Company C, 7th South Carolina Volunteers and served as their agent. *Kershaw's Brigade*, p. 559.

48 Robert Hester, brother of Captain Samuel Hester of Company D, 7th South Carolina Volunteers. *Kershaw's Brigade*.

VIENNA, VIRGINIA
August 9, 1861
No 5

My darling wife

It is most too early to see how to write but I can write with more ease early in the morning, so in future I intend writing early every morning. I find that Ed has not joined Capt Perrin's[49] Company, but still wishes to come on and join our Regt. so I intend sending on his papers by the next mail, and whatever you have to send me you can send by him. I wrote to you giving a list of the clothes I wanted. A part will do now as there will be frequent opportunity of sending on clothes &c. One pair of drawers, two pair of socks, two dark shirts, will do now, but Ed can buy them in Columbia just as cheap, if you have not already bought the clothes &c. I will tell Ed to write and let you know when he intends coming and I will ask him to go down to see you a day or two before he starts. Get me a bunch of thick white envelopes like those DeWitt[50] sent The, and send on by Ed. Tell Ben Andrews[51] to have my boots fixed and shoes made to send by Ed. It is reported that our Brigade will be moved back to Centerville or Bull Run and another put in the advance owing to the great number sick. The surgeon told me yesterday that there were at least 400 unfit for duty, the other Regts are in the same condition. Some think there not more than 16 or 1700 in the four Regts together who are fit for duty. One of Capt Hester's men, Maulden, died last night another will die, several of ours are in a bad way, and some in the other companies. Zeke is still on the mend. He has not opened his mouth that I know of about a discharge since I talked to him the last time as I did. We are having exceedingly warm weather, days and nights. How is it in Carolina? I wrote to you on yesterday, and if there are any in the Regt who writes oftener to their wives than I do to my wife, I don't know who it is. When I write to you so often my letters will be short, but should we move back in a few days as it is said, it may be several days before I write again. However as we are to go on picket this evening I will write tomorrow, Saturday, but may not have an opportunity of mailing it before Monday. I will get a letter from you this evening I expect. There is nothing new in camp, no news from the enemy, all quiet and will remain so I think for some time yet. Joe Link is still in the same condition. One of the Drs told me yesterday that there was not much hope for him. I am very sorry for Joe is a very clever fellow, makes one our best soldiers and is very popu-

49 Abner Monroe Perrin (1827-1864). Born in Edgefield, SC, was a Captain in the 14th South Carolina Infantry. Promoted to Brigadier General in September 1863 and was killed in action at Spotsylvania in May 1864. *Find a Grave.*

50 Believed to be DeWitt Huckabee, brother of J.P. Huckabee of Company D, 7th South Carolina Volunteers. *Kershaw's Brigade*, p. 559.

51 Ben Andrews was a shoemaker/overseer at Calhoun Mills.

lar. When the postage on my letters are not prepaid you are not made to pay anymore than 5 cents are you? I can not or may not find it convenient always to get silver change. Jim Covin does not require you to prepay does he? I thought he charges it and you pay quarterly. I dream of you and Fannie and of Battles very often. Give my love to your father, mother, Carie and Sam, the Esq. and Mrs. Noble and a kiss to Fannie. I will close as I wish to write to Ed this morning and finish a letter I have nearly completed to father. Write often, long and affectionate letter to your Fond and loving Husband

JOHN F. CALHOUN

CAMP NEAR FAIRFAX
August 1861
No 7

My Dear Wife

I wrote to your father this morning and mentioned that I would not write to you until day after tomorrow, but as there is some talk of moving camp this evening or tomorrow, and fearing in that event I may be prevented from writing I have concluded to write today, but will not mail it until tomorrow so I can put a postscript in before mailing it. You see <u>my darling</u> I am <u>determined</u> to carry out my promise about writing twice every week and three times when I can possibly do so. Although by writing three times a week I will <u>spoil you</u> for you will always expect three letters and should you receive them you will be uneasy. The week the Esq. Rec'd two letters from Zeke and you got only one from me, you said that you were very uneasy for fear I was sick. You must never be uneasy even should you get but one letter from me a week or even should you fail to get any as it will sometimes occur owing to the irregularity of the mail, and it may sometimes happen that I may not be able to write more than one letter a week. We may be moving. I may be sent off upon detached service, and many other things may happen to prevent my writing. Were you acquainted with camp life you could then see how it is, so in future never feel uneasy, you may feel <u>disappointed</u>. I did not have much to write to your father for I write to you so often; I had nothing left to write about. It is not like writing to <u>you</u> for I can write nearly all day to you in a <u>strain of affection</u>, <u>tender</u> and <u>loving</u> expression can't I darling? We are likely to have a little holiday from what I can find out, as we have always been in the advance, and have been kept all the time moving and working and nearly all the Picket duties and now our Brigade is in a crippled condition from sickness and the duties on those who are well will necessarily be heavier neary double. I must say that I am entirely unable to tell why we move camp every two or three days, and only a mile or two at a time. It is very troublesome packing & unpacking so often. We buried Jos. Link yesterday evening. He remained unconscious to the last. Sam Link has the measles at the same hour but is doing well. You had better write down in your memorandum book the number of your own letters and the date, for you may sometimes forget the number of the last, note down mine & date and always in replying let me know the <u>No</u> and <u>date</u> and should two reach you by the same mail mention it and then I will know if any are miscarried and which ones have been received, and never fail to read them over and reply to all the <u>questions</u>, in other words reply in the full meaning of the term to my letters. Continue to direct to Manassas until I direct otherwise; at present we are in sight of Fairfax, but may not remain here another day. I may sometimes mail my letters first at one place and another; someone is always going to Richmond, Manassas, or any village we happen to be near, although Manassas will be the office where we will have our letters directed for some time to come. If are moved back and rested for a month or so, the volunteers will get more than ever particularly those who have sweet wives. I know that any one who had a kind, loving, precious wife and a sweet sprightly pretty little daughter will get awfully homesick. It is dayly (sic) punishment to me to be kept away form you. I would rather live in a dungeon with you than in a palace without you. Sometimes I feel as if I would give all that I am worth if it would bring the war to a close so that I could return to the arms of my darling wife. I will appreciate home should I ever get to it more that I ever did before, although it was always delightful with you it will be doubly so hereafter. If it can be possible I will love you my darling more tenderly than ever and I feel like I could not so far forget myself as to speak a cross word to you as long as I live. I expect you will save this to show me like you did one I wrote during our engagement. I will write more if I have a chance in the morning. Give my love to all and kiss my sweet little Fannie. Fondly and Devotedly Thine own Husband

JOHN F. CALHOUN

[*Overwritten on first page*]

I will mail this letter this evening as I will have an opportunity of sending it to Manassas immediately. I will write again on Wednesday morning. This is Monday---one o'clock. Good bye. Write me how many letters have you received from me since I have been in Virginia. Devotedly

YOUR HUSBAND
JOHN F. CALHOUN

Camp Near Fairfax C H VA
August 15th 1861
No 9

My dear wife:

I received yours of the 5th inst written from the Mills and replied to it on the same day 13th and as the mail leaves tomorrow I will have another ready to send. I have several single sheets and I will use them in writing to you today but don't think I am scarce of paper. I am only economical and as it may be scarce before long I don't intend wasting more than can prevented. I am nearly out of letter paper. I think this is the last but I have a supply of very choice fools-cap. Capt Brooks and I have sent on to Columbia for paper and envelopes and they will be here in a few days. I forgot to mention that the Yankees came in ten or fifteen minutes of capturing General Beauregard a few days since. He and a body of cavalry as an escort went to or near Mt. Vernon reconnoitering and being fatigued they halted to rest and Gen B and a few others rode round the vicinity and while he was gone the cavalry of the enemy surrounded those that were left and took every one prisoner. It seems providential that Gen Beauregard rode off when he did, another remarkable instance of the Divine Interposition in our behalf. Just if he had been taken what would have been our condition? It would have compensated for the battle or at least the defeat of Bull Run, the enemy would so have regarded it. The weather here for the last two or three days has been very cool, the nights particularly. I sleep under two and three blankets and my feet are cool all night at that. If we are to spend the winter here I intend writing to your mother for a stout home made blanket for our blankets are not long enough. I very seldom find any long enough to cover my feet and I know I will be cold when winter comes unless I can get blankets long enough to cover me up thoroughly. I do hope we will have to stay longer that the first of December. I am getting very tired of camp life still I must remain and do my whole duty. It is bright and pleasant this morning and we have nothing to do now and I will find it impossible to fill out four pages every letter and three letters a week, twelve pages a week. I mean I will not be able to write much more as every thing is so quiet at present and no news [*Letter ends.*]

CAMP NEAR FAIRFAX CH, VA
August 17th 1861
No 11

My dear wife

I wrote to you on yesterday and was somewhat hurried in finishing it to send by mail on yesterday evening, and this I will begin and have ready for Monday's mail although I may have an opportunity of mailing it or sending by private hand to Manassas. As I said before there is a regular mail every Monday, Wednesday, and Friday and I always write my letters a day before and very frequently I have an opportunity of sending by private hand to Manassas so I am unable to say what days I will write. The best plan will be to have no regular day for writing but to write as often as I have an opportunity to write and anything to write about. This is Saturday the 17th and just one month ago today we were in full retreat from Fairfax to Centerville, thence to Bull Run and on the 18th we had to face their Batteries. How things change. I got up this morning feeling quite unwell from the effects of cold, my cough is not so bad but my head was stopped up and my jaws pained me but I am feeling much better and if the weather was only pleasant I think I would recover from the cold. It is still cool and drizzling, everything is so wet and we are encamped in a pasture and the weeds and grass are nearly knee high. It is a delightful camping place in dry weather. Dr. Hearst had a few pair of shoes made in Culpepper for some of our men and they charged him for kipp skin, coarse, stout soles, stitch-downs with some of the stitches quarter of an inch long, for such shoes they charged him $3.00 a pair. No one complained. I merely mention it to show you how high everything is. Some of the officers were talking about it this morning and all agreed that shoes would certainly be very high, some have concluded to write home now and engage their negro shoes in time fearing that they cant' be had scarcely at any price. We will have to charge $2.00 "plantation around" this year and then that will be low compared with the price here. I dislike charging so high but everything is high and everything else has risen. I see no reason why we must not rise with the demand. If I were only at home now to attend to the tan yard and shoe shop I could get out of debt in one or two years. If I could only have it pushed ahead for a year or two a <u>small</u> <u>fortune</u> could be made. I intend writing to Mr. Rogers to rush it ahead and if he can get leather out fast enough to employ another good shoe maker. He ought to have the Bark Mill running two thirds of the time and the yard kept all the time full of hides. I wish I know how much [tan?] bark our hands gathered last spring. Is Henry hauling bark? How much has he hauled and is there much under our sheds? Was much brought in from the neighborhood? That must be my dependence for getting out of debt. Caution Clarissa[52] about not wasting the provisions particularly the sugar and coffee. Tell her to use milk as much as possible. I would notice how much they consume in a week. The sugar and coffee ought to last until next June. Tell Mr. McCrevan not to lend out a pound of either sugar or coffee. I can't lend any for soon there will be none to be had. Coffee is selling at 33 1/3, sugar the commonest kind of wet dark sugar is selling for 16 cents per pound. Our sugar ought to be worth 20 cents, perhaps more, there is none of that kind to be had. You may sell that barrel if you wish, it would be much better to sell it as you could no doubt get 20c. Be sure and save enough to last us until June or July next McK___ owes me and tell Mr. McCreven to make him return it and not to pay for it. Tell Mr. McC also for me to make Clarissa saving with the coffee & sugar. You can easily sell the sugar in a month or two if not now and make whoever buys it pay you very soon. I find that my letter of yesterday was not mailed as I expected. I will get it and enclose the two in the same envelope thereby saving 5 cents. They must count as two letters. I will write again Monday. Give my love to all and many kisses to Fannie. I dreamed about you last night but I can't write what it was. I hope it soon comes to pass. Believe me my darling, most lovingly your husband

JOHN F. CALHOUN

52 Henry and Clarissa were married Negroes at Calhoun Mills

CAMP NEAR FAIRFAX CH, VA
August 18th 1861
No 12

My darling wife

I wrote to you on yesterday and sent the letter by The Rogers who went to Manassas in a wagon for articles that Dr. Hearst had purchased but had failed to reach us. I sent you enclosed a piece of Cedar from a tree cut down by one of the first cannons fired by the enemy on the morning of the 17th of July at our retreating Pickets. I was whittling upon the piece of cedar trying to make a pen staff and spoiled it and just thought I would send I to you as there was an association connected with it. Just one month from today we had the first battle on Bull Run and it was then and there I had the first cannon fired at me, the first shell to explode near me. I had a long conversation in Capt Brooks' tent yesterday evening with Captain JW Harrington[53] of Col Cash' Reg who was in the Battle of the 21st and he said that he was more alarmed on Thursday than he was during the battle of the 21st and remarked that we had more to stand facing the enemies batteries as we did than we would have had in the battle that he was not under fire more than half an hour in all on the 21st and we were bombarded all day. He said he doubted that we would ever get credit for what we did and the manner in which we acted. If you have read all the accounts in the papers of the battle, Hampton's[54] Legion gets more praise than any of the SC Regt's that is all humbug many suspect some of the officers in the Legion of getting up all of that humbug and praising themselves. Many of them ran one entire company so Capt H told me and they were awfully scattered in the fight and undoubtedly fought to a great disadvantage. Gen Beauregard dashed up and led them upon one occasion and no doubt they were faltering at that time. Sloan's Regt, the Georgia 8th, and Alabama 4th were exposed nearly all the time and fought if anything better than Hampton's Legion certainly to far better success and in better order. I bathed my feet last night and this morning I am feeling much better. I have had a cold for near two weeks. This morning is cloudy, damp and disagreeable. It has been an awful spell of weather. Another one of our men died in Richmond a

53 Captain J.W. Harrington of Company G, 8th Regiment South Carolina Volunteers. Served under Colonel E.B.B. Cash and had been ordered to Fairfax Court House, VA on August 14, 1861. *Kershaw's Brigade*, pp. 38, 565.

54 Lieutenant General Wade Hampton, III (1818-1902). Born in Charleston and spent his early life hunting, riding, and enjoying his family's summer estate in North Carolina called High Hampton. Graduated from South Carolina College and trained in law, but never practiced. Elected to the S.C. General Assembly in 1852 and served as a State Senator 1858-1861. Governor Francis Pickens made him a Colonel in the S.C. militia. He went on to organize and finance "Hampton's Legion" which included 6 infantry units, 4 cavalry units, and 1 artillery unit. After the war he re-entered politics serving as S.C. Governor and U.S. Senator. *Find Grave*. *Biographical Dictionary of the U.S. Congress*.

few days ago. Cook[55] from the Range I think making two from our company and Bosworth I suppose will die. It will be a long time before our Brigade will be ready for active service again. Captain Harrington says there are not more than 350 or 400 the outside in his Reg reported for duty so there must be near 500 unfit for duty. Some think that it will be two months or more before there will be any more fighting but that is mere guess work. It will no doubt be some time and I don't think they will ever make another advance in this direction; the next fighting will be in the western part of Virginia or near Occoquan[56] creek south of this. If I am to spend the winter here I think flannel drawers would be the best kind of drawers for me to wear. Don't you think so too my darling? If so make me two pair out of red flannel I feel sure that The will bring me a letter. It appears like five or six days since I received one from you, but upon examination I find that it has only been three. I note down the number of your letter and the day I receive it. You began numbering before I did and as well as I remember you had written or at least your 2 or 3 number had been recd before I had commenced numbering and I told you that I would not be behind very long. This is my 12th letter since I began numbering last and I have only recd your 6th when you had two or three the start of me so you see I more than double you darling but I don't doubt you in affection, do I my darling. No I am well assured of that fact. You are as true and devoted as any wife can be. I dreamed again about you last night and strange to say it was just the same as the other dream. Isn't that singular? But no, it is not either, it is very natural. I do hope for more than one reason that it may come to pass even in two months. Do you ever dream of me darling? If not I know you think often of me. Oh my darling how I long to see you years, years could not sever my affections from you. "Home sweet home there is no place like home." Sincerely can I express that sentiment. Mr. Carlisle has procured a furlough and will start home tomorrow and I will send this by him. I don't know how long he intends staying. If we are to remain long in the inactive state I expect many a one will try to get a furlough, but it is a very difficult matter to get one and perhaps it would be worse for us to spend ten or twelve days at home and then return to our post again then the parting again would be painful. What do you think of it darling? Many of the officers wives are with them some are at Culpepper some in Charlotte and others in Richmond. There are not more than two or three of the wives of any of the officers of our Regiment in Va. Suppose you come on to Charlotte[57] and assist the other ladies from SC in attending to the sick? I expect I would soon get sick and go down if you were there. You think you could nurse me well don't you?

55 Could be any of a number of Cook's in Company C, 7th South Carolina Volunteers. The "Range" refers to an area of old Abbeville District where the town of McCormick is now located. *Kershaw's Brigade*, p. 559.

56 Occoquan Creek (river), a tributary of the Potomac River. Bull Run creek enters it east-southeast of Manassas, VA.

57 Should be Charlottesville, VA.

A box of clothes from Abbeville reached the hospital a day or two ago and I looked at them and though you dear fingers did some of the sowing. There were two or three dark comforts in the box. It is getting a difficult matter to get sugar now. We have been drinking coffee for two day without sugar and now there is no coffee in the Commissaries department. Still now one grumbles or seems to mind it. We get accustomed to privations and hardships. We will get on some sugar and coffee in a few days I expect. The finest Irish potatoes I ever saw are raised in Va and they are so "mealy" and nice. Don't forget about writing me fully about my crop, corn, & peas when you go down again, and make arrangements about having any of our negroes who should take sick well attended to. I will now cease writing until The Rogers comes from Manassas for I feel sure he will bring a letter to me from you and I will reserve space to reply to it in the morning. Sunday night The brought me a letter from sure enough No 7 and you cant imagine the delight it gave me. Dr. Link came on with The. It will not have time to reply fully to your letter as I must finish tonight but I will write in a day or two and will reply more particularly. I know Fannie must indeed be sweet and smart. How I wish I could see her. If you have made my drawers save them and make me two pair of flannel drawers and there will be time enough to get them before winter. I am afraid cotton will be too cold. I will write you fully tomorrow and mail it the next day and both may then reach you by the same day. Give my love to all and give many kisses to Fannie an make her say "papa." I am writing by a miserable tallow candle and I can't half see. Do write often and long letters to your Most loving and Devoted Husband

JOHN F. CALHOUN

PS Monday Morning August 19th

It is raining still. I am nearly over my cold feel warm in the morning than any other time. You have never written whether or not my wheat box has been made and if mr. McC is giving any to the negroes. He ought to give them ½ allowance sometimes. Col Wynder[58] is the Col of the new SC Reg near us, an old classmate Tom Woodward[59] is Maj. I will write again tomorrow. Your constant and Devoted Husband

JFC

58 Colonel Charles Sidney Winder (1829-1862) . Appointed Colonel of the 6th South Carolina Volunteers in July 1861 and was Captain of Artillery prior. Had been promoted to Brigadier General when he killed at Cedar Mountain in August 1862. *Find a Grave*.

59 Major Thomas W. Woodward of 6th South Carolina Volunteers. Received serious wound at Dranesville in December 1861 and was dropped from the muster roll. Later returned as a quartermaster in Kershaw's Brigade. Woodward was a classmate of John Francis Calhoun at South Carolina College. *Kershaw's Brigade*, p. 576.

CAMP NEAR FAIRFAX C H, VA
August [20] 1861
No 14

My Dear Wife

I wrote to you this morning and as Dr. Link will start in the morning for home, I will have another ready in time to send by him. Mr. Carlisle started this morning for home on a furlough. He told me a few days ago that it was important for him to be with his wife about the first of September. What a good excuse to go home. I wish it was me, but I suppose it will not be my luck to obtain a furlough upon any such plea. This letter must necessarily be a very short one as I wrote this morning and I have nothing to write about this evening. I will send my two summer vests back by Dr. Link and in the pockets or among them you will find some pieces of that famous cedar tree and the large piece you can have made into something as a relic. The officers and men of the Brigade have used the tree entirely up, even to the ground, and in my leisure moments I made some pen handles &c. I expect Sam Link will go home with the Dr. It has cleared off at last and I am in hopes we will have clear weather for a while for it has been one of the longest rainy spells I ever saw. I requested Dr. Link to get me a few gallons of choice old Apple Brandy in Culpepper if he had time and take on as a present from me to your father. I don't know whether or not he will have time to shop there as he is to take charge of some of the sick from our Regt who will be sent there or to Richmond or Charlotte. I hope he can get the Brandy. I sent by him for five gallons if he can get that much and can carry it on with him conveniently. As Dr. Link will be fresh from the camp it will be unnecessary to write as fully as I would otherwise as you will soon hear all the particulars from our camp, rumors, &c &c. Send me a lock of Fannie's hair and the first opportunity have your and her Ambrotypes[60] taken and send on for me to look at in my lonely moments. Now don't forget. Do you need any more money, if so don't hesitate my darling to let me know and let me beg and insist that you deny yourself nor Fannie a thing that you need or want. My wife and child must have anything they want so long as I have a dollar. Have our negro shoes selected from the best of those we have on hand and I want Cupe[61] particularly to have a pair of those Mr. Chapman[62] made and if they are not all taken I don't care if you let all have a pair apiece of them. I am willing to pay 225 cents a pair for my negroes all around, get a pair for Cupe at any price they are worth $2.50 a pair. Those that I am wearing made by Mr. Chapman for Ed are the best shoes I ever wore. They have not commenced wearing out

60 Type of photograph made on glass. Replaced the Daguerreotype in the 1850's.

61 Cupe or Cupet was a Negro foreman or lead man at Calhoun Mills. Mentioned frequently.

62 Mr. Chapman was a shoemaker at Calhoun Mills.

and therefore I say that those negro shoes made from the best leather are worth 1.00 a pair more than the others and I am willing to pay that difference. I will now close for the night and finish in the morning.

Wednesday 21st A beautiful bright morning cool and clear. Memorable day just one month ago the great battle of Bull Run, or "Manassas Plains" as Gen Beauregard calls it, was fought. I will never forget the 21st and on the 24th my darling little Fannie will be one year old. I will think of you all of that day and on the 29th too. I wish I could send my Minnie rifle to your father, but I will carry it through the war and then it will be a more valuable relic. Brooks sent on to Columbia for a good pistol both for himself and for me and they are very nice- a strap goes around the shoulder, over the shoulder I mean throwing the weight on the shoulder. Zeke and Gib are both well. Sam is complaining but I think and others too that as Billy is going home he wants to get off too. You may think me childish in sending you little relics in the way of pen staffs &c. I merely send them, as I whittled them with my own hands and on account of the association connected with it. I intend going to the Battlefield and cutting a walking stick for your father as near some noted spot as possible where Bee, Bartow,[63] or Johnston fell, or where Beauregard led the Hampton Legion in their charge. If there are any relics that any of you wish let me know, for it is only once and awhile I think of any thing of the kind. Well I must now close as this will be enough for this time. I will write again in a day or two. Don't you think I write often enough my darling? Give my love to all and tell your father I said look for his letter about the last of this month. Many kisses to my sweet little Fannie and a world of ardent love to my own dear precious, darling wife from her own true, faithful, constant, and Devoted Husband

JOHN F. CALHOUN

---

63 General Bernard Elliott Bee (1824-1861). Born in Charleston, graduated from the U.S. Military Academy and served in the U.S. Army. Resigned his commission in March 1861 and joined the Confederacy as a Lieutenant Colonel. Was promoted to Brigadier General in June 1861 and sent to Manassas under the command of Joseph E. Johnston. Gave the nickname "Stonewall" to General Thomas J. Jackson. Bee was killed at the battle of 1st Manassas in July 1861. Bee Historical Marker Database. *Find a Grave. Kershaw's Brigade*, p. 63.
Colonel Francis Stebbins Bartow (1816-1861). Born in Savannah, GA and was local attorney turned politician. Served two terms in U.S. House of Representatives. Resigned from Congress, returned to Savannah and formed the Oglethorpe Light Infantry. Bartow and his unit were sent to Virginia where they fought in the battle of 1st Manassas. He was killed in action there in a gallant fight to assist General Bee's Brigade. *New Georgia Encyclopedia. Find a Grave. Kershaw's Brigade*, p. 63.

PS

I send a Haversack taken from the Battlefield. You can give it to Sam as a present from me or if you think it will suit you or Fannie you had better keep it and I will save the one I am using for Sam, there are Yankee marks about it.

Your own

CAMP NEAR FAIRFAX C H, VA
AUGUST 22D 1861
NO 15

My Dear Wife

I wrote to you on yesterday by Dr. Link and will write again today as the mail closes this evening at three o'clock and then there will be no opportunity of mailing a letter again before Monday. The Brigade mail arrangements are continually being changed, now the mail closes this evening before it starts to Manassas at three o'clock and then it lies over here until the following morning, so hereafter I must write my letters the day before I mail them that is when I depend upon the regular mail. Yesterday was clear nearly all day but this morning it is raining again. I never saw so much rain in my life. I am "officer of the day" and not having much to do excepting to wear my sword and sash as a distinguishing mark, I have determined to spend as much of my time as possible in my tent writing at least. I intend finishing this letter. I sent my two summer vests back by Dr. Link and also a Haversack left upon the Battlefield by the enemy. It may suit you to carry Fannie's clothes in, if so, you had better keep it. I wrote you to give it to Sam as a present from me, do so still unless it suits for what I mentioned. I have another which I will save for Sam if you want the one sent home. We have very encouraging news in from Missouri and if Gen McCollouch[64] has routed Gen Lyons as reported and Gen Hardee has taken Gen Ziegler[65] and command I think they will soon make peace. The Federalists have been defeated upon every hand and another defeat will end the war. I think particularly if we can draw Gen McClellan[66] out and get him to meet Gen Beauregard. He is their strongest general. There is no important war news now afloat, everything remains quiet and the camp is very dull, getting more and more so. I can't find material enough to fill up a letter with and write merely to let you know I am well. I am looking for a letter from you this evening but will not get it in time to reply

64 General Benjamin McCulloch defeated Union General Nathaniel Lyon the Battle of Wilson's Creek (Oak Hills) Missouri. Lyon was killed in this battle. *ORWR*, Vol III, Chapter X, pp. 104-107.

65 German born Union General Franz Sigel (1824-1902) lead the retreat from Wilson's Creek (Oak Hills) after General Lyon was killed. His career was filled with controversy . After the defeat at Wilson's Creek he was ridiculed as being, "superior in theoretical tactics, incompetent in battle, and hell in retreat." Although the Federals were defeated, Missouri remained in Union hands and Sigel was later promoted to Brigadier General. Confederate General Hardee had a small role in this battle. *ORWR*, Vol III, Chapter X, pp. 93-95.

66 Union General George B. McClellan (1826-1885) was commissioned Major General of Volunteers. He was opposed to any interference with slavery but opposed secession. He was made Major General of the Regular Army and outranked everyone except Winfield Scott. Always demonstrated extreme caution and consistently over-estimated enemy forces. After the Union defeat at 1st Manassas he was reluctant to mount further attacks along the Potomac. Lincoln relieved McClellan of his command in March of 1862. Two years later, McClellan ran against Lincoln as a Democrat while still in the Army. He resigned his commission on election day, November 8, 1864. *ORWR*, Vol V, Chapter XIV, p. 567. *Find a Grave*.

before the mail closes. Sam Harris was sent to Charlotte[sville] or one of the other hospitals yesterday evening he was only a little unwell and wanted to get off. Zeke and Gib are well. Our men I think are getting too fond of going to Charlotte, Richmond & as they are well provided for and fare well down there and when they get well and are discharged by the Surgeon they hang on and sometimes stay until they are sent after. Write to me a great deal about Fannie in every letter. Tell me all about her sweet little tricks. Does she know our ambrotype? Learn her whose it is and make her say my pa. I want her to be able to call me pa when I come home. Will you father permit you to whip her? Do you ever do it? It has cleared off again but is warm and looks like the rain is not yet over. Give my love to all and many kisses to my darling little Fannie. Write often and long letters my darling. It is half of my existence here and I am getting more and more anxious to get letters from you. It always seems a long time from the receipt of one letter to another. Good bye my darling.

Ever your Devoted Husband
JOHN F. CALHOUN

CAMP NEAR FAIRFAX C H, VA
AUGUST 23RD 1861
NO 16

My own darling wife:

I received a letter from you on yesterday evening dated "Gibert Mills Aug 12th No 8" and my darling it was a long interesting and affectionate letter and gave me much pleasure. I am sorry one of my letters enclosing the one to Mr. McCrevan did not reach you, however by this time I hope it has been recd. I am glad to hear that my corn and peas are very good and hope that I may yet make a good crop and I am also truly glad to learn that your father has such a good crop. I shall look anxiously for his letter and hope that mine may reach him before he closes his letter. Tell Carie I am truly glad to learn that my letter reached her safely and that she intends replying to it soon. The Rogers received a letter from Mrs. Rogers dated the 16th and she writes him that the check he sent had reached here so I suppose mine went safe as they were both mailed together and went the same rout[e]. I am sorry you think Nettie can never be gentled and as soon as the colt is large enough to wean if you sell her for the sum I gave, do so. Mr. Porcher might engage to buy her in the fall. I hope Mr. Rogers will engage another tanner immediately. I wrote to him requesting him to see that everything was rushed ahead. Ben Andrews wrote me a doleful letter about the way things were carried on complaining all the way through of Mr. McCrevan his never going to the field, permitting the negroes to do as they please, and waste the sugar, coffee and everything, meddling with the tan yard and causing the tanner to become dissatisfied and customers to leave &c. He says the customers want him to superintend &c &c. I write this to show you what a grumbling malicious rascal he is. He you know he was always letting me some thing to annoy me and now he thinks if he can succeed in running Mr. McCrevan off he will be superintendent and Mrs. Andrews can be mistress of the house. I understand him perfectly and like him far less for his tale baring. I am fully satisfied that everything is not carried on as I could wish and as it was when I was there and no doubt I would find great complaint, still, I don't believe it is near as bad as he represents and the motive is another thing I look at. He says the coffee is nearly out. I don't believe it for you have been going down every week and of course examine in to everything of the kind and can tell whether or not they wasting or not. I bought 50 lbs of coffee in Jan, the middle we recd it and you and I drank tea nearly all the time until I entered the Army. I would look into these things and if you find that they are squandering I should tell Mr. McCrevan very plainly about it. Tell Cupet that I hear they are neglecting things. I may slip home sometime when they are not expecting me and I will remember those who are unfaithful. It will be well to give them a caution, I am very fearful my affairs are not going well and I am truly sorry that nothing can induce my own father to take an interest in my business. I regret deeply and am ashamed and mortified to think that he seems so insensible of my promp[t] discharge of duty in volunteering at the first call involved as I was in debt, but dedicating myself and my all to the service of my country to sustain the reputation of an honored name. I thought he would appreciate the act and that whilst I was periling life upon the field of battle he would at least assist me in my pecuniary affairs. Attention is all I have asked to my affairs. Let Ida see this I don't care a cent. Poor men are even lending and giving, some half of their yearly income to the Government to aid in carrying on the war. And knowing my situation as he does, I thought it was doing but little to aid and overlook my affairs and write to me occasionally about it.

Saturday evening August 24th

The mail this evening brought me you letter of the 15th No 9 containing the note of Idas. I was so delighted to get it and was greatly cheered by it. Ida mentioned that the check had been received but said nothing about the $10. I suppose it was received as you received those the same mail. You have done wisely about the shirts and drawers in making them out of thick flannel, however if the calico is suitable make me two or three for if the winters are as cold as I hear they are I will sometimes wear two flannels shirts and a calico one over them. I am glad to hear we have had an abundance of rain and from the way you write your father must have an excellent crop and I am truly glad to hear it and hope the yield may even exceed his expectations. I don't know that I feel a greater desire for my own fathers success than for yours. The better I know your father the better I like him and I feel sure that he loves me and feels as much interested in me as if I were his own child and I look upon his [*sic*] nearly as my own father, your mother also. I expect he loves Fannie today better than he does any of you for she is the youngest child. So he intends giving her a silver cup. We must name the next child after either your father or mother as the case may be I hope a son. You must not forget to send me a lock of Fannie's hair and I will preserve it and carry it in my pocket book. I know she must be smart and I will say pretty notwithstanding her red hair. I know it is not red but Auburn. She is pretty any way. General Bradley and Dr. Hearst borrowed Col Fair's horses and visited the battle field today and the Gen according to my request cut me a cedar walking stick for your father and he said it was cut upon the part of the field where General Bee was killed, the nearest tree to the spot where he fell. It is not a very pretty stick but the Gen said the best he could get. I will leave it long with the [g[nots and everything just as it was cut and the first opportunity will send it on to your father. I will get letters enough next week, two from you and one from you father. I suppose Carie will not write until the next week. It seems that very frequently two of my letters reach you by the same mail. Do you often receive one by each of the three weekly mails? I have written often enough the last three weeks for you to get one every mail. Tell Ida that I will write to her soon but she must not wait every time for me to reply for she has much more time, as we are now drilling twice a day again. I am glad you did not mention anything to your Aunty about Zeke's conduct for it would mortify and distress her as you say. He is now entirely well and satisfied and doing well again. I kept him from getting the discharge that he was applying for, I talked very plainly to him and he saw that my patience had been exhausted and that I was done with him. He was no doubt mad, in fact I heard that he was but he said nothing about it to me and got over it all very soon and may thank me for keeping him from nearly disgracing himself. I will still try and keep him straight. He and Gib are both well. They are with The on Pickett duty. Cothran and I are alone in our tent tonight both writing to our wives with the point of a bayonet in the ground the socket acting as a candle stick. The officers have two tents now between them. I do not know who mailed my letter in Cheraw. Some one I suppose that I sent it by to mail on the way to SC and they forgot to mail it at the proper place. This is Fannies birthday and I have thought offten often [*sic*] of you today and just about this hour 8oclock I first beheld my first child. Yes at this hour one year ago I was seated by your bed side and now I am far, far away. Say nothing about what I wrote about Father's not taking enough interest in my affairs. I was rather low-down at the time and am sorry that I wrote anything about it. The weather is quite cool here and the mornings feel cool enough for frost. I sleep under two blankets every night. I fall to sleep nearly every night thinking of you and Fannie and I will now cease writing and prepare for bed and hope I will dream of you my own darling wife. I will finish this in the morning. Good night and may guardian angels watch over you my darling and my sweet little daughter. Sunday morning August 25th This is a beautiful bright sunny morning and I have just risen from my blankets after a good nights sleep. I will finish this letter to send of[f] this evening. Darling I wish you to make me a thick comfort and send on for the blankets are not long enough. You can have many opportunities before fall. I am needing a vest very much and hope you will soon send one on. If you have any chance send word to Jim Shehto to send down my uniform to you and you can make it well enough. He will not get the cloth before the 1st of Sept I don't expect. Our little Fannie has now entered her second year bless her dear little heart, how I wish I could see her. Give my love to all and many kisses to Fannie. Everything is quiet and there is very little news. I will write again the middle of the week and then the last. Good bye my darling wife, write often to you Ever fond and devoted Husband

JOHN F. CALHOUN

CAMP NEAR FAIRFAX, VA
Aug 27, 1861
No 17

My Dear Wife

I received you[r] last, No. 9 a few days since and replied to it, and I write today not that I have anything of importance to write but because I have promised to write three times a week and I intend doing so whenever I can if it is merely to let you know that I am well. The dullest time we have yet had is just at the present juncture. and as to news there is none. We have commenced having Brigade drill and the evolutions of the line is something new to me. On yesterday evening was our first drill, and I thought all of our Cols as green as any of the company officers in fact more so for the Cols were merely acting somewhat like a Captain on Battalion drill and the Capts in the capacity of Lieuts. Bonham did far better than I expected. The four Regiments of our Brigade were all out, and when they were first mustered into service they numbered 38 and we only had 12 or/300 yesterday. Ours was the largest Regiment by at least a full company. Today we had a miniature imitation and I had the command of Company C and as Capt Brooks' Company was not out, I had the color company and he sent to his camp for his colors and color guard and attached them to our company. Capt Bradley seldom drills. Cothran and I have it to do, all of our company officers do not appear upon drills not once in twenty times. I have just rec'd a letter from you dated Sunday 18, No 10 and one from aunt Lou same date directed by JLC to Fairfax CH. Who authorized him to direct to Fairfax? It reached me sooner by that route but I don't know how how (sic) [long] we may be here. I will write on tomorrow or next day and reply fully to your letter. I am writing with a gold pen and I can't bear to write with one. Give my love to all and many kisses to Fannie. Most Devotedly your own loving husband

J.F. CALHOUN

CAMP NEAR FAIRFAX C. H. VA
AUGUST 29, 1861
NO 18

My dear wife:

I received you[r] last letter dated Sunday 18th No 10 on the 27th and I replied to it on the same day, and as it is my birthday I will write again. Have you forgotten that this is my birthday, and did you think often of me? I might know my darling without asking that you did. I received a letter from Ed written from Willington, in which he says that he has had another attack of Liver complaint, but he says he intends coming on as soon as he gets stout and well I have written to him advising him not to come if his health is not good for we have hardships to undergo sometimes and a winter campaign will be severer still, so it is no place for one subject to such a disease. Should you have anything to send to me you can send by some from our company who have gone home on furlough....several from the neighborhood of Calhoun Mills. Brown, Brough and Lyons, and I expect Sam Link has gone on. They will start back between the 10th and 15th of Sep. Get your father to inquire. Don't forget to inquire when they start and send the shoes that I wrote you to send me. Our forces are being ordered forward gradually so as to confine the enemy to the Potomac. Elzey's[67] Brigade is entrenching Chestnut Hill which is in two and a half miles of the chain Bridge across the Potomac, and Gen Longstreet's Brigade is now at Falls Church, and the whole army this side of Manassas is moving forward. Gen Bonham's Brigade, this time is being held in reserve having been always in the advance before this. We have just received orders to be ready to move forward as Gen Beauregard has rec'd a dispatch from Gen Longstreet[68] saying that he would be attacked today or tomorrow but I expect it will be like all our rumors. The enemy are lining up very fast on the Potomac and of course they don't want to go back on the other side but wish to come out several miles on this side, so I expect Gen Beauregard's plan is to keep them confined to the Potomac. Our forces will

67 Arnold Elzey (1816-1871). Born in Maryland, graduated from the U. .S Military Academy in 1837. He was commander of the Augusta, GA arsenal in 1861. When Georgia seceded, he surrendered the arsenal to the Confederates and resigned his commission. Elzey went to Richmond and joined the Confederacy with General Kirby Smith. When Smith was wounded, Elzey took up the command and was battle field promoted to Brigadier General for his service at 1st Manassas by President Jefferson Davis. *Find a Grave. ORWR*, Vol II, Chapter IX, p. 496.

68 General James Longstreet (1821-1904). Born in Edgefield, SC. Attended school in Augusta, GA and later the Academy at West Point, graduating in 1842. Appointed Brigadier General on June 17, 1861 and reported to General Beauregard in Manassas. He was one of the Confederacy's foremost generals serving under Robert E. Lee as Corps Commander. Said to have served in the wedding of Union General U.S. Grant and Julia Dent, Longstreet's 4th cousin. *Encyclopedia Virginia. Find a Grave.*

extend several miles on the river, and will entrench and then advance and entrench again, and in this way we may get entire possession of all on this side of the river, but no one knows Gen Beauregard's plans. It drizzled rain all day yesterday and today it looks like it will rain all day again. I received a letter from Rosa[69] on the 27th in which she said that she would write to you in a few days. You must reply to her letter promptly. Aunt Lou[70] wrote me a long and interesting letter a few days ago. She seems fond of us. She said Fannie was smart, pretty and cunning as a monkey and petted by everybody. The box has not yet reached us but will in a day or two I expect if you started it on Thursday as you expected when you wrote to me. I am looking for a letter from your father by the next mail and then in a week or two from Carie. Every letter that I wrote when I wrote to her has been answered. Aunt Lou and Rosa by the same mail, and in Aunt L's reply she says "Your very kind letter I received some two weeks ago" so Carie has permitted my letter to remain unanswered at least three weeks already and may leave it three or four more for aught I know. Give my love to Aunt L and tell I will write to her as soon as I can have time. We may be very busy for some time, moving, entrenching &c so that I may not have much time for a while. Zeke and Gib are both well, Sam I have not heard from he is still at some of the hospitals. Give my love to all and many kisses to my darling little Fannie. Write often my darling to your Fond and loving Husband

J. F. CALHOUN

69 Rosa Calhoun, sister of John Francis Calhoun. She was 13 years old at this time. *Calhoun Family Genealogy.*

70 Louisa (Jones) Calhoun was the wife of Francis Augustus Calhoun, aunt and uncle of John Francis Calhoun. *Calhoun Family Genealogy.*

FLINT HILL, FAIRFAX, VA
AUGUST 31ST 1861

My own darling wife

I received two letters from you yesterday, one in the box. No 11. August 21 the other No 12. Aug 22. I am so glad the box of clothes came and I am very much pleased with all my clothes although my vest which I needed most is entirely to short. I will not be able to wear it. I suppose you forgot and cut it by The R's pattern and I am at lease half a head taller, his vest is even too short, still as his pants are long waisted he can wear it. My vest will not do for me, so get some cloth of the same kind if you can and make it exactly like the other one, buttons and all and send to me by John Brown or some of our men. Make the vest at least one and a half inches longer and a very little larger as I will have on thick undershirts in the winter and it is full tight now. I am so sorry it is too small for it does not look like a home made vest. It is so nicely made and I am very much obliged to your mother for making it. I regret it not fitting me on her account nearly as much as my own. I will take care of it and bring it back to your father or Sam, it will fit either of them. I expect I have not tried on my drawers but I like them very much. I suppose they are larger than The's his are rather light for him. My pants fit beautifully, no fault shirts as were socks too. I have on a pair now. I wish I had four pair of them. Make me two or three flannel shirts long nearly all the ready made shirts are too short. The shoes Ben Andrews sent me are too tight across the toes. I have sold them, tell him to make me a pair immediately and make them broader across the toes and not across the eye seams and not so large in the heels, my foot slips up, or at least my heel slips up in them. The soles are just right, heels too high. I want the stoutest calf skin and tell him to double it so as to make them as near water proof as possible. Send them when you send the other things. The express company charged $7.70 for delivering the box at our tent. All will divide the expenses. My darling I was delighted to get such an affectionate letter as you wrote me and sent in the box. I did my heart good to read and I read it over two or three times and intend reading it again. I am glad that your father received my letter and shall anxiously await his reply and hope to get a letter from Carie before I return home. I don't doubt that she loves me, but some love when it puts them to no trouble. I prize the little lock of hair which you sent me of Fannies. It is by no means red. It will be nearly black when she is grown. I kissed the precious little lock and folded it in a piece of paper and put it in my pocket book. I am surprised at William Tennent not volunteering when his wife is so anxious that he should. As for Aleck I am not at all surprised at him, just what I would expect of him. I expect we will soon have to pay 10 cents soon on all letter from Va to SC. I will write just as often as I would if it was three cents, although it is so dull here now that I find it difficult to write three pages every time. The letter paper and envelopes were received and I very much gratified that you thought of me. I would send again to Mr. Burt and tell him to take away his pigs. I want them away and if they are not already taken away tell Mr. McCreven I want them separated immediately and let Mr. Burt know that I will not be responsible for them. You ought to remove anything that you don't wish them to consume at the Mills. Don't let them use your sperm candles make them use tallow. Don't be backward in examining into everything at the Mills. It is your right and duty. Ask Mr. McCrevan how much wheat do they use weekly, negroes I mean. Tell him to have oats saved for me to feed on in the spring and I want 30 or 40 bushels of seed saved. I am afraid but little good fodder was saved this season as there has been so much rain. Will there be much hay? Ask your father. How are our potatoes? I must close I will write again in two or three days. Give my love to all and many kisses to Fannie. Thank you for making my vest and Mrs. Rogers for her kindness. Tell her I will take care of Mr. Rogers. Thank your aunt Betsy and love to her and aunty & all. Gib, Zeke are well. Write soon to your most loving and devoted husband.

JOHN F.C.

September 1861

FLINT HILL, NEAR FAIRFAX C H
Sept 2nd 1861
No 20

My own darling wife:

I received your last letter on the 30th of Aug. and replied to it on the 31st and as you always expect three letters from me every week, I suppose I must continue to write three a week to prevent my dear little wife from being disappointed although I should not be surprised if I did not get to soon writing only two a week, as everything is quiet and dull here and when the weather turns cold it will be inconvenient to write unless we go into winter quarters and build huts. The weather is getting quite cool, but the days are still warm. The nights are cool enough to sleep under three blankets and if it increases until the middle or last of Nov I don't know how I can stand the winter. Make my flannel shirts thick, loose and long. If it gets too cool I will wear two flannel shirts at a time. What you have to send, you can send by William Darricott[71] who went off sick and we heard he went home on furlough. I received a letter from Sallie[72] a day or two since. She said that Ed was in bed and requested her to write to me saying that he was in bed sick with what he feared was liver complaint – but still intended coming on in two weeks if he was able to come by that time. I wrote to her and advised that Ed would abandon the idea of coming if his health was not good, for the camp was no place for an invalid. Ed wrote that my corn was good, and everything going on very well. He said that he counted fourteen – 14 large shoats that I would have to kill. Surely if they are attended to they will make bacon enough. I will kill the three old sows and perhaps save two or three of the smallest of the shoats if I think them too small to kill this fall. Tell Cupet to be sure and attend to them closely and let nothing happen to them. Tell Mr McCrevan that when any of the negroes are sick to send for the Dr. I don't want any of them to be sick and have no attention. Give any directions you may think proper about it or anything else. You must not stand back like nothing belongs to you. It is all yours my darling so order everything as you wish. Tell Clarissa I have heard several times that she is getting lazy and careless and was wasting the sugar, coffee and everything. I have heard that she had not attended to things as I directed. I heard that she let the garden run away with grass &c. Tell her I know how they are doing and if I ever get home I intend settling up with all of them

71 William Tennent, 1st cousin of John Francis Calhoun and from the Willington area. Aleck Houston, brother- in- law of William Tennent. *Calhoun Family Genealogy.*

72 Sallie Smarr Tilman (Calhoun) wife of Edwin Calhoun, John Francis Calhoun's brother. *Calhoun Family Genealogy.*

according to their deserts. Tell Cupe I don't want to ever hear of his being unfaithful. I hear often, tell him from home and some that I had confidence in are not doing as I expected. Our troops are drawing nearer and nearer the Potomac. they frequently see Washington from a high hill on this side of the river. I heard the federalists took two Batteries and 500 prisoners on the coast in NC[73] a few days since, very unfortunate, but it will make us more watchful and this keeps them from taking some place of more importance. How many pair of socks did you send me? I only got two pair, you said you would send four. Give my love to all and many kisses to my darling little daughter. Zeke and Gib are well. I got Gib the appointment of Corporal a few days since. Write soon my own precious wife to your Ever devoted Husband

JOHN F. CALHOUN

PS Let Mr Burt know his pigs are old enough to wean and he must take them away. They may die or something happen and then it would be my loss. Don't forget and attend to it immediately. It ought to have been attended to long ago. Yours

Tuesday night September 3, 1861

The mail from Manassas was brought in late this evening and to my great joy I received two letters. I may say three. One from Carie dated Aug 26 one from your father dated 27 and enclosed in same was one from you, No 13 dated 27 and mailed 29th. We were all seated at supper and as soon as I finished I retired to my tent and read them. I opened them before I lighted my candle and took up yours first. I was indeed greatly cheered reading those three letters and feel if anything in better spirit than I have been in for a long time. You say you received No 10 & 11 of my letters and then no more until you received the one sent by Dr. Link No 14. I have no doubt the other two have been rec'd before this. You did not say whether or not you had rec'd the Haversack and my two summer vests which I sent by Dr. Link. I suppose of course he carried all safe. I am glad to learn the tanner has returned and hope everything will be rushed ahead. It is a fine time for making money on the tan yard and shop. I of course would not expect the damaged shoes sold any higher than such an article is worth at home. I was too high. I mentioned what shoes were bringing here. I have such poor light to write by that I will wait until morning and then finish my letter so good night my own darling wife.

73 Surrender of Confederate coastal Forts Hatteras and Clark at Cape Hatteras on August 28-29, 1861. Heavy fire from Union warships off the North Carolina coast forced the surrender of these two forts and the capture of more than 600 prisoners. *ORWR*, Vol IV, Chap XIII, pp. 592-593, 637.

WEDNESDAY MORNING SEPTEMBER 4, 1861

I will now finish my letter to you my darling and send it off today. Fannie must be sweet and smart. I can scarcely realize that I have a daughter walking and talking, bless her heart. How I wish I could see her. I hear Carie and Edward Yarbrough are taking on at a great rate, visiting together &c. Tell her she is too young yet a while to think of marrying is that is their notion. That accounts for her not writing me sooner. From what your father writes I will make more than enough corn and if my shoats continue to improve, I will have more pork than we can consume. Tell Cupet to watch them closely and he must go over once a week, call them up and give them some corn so as to gentle them. He must count them every week. See that the wheat is not wasted, that together with my corn should my Graves place make 450 bushels and the low ground which your father did not see 100. We ought to have 150 bushels, more than enough to do us. I want a quantity of peas gathered. Have you had old Ben to make those baskets for gathering peas? See that the baskets are ready in time and get your father to select some place for gathering the peas. Ask him to see if the upper part of the carriage house won't do. It can be fixed, it may also need covering, if so, Mr. McC could get old Ford[74] to make enough boards in a short time. You have never written to me where my wheat is kept. I wrote two or three times to know if Mr. McC had a wheat box made. Do let me know. Tell him to give the mill hands half allowance of wheat as I hear that there is a great deal of wheat on hand. I want them to have it anyway. Have you ever rec'd our negro cloth from the factory? You can take half if you wish and sell what you don't want. I am very glad to hear your father has such a good crop. He will no doubt make a year and a half supply of corn. Tell him by all means to clear 20 or 25 acres on the branch where he made a commencement. He ought not to plant any but good fresh land having as much good woodland to clear. He has one grand child now and there is no telling how many there are behind. Fannie is merely a beginning. Tell him to clear up 10 acres for little Andrew, in prospective and so on every once in a while I will not have time in this to reply fully but will wait until the next mail. Tell your father I read his letter with much interest and will reply soon. I am glad he wrote so fully as he did about the crops and everything, just as I wanted and I knew he would. Tell Carie I am truly obliged to her for her kind letter and I will reply soon. But in the meantime let me beg as I did before of her not to wait for a reply but to write again if she cares anything for me. Troops are still passing on towards the Potomac. I heard cavalry and infantry and some said artillery passing for some time last night after we had gone to bed. We are still here and may be intended for one of the divisions or

74 Old Ben and Old Ford were Negroes at Calhoun Mills.

columns to cross the river into Maryland. Some great movement is on foot, I am sure, we are on the eve of some great event which will shake the world to its center. The death struggle is near at hand, and from the late timid conduct of the Lincoln government, they are backing down. They dread us, no one however can tell what is to be done, but I am sure something will soon take place. Give my love to your father, mother, Carie and Sam and many kisses to my sweet little daughter. Make her say "Pa." Love to your uncle and aunty and tell him I am much obliged for the share in the grapes. Love to Ida and tell her to write to me. You write often my darling and I love you more for it, my own darling precious wife.

Fondly your own devoted Husband
JOHN F. CALHOUN

FLINT HILL, NEAR FAIRFAX CH, VA
SEPTEMBER 9TH, 1861
NO 24

My Own Darling Wife

Whilst at supper this evening, mail was brought in and a letter handed to me from the dearest thing being on earth to me, my own loved Rebecca, a kind and loving wife she is too, I am happy and proud to say. My darling I can but think that we must love each other more fondly and tenderly than most husbands and wives, do you not think so? I regret very much that you should ever be disappointed in not receiving a letter from me when you expect one and I will write three or four times a week until I get a reply to this and in your reply let me know how often must I write. As you now have your own and my postage to pay, it will be wise to write only twice a week particularly as there is no excitement or any prospects of any movement soon. Again it seems that when I write three times a week two of my letters reach you by the same mail. Don't you think under the circumstances two letters a week will do? I am willing to write every day my darling if it will be any gratification to you love. Anything on earth to make my dear wife, anything, to add to her happiness. My dreams about you are always pleasant and as to yours you know they go by contraries. I am glad to hear that you dream so often about me, it shows that you think often of me. I am glad to hear that my vests reached you safely, but am truly sorry that you did not get the haversack. I cautioned Dr. Link about it and Sam too. Billy Harris and the Dr. had their lunch in it and I cautioned all about it, Billie's boy Charles too. He may have taken it. Ask the Dr. and Sam Link both about it and find out what became of it and if Billie's boy has it you can get some of the family to get it. I wish you could get it as it was a very nice one indeed. I have heard that James Wideman has purchased the cloth for our uniforms. Dr. Hester made a "slow trip" this can excede nine out of ten. Wait until ---- ----- never mind now, you know sweetness. Your father is perhaps insisting upon my needing wool socks. I do not like them but the weather is so intensely cold that they may suit me best. I could make out with two pair, three anyway, to wear over my others in very cold weather. Sometimes the Potomac is frozen so hard that wagons cross backwards and forwards for a long time, so the citizens say, so you see I have cold weather to pass through. My darling I am getting more and more anxious to see you too. It will be four months since I saw you on the 23rd of this month and just to think of passing through two or three months of absence from your tender embrace. It must be endured my country demands it, and I will be thankful if we may be permitted to see safely even then. I would like to see Fannie trying to walk. Teach her to be smart. Is she growing? How large and fat? We had a long and fatiguing Brigade drill this evening. I commanded a company but only six or eight of Company C., some from Captain Brooks and Hards[75] Co. Gen Bonham complimented us highly and said he was gratified that it was witnessed by one who stood high in the military line in SC, Col I. D. Wilson.[76] Three cheers were given for him and for Bonham. All is quiet here and it is impossible to form an idea of what is to be done. It does seem the enemy are completely cowed or they would not let us remain in sight of their Capitol. I think they will try to annoy the southern coasts with their fleet. I feel sure they will never try to invade us as they did before, not through this country anyway. Delay will injure them much more than it will us so we can lose nothing by inactivity.

Sep 10th This is a beautiful bright morning and I hope will continue so. Capt Hester told me yesterday that he wanted a pair of my pigs if he ever got home, so take care of Bess. Zeke got a letter from home last evening. He and Gib are both well. Send me a pair of wool gloves. I will write again on the 12th and 14th. Give my love to all, many kisses to Fannie. Write often and long letters to your Constant and Devoted Husband

JOHN F. CALHOUN

We have been at this camp just four weeks this evening and nothing of any importance has happened. I heard heavy firing to-day towards the chain bridge, cannonading is of such frequent occurrence that it produces but little or no excitement. J.H. Wideman the Agent of our company to whom is entrusted the selecting of cloth and having a uniform made for our company writes that he has the cloth and will get Shelito to cut and make the officers uniforms and sent them to the Ladies sewing Societies as patterns to have the others made by. Some Tailor in his neighborhood will cut out all of the privates uniforms. Ours will have shoulder straps &c put on here I expect. Have we a good stand of turnips? If not they can be trans-planted, have it attended to. How much and when are they planted? How is the corn in the bottom neart to the Tan yard looking? Are there many pumpkins? How did the sugar cane for forage turn out?

Sept 9 I have asked so many questions in my letter that you will not answer half I am afraid so I will stop. Zeke and Gib are both well. Give my love to your father, mother, Sam and Carie, your uncle and aunty. Tell Carie I heard sure enough of her courting and it accounts for her neglecting me as she did. I will try in future to give her less trouble. Kiss Fannie and teach her to say "pa". Howdy to all the negroes. Tell Mr. Andrews to teach Henry to

75 Lieutenant J.S. Hard, Company F, 7th South Carolina Volunteers. *Kershaw's Brigade*, p. 557.

76 Isaac D. Wilson of Darlington District SC, a signer of the Ordinance of Secession.

cut and to make <u>fine</u> <u>sewed</u> shoes. Write often my darling to your own Fond and loving Husband

JOHN F. CALHOUN

FLINT HILL, NEAR FAIRFAX CH
September 11, 1861
No 25

My Darling Wife

Ed arrived today looking somewhat badly but says he is feeling much better than he has felt in several weeks. He brought me a letter from you to which I will reply tonight my love. I am glad to hear everything is getting along so well at the mill, and, from what Ed tells me I will make a good crop of corn and peas. He reports my stock looking finely, the colt a perfect beauty for which he says he will now give me $100. Ed says from what Mr. Mitchel[77] said to him he thought he would give $250 for Nettie. I am willing for him to take her at that price as soon as the colt is large enough to wean. Ed says Mr. McCrevan has my wheat in the mill and stirs it to prevent weevils, if your father thinks that will do you need not have it put in the wheat box but have it fixed with hinges etc. Surely Mr. Andrews and Henry will book upwards of $2000 this year, and surely several hundred dollars worth of leather will be sold we ought to book near $3000. Ed is a noble hearted fellow. He said that he only owed 4 or $500 and he would make enough at fathers to pay that beside 20 or 25 bales at Mr. Tilmans[78] and he told father he might have it appropriated to my debts. I will be able to get out easily now unless some misfortune happens. If Mr. Burt sends for his pigs and does not pay you soon, remind him of it for I paid cash for them. Capt Hester told me again today that he wanted to engage a pair. He said Dr. Yarborough[79] had pigs and was greatly pleased with them. So take good care of Bess, you can dispose of them as fast as you can raise them. Dear little Fannie, she must indeed be sweet and will be mischievous and I hope I may be permitted to see her in two months. Tell your mother that it would indeed be most gratifying to me to have her write to me and the reason I did not request her to write was that I did not think she would write. Tell her to write to me and I assure her that it will be highly appreciated and it will be immediately answered. I will certainly expect a letter now. Tell Carie I will reply to her letter soon, all my time is taken up in writing to you my darling but I will occasionally take time to write to a few others. Ed says father seems to take more interest in my business than in his own. I will write to him to sell Nettie and if you wish a buggy horse before I come home my darling, you have only to intimate it. I think I ought to buy one for you as old Charley is getting old and you are living with your parents. Then they might have the use of their horse. What do you think of

77 Edward Mitchel, farmer and resident of Willington, SC.

78 Edward Tilman, father- in- law of Edwin Calhoun. Tilman died in 1855, but his widow (Catherine Calhoun Tilman) was able to keep the family farm. She died in 1887. *Calhoun Family Genealogy.*

79 Dr. Yarborough of Wilington, SC, father of Edward Yarborough, who had been courting Rebecca's sister Caroline (Carie). Mentioned in letter of September 3rd.

it? Remember darling anything that we have and your parents may need, let them have. Should they wish any sugar let them have our barrel and let your mother have a supply of our table salt. Our cows ought to be turned in with fathers cattle occasionally. I want to raise more Durhams. How many pigs have we? Can I have those three sows fattened in time to kill this winter? Even by the first of January? I want about 15 or 18 pigs to turn in my pasture when I open it in Oct and if I haven't that many buy me enough to make the number. How many stacks of fodder did Mr. McCrevan gather? How much oats have we on hand? I am much obliged to you for the cotton it is fine but the zipporah not so fine as the other. Tell Ida I am much obliged to her for the cap, it will be the very idea for winter. I will reply to her letter soon. If Sallie is in the neighborhood give my love to her and tell her I will take good care of Ed. You need not knit me any gloves. Ed gave me a thick warm pair out of cashmere. I am writing at night and will finish in the morning.

Thursday 12th It rained hard last night but this morning is bright and clear. Ed gave me a vest that he had been wearing so if you have not made me one you need not do so. Keep it until I come as I will not need it soon. Give my love to all and many kisses to Fannie. Write regularly as you have been darling to your fond and loving husband.

JOHN F. CALHOUN

FLINT HILL, NEAR FAIRFAX CH
September 13, 1861
No 26

My Darling Wife:

I have received and answered the letter which you sent the 4th inst by Ed and will write again this week making four that I have written with the last six or seven days. Now my darling, have I not written often enough? Too often I expect, and in writing so often you will not certainly expect me either to write long or interesting letters. In future I think two long letters a week will be entirely satisfactory will it not? Times are hard, postage high, news scarce but love as abundant and sincere as ever, so if you desire, I will continue writing three times a week. Ed wrote to Sallie and directed to Mt. Carmel on yesterday and received one from her this evening with a short slip from Ida. He wrote to Mrs. Tilman this morning. I commenced a letter to Ida yesterday but did not finish it so I will postpone writing until the 15th when I will be in command of a detachment from our company of picket and will have ample time to write to Ida, Carie and the "idol of my heart." I forgot to mention in my last that Ed brought two comforts, one for me so you need not send any. He gave me a thick warm pair of woolen gloves knit from cashmere wool. You need not send me any. We are still going on in the same old way, no news, everything dull, no prospect for a battle but a fine prospect for a long stay at this place. As I said before it is impossible to form any idea as to future but from the signs of the times I cannot think that the enemy intend trying another invasion. They will annoy our coasts, make sudden attacks upon exposed points, pilfer and try to starve us into submission. There was a small battle if the enemy stood it for long enough to dignify it by that term a day or two since at Louisville.[80] About 3000 of the enemy were hovering about there selecting an encampment so it is said in order to escape the sickness in this present camp on the Potomac when three or four companies of infantry one or two of cavalry and four or five pieces of artillery under the command of Col Stuart[81] of the cavalry met them fired upon them drove them from the place killing five or six taking a few prisoners, guns etc. The confederates did not loose a man....the enemy retreating at the first fire. There is little skirmishes continually taking place but of so little consequence I rarely think of mentioning them. They are of daily occurrence nearly and produces no excitement. I received the notes which you sent in your letter. If I can't get $250 for Nettie

80 Skirmish at Lewisville, [WEST] VA on September 11, 1861. *ORWR,* Vol V, Chapter XIV, pp. 183, 184.

81 James Ewell Brown "Jeb" Stuart (1833-1864). Born in Virginia and graduated from West Point in 1854. Resigned from the U.S. Army when Virginia seceeded. He was the commander of the Confederate cavalry in VA.. Stuart was a master at reconnaissance and the use of cavalry in supporting offensive military operations. Was mortally wounded in the Battle of Yellow Tavern (outside of Richmond) in May of 1864. *Encyclopedia Virginia. Find a Grave.*

what say you to keeping her and raising another colt? It would pay us well for the one she has now would bring us $200 in a year if it continues to improve. I do not wish the colt weaned until the middle of October or later if your father thinks it better. Have you asked Capt Rogers to save me those two pigs that I wrote to him about? Tell him not to forget them and if there are any half-breeds at home suitable tell him to select a pair in exchange. I am anxious to get a cross between my Chester and the Essex. Ed says Jim is a very fine hog, far ahead of Billy, father's hog. Don't forget to have a grazing lot sowed for your colt and calves for spring. Whenever the hands have leisure, ask Mr. McCraven if they had not better thrash out some oats for seed. If your father wishes any he can have them. Ed says he and father both want some of the kind that I got from Capt Sale, they won't [shatter?]. Your father ought to have some of them saved for himself. Which kind of the wheat does your father like the best? Have some of the white Lams wheat ground up for your mother. Do you wish me to subscribe again to the Dispatch, if so, let me know. We have a band now and the nine o'clock drums have just beat tattoo and the band always plays two or three pieces, they are now playing "Sleeping, I dream Love." I always think of you every time the band strikes up. I will finish in the morning. Good night love, my darling wife and sleeping "I'll dream love, dream of thee."

SATURDAY MORNING SEPTEMBER 14TH

I have been writing all of my letters at night for the last ten or twelve days and always have a few lines to write the next morning to let you know how I am as the letter leaves. I will mail another letter to you on Monday. Let me know when they reach you and if two come by the same mail. Ed is improving every day. Gib and Zeke are well. Give my love to all and to your aunty and uncle too and Ida and Sallie. Many kisses to my darling little Fannie and believe me dearest, most devotedly,

Your own fond and loving
Husband
JOHN F. CALHOUN

PS The boys to be remembered

FLINT HILL,NEAR FAIRFAX C. H.
September 15: 1861

My dearest Rebecca

I was disappointed this evening in not getting a letter from you but I know full well there are several on the way. The last I received from you was dated the 5th the one sent by Ed. I went out on Picket yesterday evening and Edwin went with me and stood it very well indeed, he is improving although he is unwell tonight somewhat and unless he continues to improve from this on I am afraid he can't stand it. Service in the Army is no child's play. Col Bacon sent out for me to withdraw my Pickets as he was ordered with his Regiment to Munson's Hill. I came in a hurry but feeling somewhat unwell. I concluded to put off going until morning. Col William's Regt. is to occupy Mason's Hill and we are all to remain and hold those hills until Gen Longstreet moves up his Brigade. Mission's hill is ten miles from here and I am to foot it and perhaps alone for we may only remain one or two days. I will advise Ed not to go as he can't stand the walk. We leave all our tents here. I will write to you from there with Washington, Alexandria and the Potomac in view. Tell Carie I will write to her from there. I did intend writing Carie today but was not well. I intend sending home in Ed's valise by one of Capt Hester's men, some of my old socks, an old pr of pants that will do for some of the negroes, two shirts, that vest that you sent me, two sugar crushers made by me from that famous cedar, pen handle &c. the fork was made by one of Capt Bland's men. I have sealed up some of your letters and directed them to you, don't destroy them for I prize them highly and if I am spared to survive this war I want them to read. They are some of my jewels. Ed will write to Sallie to send them down to you. We are sending back some things together. I told him he had better send his valise back and keep his carpet bag, and as it was going empty I thought I would send some thing back. Give Carie and Sam a pen staff or some of the relics. I may not have an opportunity of mailing a letter before Wednesday or Thursday so don't be uneasy if you should not get a letter for four days after you get this. I will write if possible. Give my love to all and many kisses to Fannie darling. Time is passing away and may it fly by until we meet which I hope will be in two months. Good night and may guardian Angels watch over you and my darling child, dearest is the prayer of your Fond and Devoted Husband

JOHN F. CALHOUN

MONDAY MORNING SEPTEMBER 16:1861

I will write a few lines more this morning. Dr. McComb[82] has procured a discharge from the surgeons of the Regiment and has to go before the board or Medical Director and if approved he will start on home tomorrow if he goes I will send that cedar stick by him and if he does not get off I will send it by young Huckabee to carry on and lean with fondly. I doubt that he will ever get it but I can take care of such things in camp. Love to all and many kisses to sweetness.

Most Devotedly Your
Own fond Husband
JOHN F. CALHOUN

82 John F. McComb of Company D, 7th South Carolina Volunteers. *Kershaw's Brigade*, p. 559.

FALLS CHURCH, VA
September 18, 1861
No 29

My Darling Wife

I received a letter from you today No 17 dated Sept 8th leaving no intermediate one out and from yours I judge all of mine have been received although they must be detained unduly on the way and sometimes reach you irregularly still I am glad that all reach this destination for there are many complaints. I am pained to hear that our darling little Fannie is sick but hope that she has recovered before this. Darling when she seems much sick always send for the Dr. never put off sending until you think she is ill. I wrote to Ida a few days ago and told her to say to father that he might sell Nettie if he could get $250 cash but tell him as soon as you see him that if anyone wants her they must go to you as I will give directions to you and no one shall be authorized to sell her but you. My object is this, I wish to leave the matter entirely in your hands the price and all $250 is my lowest mark, she ought to bring 300 and you may hold her at that. I can soon make that from her raising colts and as my part, I don't care whether you sell her or not. We are still at the same place. Today I went to Munson's Hill again saw Col William's Pickets firing away at the enemies, they replying, soon a white hand kerchief was raised and answered and they met half way and chatted more than an hour. Another was raised opposite and near the Hill and they also met and many of both parties came out into the road they met without arms. The Yankees, New Jersey men said they were tired of the war, thought it hard to be shooting brethren, but thought we would soon have peace and the union would be reconstructed, our men, they were two Louisiana scouts told them we of the south would rather die than live under Lincoln's government. They said yes they were aware we had such feelings but still they thought that the Union would be reconstructed. Col W did not like this meeting and said he would reprimand the officers commanding the picket for permitting it. He said they might admit Gen McClellan himself without knowing it. I met Col. Stuart of the cavalry going dashing down and I heard him say he was going down to find out what that "palavering" was about, he is in command of all the pickets and I expect will put a stop to this meeting and conversing. A short while since Gen's Longstreet, Beauregard, and Johnston with their aids and an escort of cavalry came dashing along on the way to the Hills. Gen Johnston[83] is the most military looking Gen that I have seen, tall, well made, erect, every

83 General Joseph E. Johnston (1807-1891). Native of Virginia, graduated from the U. .S Military Academy. Resigned his commission Brevet Brig. Gen. when Virginia seceeded and was arguably the highest ranking U.S. officer to join the Confederacy. Died of pneumonia contracted while serving as a pallbearer at the funeral of Union General William T. Sherman during inclement weather. *Encyclopedia Virginia. Find Grave. Biographical History of the U.S. Congress.*

inch a military chieftain. He is quite gray wears a moustache, side whiskers and imperial. He raised his cap from his proud lofty head as he dashed by us. He ranks Gen Beauregard who rode on his right, Gen J in the middle and Gen L on the left. I have no doubt but that Gen Johnston is fully equal to Gen B. I think could conduct a fight as well if not better. I have a very high opinion of him. I met a Major Gantt[84] of one of the Va. Regt's this morning at the Hill and he made very particular enquiries about Maj Hammond,[85] son of Senator H. He asked me if he was dissatisfied and if the family were wealthy and seemed so much interested and asked so many questions that I could see that it was some matrimonial affair. Something may take place soon as four Generals, some I did not name, have been here in the last few days. They are examining everything around here. The enemy I am sure will never advance and I can't think they will attempt to take Arlington &c or our post. Gib and Zeke are well I have written you all the news I know of. Give my love to all and many kisses to sweetness. Have you received all of my letters? Write often dearest,

Most Devotedly your Husband
JOHN F. CALHOUN

THURSDAY MORNING 19TH

I will write a few lines more this morning as I may not have an opportunity of sending this before tomorrow. I have not yet heard when we will return to camp. Tomorrow I expect. Many troops are collecting around here. Sloan's regiment came in night before last, a Virginia and a Georgia Regt and there were eight to ten around here before. I don't know that any movement is to be made. How are our turnips looking? Do have them well worked and don't forget to have a grazing lot for your calves and colt. Tell Mr. McC to make you as large and rich a lot as possible. It is time now to sow it and the last working of the turnips you might have grain sown in them. Tell Mr. McC to have as much hay gathered as he can possibly gather and tell Cupe also and tell them to gather peas as long as there are any to gather and when there not enough in my field to get father to let him gather in his field as he has a great many. I wish he could save me 200 bushels. Where are they putting the peas? See that Clarissa and John are kept employed. Mr. McC might make her and John & uncle thrash out thirty or forty bushels for seed, eating &c put it in the wheat box. Are you having the wheat from the smut machine saved? This will be three letters this week and I will write another on

84 Henry Gantt of the 19th Virginia Volunteer Infantry. He was shot in the face at Gettysburg and lost all of his teeth. He survived the war and died in 1884. "Colonel Henry Gantt of Valmont" by Richard L. Nicholas. *Scottsville, VA Museum.*

85 Major James Henry "Harry" Hammond (1832-1916), son of Senator James Henry Hammond of South Carolina. Harry served as Quartermaster with General Maxcy Gregg. *Find A Grave.*

Saturday. Don't forget to deliver my messages to Mr. McC and always enquire and find whether or not my orders are attended to. Good by my own tenderly beloved Rebecca. Ever thine own true and devoted Husband

JFC

FALLS CHURCH VIRGINIA
SEPTEMBER 20, 1861
NO 30

My own darling wife:

This will be the fourth letter that I have written this week and if we return to Flint Hill Saturday I will write another by Sunday's mail. We are still here some say held in reserve so as to give assistance should the enemy attempt to break through our lines; we will surely return Saturday, day after tomorrow. Every day shows more and more clearly the great deficiency of our field officers. Bacon is a kind generous hearted man but entirely unfit to command a Regiment and as for Fair, he is a perfect failure, a good drill officer, but too abominable lazy to do anything. He is a nuisance in the Regt and gives no assistance at all to Bacon. He has not been seen fifty yards from where he is encamped since he has been here, five days. He gets more and more unpopular every day and after our time is out should our Regt again volunteer not one of our present field officers would be reelected. Brooks came into our camp last night and asked me to go down and spend the night with him. We slept up stairs in a large house which he is occupying. There is a plump little yankee woman and an Aunt in the house where we are staying. They are so entirely different from our ladies. The girls allow too many liberties and are too bold and familiar. I have but little to say to them. I dreamed about you and Fannie last night and I dreamed that Fannie kissed me and said "my pa" so sweetly. All the volunteers from every state as far as I can learn are tired out of the war, although all are willing to stay and see "it out" but such an army has never before been brought into the field in any age. Such a large proportion of business and married men. A Balloon was seen a few moments ago in the direction of Washington and it did not seem to be more than two or three miles. We could see the cord with the eye very plainly. We are drawing very near each other, the two armies are facing each other, but I have no idea we will ever attempt to take Arlington or Washington unless our division cross the river above and below Washington and get in the rear and approach from the other side. It would cost thousands and thousands of lives to take Arlington or to even cross the Potomac near Washington. You can see with the eye from Munson's Hill a line of fortifications with flags flying for miles along the Potomac. The enemy will never make another invasion like they did before. They may sometimes move out a few miles from the river to attack any unprotected point or to make a surprise if they think they can be successful, but it will be always in a small way. They will be satisfied now if they can hold Washington and I think they fear the Confederates contemplate attacking it. And when Professor Lowe[86] of Balloon notoriety reports the

86 Professor Thaddeus S.C. Lowe (1832-1932). Known as the father of military aerial reconnaissance. Lowe was appointed Chief Aeronaut by President Abraham Lincoln. At this time he was reporting on

number of troops on the Hills around here and in and around Falls Church they will think we are intending to make an advance. The Hills are 1-1/2 and 2 miles from here. I wrote to Mr. McCrevan giving him the same instructions I wrote you but you must tell him any way and then he may attend to them. I wrote to you that I sent some clothes home in Ed's valise by DeWitt Huckabee, who came on a visit to his brother and other relatives in Capt. Hester's Company. I sealed up some of your letters very securely with mucillage and sent them among my clothes and Ed wrote to Sallie to take particular care and hand them to you herself. He sent the key in a letter by Huckabee to her. Preserve them for me darling as I want them should I ever return as tokens and precious ones they are. Ed has not paid for the saddle &c. He will pay that bill. Where is my saddle and bridle? Take it home and take care of it. Tell Cupe to take care of all my gear &c lock them up. Keep my wagon well greased when they use it and when not using keep under the shed. Tell him nothing must be loaned out. If you will always, see Cupe and tell him what I wish to have done and let him know that I depend upon him he will take an interest. Give my love to your mother, father, Carie and Sam and to Miss Calhoun my daughter with innumerable kisses. I have not rec'd any letters from Mr. Porcher, send him word and tell him if he wishes to buy Nettie she is yours and you will sell her. Write often and long letters dearest to your Faithful and ever Devoted Husband

JOHN F. CALHOUN

Confederate troop positions and movements along the Potomac River. *http://thaddeuslowe.name/*

FALLS CHURCH, VA
September 21, 1861
No 31

My Dearest

I am seated in a shade by the side of a fence a few hundred yards from our camp and The Rogers is with me, both of us devoting the morning in writing to our wives. he received a letter from his wife this morning but none came for me, but I know you write regularly twice a week for you promised to do so. We are still at the same place and have been kept doing nothing being held as a reserve. Col Kershaw's Regiment came in yesterday and I met with Mr. Dwight. I thought he was a Lieut in Haskell's[87] Company but he said that he was unable to get off. He introduced me to an elder brother who talks through his nose and is somewhat "hair liped." Kershaw's Band serenaded some of the officers last night and they played some very good pieces. Gen Longstreet's Head Quarters are near us. He is in command there. Bonham is at our Brigade encampment. Gen Bonham is the fifth Gen in point of rank. Lee, Johnston, Beauregard, Bragg, Bonham &c - old Gen Johnston from what I now know of them is my favorite if not before, certainly next to Beauregard and in a desperate fight, to conduct a retreat or pursuit, to make a gallant charge or in a "rough and tumble" fight or in a battle where quickness is required, I don't know but that he would surpass Gen Beauregard at least that is my opinion. Gen B can plan a campaign or the storming of a fort &c construction of fortifications, besieging a city, conducting a slow and continuous campaign, and no doubt may be Johnston's equal to the qualities which I attribute to him, still there is such promptness and boldness in Johnson's movements, something so gallant and dashing about the old fellow that I have a high admiration for him although from what I can learn he is strict in discipline. B is too. Cothran, The, and I went out yesterday evening to get some Hazelnuts. they grow abundantly here and the finest Irish potatoes I ever saw, in fact vegetables of nearly every kind grow well here. This section is nothing but gardens and orchards, Washington and Alexandria were the markets before the war. Buckwheat grows well here. I will put a few grains in this letter for you to see how it looks; there is a patch near where I am writing. You ought to have all the garden seed that Mr. McCrevan saved well sunned or the worms will destroy them. I did not send the shoes by Dr. Link. Did he say what became of the Haversack? Did Dr. McComb give you father the stick which I sent him? Whenever you write always let me know about the

87 Colonel John Cheves Haskell (1841-1906). Born in Abbeville, SC and attended South Carolina College. Enlisted in the Confederate Army in 1861 and was 2nd Lieutenant of artillery and later served as staff officer for General Joseph E. Johnston and General G.W. Smith. He married a daughter of General Wade Hampton, III after the war. *Find a Grave*.

weather and the crops as I feel a great interest. How many small pigs have those three old sows? I want to get enough to bring the number up to 16 or 18 as some may die or be lost by this fall year. I wrote to Mr. McC to get me some by the time my pasture is open and as he is so slow you might get you father to speak to someone for a few pigs or a good sow and pigs and I will pay for them when I come home in Nov or Dec. He may get them from some one who owes us an a/c. Don't forget to get your father to ask Capt D. M. R. to save me those 2 pigs that I spoke to him about and get them home by the middle of Oct. The weather is still warm here, but the nights cool but not cooler than they were in July. I am in hopes the planters will have fine weather for picking cotton. Has your father a good pea and pumpkin crop? is his cotton turning out well? As Fannie will soon be walking about, I advise you to be very careful or Furo will some day bite her. I am expecting nothing else and have thought often of it, but as much attached as your father is to him, he would surely part with him of [or] kill him before he would have Fannie in any danger. This will be five letters this week and as postage is so high three times will be enough here after won't it. I will write again on Monday 23 this is Sat. Zeke and Gib are well. Sam I hear has just returned to camp. Ed is there he has been unwell and is in bad health. Give my love to all and kiss our sweet little Fannie for me. My darling I feel like writing every day to you although there is no use in it. You don't know how much, how devotedly I love you dearest. Good bye love. Most Devotedly Your loving Husband

JOHN F. CALLHOUN

FLINT HILL, NEAR FAIRFAX C H VA
MONDAY SEPTEMBER 23, 1861

My own darling wife:-

Upon my return to camp from Falls Church yesterday morning I received two letters from you Nov 18 & 19 dated 13th & 15th to both of which I will reply today although I can not mail my letter before morning. I am glad you intend going up to spend a week with Sallie, but as you have nothing particularly to employ you at home I think you ought to make a longer visit. Darling you ought to visit more then your time would pass off more rapidly and would not hang so heavily. I am sorry to hear that you suspect Clarissa of dishonesty. Tell her that if I find out that she is unfaithful I will separate her and Henry and as for the sugar the other bbl must not be opened, they shall not use such nice sugar. Get fifty or sixty pounds of brown sugar for Mr Andrews and as far as coffee tell him that I will not engage to furnish it. They must mix it with parched meal as they are doing elsewhere, here in Va too. We will not be able to get any more such nice white sugar and I would not let it be used. Would it not be better to measure out a weeks supply at a time? Keep an account of the times Mrs Andrews stays at the Mills, provisions are high and in debt as we are of course we cant board any one as a favor. Have you engaged to board her at any named price? If Mr McCrevan leaves tell Cupe that I will depend upon him to carry out all of my orders and shall expect him to have the work carried on properly. Tell him that he may indulge the hands and permit them to idle and to sleep late in the morning but I warn him not to let me hear it. I will get father, his overseer, Mr A and Mr Guillebeau to notice what time they go out to work &c and report it to me, and if he is faithful I will reward him but if not he shall repent it. Tell him this. I believe Cupe will carry on everything as well as any white man I can get. Do make me two or three flannel shirts and send on to me. I am glad to hear the leather is better than it has been there before but 40 cents is lower than it ought to be sold, leather is very high and we ought to rise with every one else. Have you selected our negro shoes yet? Get the very best, if you don't get all from the ones made by Mr Chapman give Cupe a pair any way . I am glad to hear we lost but little fodder. Examine everything when you go down and let them see that you are watchful. I don't think you are answering my letters as you started to do. You have not said anything about the salt, oats, &c. Fannie must be sweet and smart, that was indeed a smart trick about the letter. She will soon yet be saying "pa pa" whenever she sees a letter. If I can get off in Nov and we are in comfortable winter quarters I will be sure to want you to return with me, so fix up with that expectation. As postage is high and we are back again in the same old camp where everything will be dull I will write only three times a week. I will send a map of the Battle ground &c. Give my love to all and many kisses to Fannie. I will write to father in a few days.

Most Devotedly Your own
Fond Husband
JOHN F. CALHOUN

PS Our company are needing blankets, &c and if your society have not sent on that box send it here. Dr. H says that he did not say that we did not need blankets and he aluded to bodily clothing but gloves and socks we will need.

Yours lovingly
J.F.C.

FLINT HILL, NEAR FAIRFAX VA
September 24, 1861
No 32

My darling wife

I received two letters Nos 18 & 19 from you on the 21st to both of which I have replied, but as this is my day for writing I must write a few lines any way. By this time, or at least by the time this reaches you, you will have returned home so I will direct to Mt.Carmel and will enclose a letter to Mr. Andrews which I wish you to hand to him when you go down. I suppose Mr. McCreven has left so I wrote to Ben A. to be watchful and to attend closely to everything. Has Mr. Burt taken away his pigs, if not send him word to take them away immediately and if he does not, and you can dispose of them to anyone else, do so for I won't be "fooled" by him any longer. Ed does not think that he intends taking them at all. Send him word that he can just pay over the $25 to you, he won't pay it unless you give him a hint. I am looking for a letter from you today and as this will be such a short one, I will write again tomorrow or next day. You must not expect but three letters a week hereafter. There is no news at all everything dull. Give my love to all and many kisses to dear sweet little Fannie. Most devotedly you own fond Husband

JOHN F. CALHOUN

"BIVOUAC" 1ST BRIGADE ARMY
OF POTOMAC Sept 28, 1861

My darling wife:-

I wrote you a short letter on the 25th and intended writing the next day but that night whilst at supper we were ordered to get ready immediately for a march and the Regt was called out in ten or fifteen minutes and put upon the march. We marched to within 4 or five miles of the Chain Bridge and Bivouacked in the woods without tents and with one Blanket for two nights and days. We built huts out of pine and cedar bushes and on Thursday night it rained half the night and all day yesterday. Why we were ordered out so suddenly no one knows. It was an order from Gen Beauregard to Bonham and Gen Jones[1] to put both the Brigades immediately on the march Capt Kemper's [2] Battery with our Brigade and Ransom Calvary Battery[3] with Jones. Last night an order was sent by Gen Beauregard to have the Brigade ready for marching at a moments notice that was about 11 o'clock and Aiken came around and delivered the orders to the commanders of Companies. I am in command of Company C. Capt B and Cothran are both at the Camp sick. We formed the Regt thinking that we were to make an attack but Gen Bonham had to await further orders after a while we were marched back a mile beyond Vienna and filed into the woods to await orders. No one knows what all this means, not even the officers, all comes from Gen Beauregard. It is said two musket Batteries have been erected on the Potomac near Ocquoquan creek in a Cedar thicket and they will command the Potomac and it is reported they will open tomorrow we may be in some way connected with that move but all is shrowded in darkness. We may not have any fighting and it may all be a cunning maneuver to deceive the enemy moving in the night as we do. I am inclined to think this is the case. If we get into a fight I will do my duty by Company C. I rec'd the letter you sent by W. Darricott it was sent out to me. It is the longest one you have yet written and as soon as I return I will give you a long reply. I will not

1 General Samuel Jones (1819-1887). Served as Chief of General Beauregard's artillery. Was promoted to Brigadier General in July 1861. Jones and other generals had written to Acting Secretary of War Judah Benjamin requesting that their army be sufficiently resupplied in order to make an advance across the Potomac and carry the war into the enemy's country. If they could not be resupplied, they would have to fall back to a more defendable position. At this time, the generals were awaiting a response from Benjamin, who had asked President Jefferson Davis go meet with them personally to discuss the options. Find a Grave. *ORWR*, Vol V, Chapter XIV, pp. 883-887.

2 Captain Dell Kemper of an Alexandria, VA artillery unit had been ordered to Flint Hill, VA in August of 1861. *Kershaw's Brigade*, pp. 54, 55.

3 Captain Robert Ransom, Jr. (1828-1892). Born in Warren County, North Carolina, and graduated West Point. Served in U.S. Army but resigned in early 1861 to join Confederate cavalry in North Carolina. Was promoted to General in March of 1862. His brother Matt was also a Confederate General. *Find a Grave.*

have time now. Give my love to all. Kiss Fannie. Most Affectionately Your own Devoted Husband

J.F. CALHOUN

III.

Letters of October, November, & December of 1861

SUMMER GAVE WAY TO FALL on the Potomac and the 7th Regiment continued to hold their position along the front line. The Battle of Manassas had given them a real taste of war and the horrors that go with it.

They began to realize that, despite that victory, additional battles would be forthcoming and the Confederate government asked for 400,000 more volunteers. The requests for additional troops coupled with increased skirmishing began to change everyone's mind, both in the Army and at home, that the war may last longer than anticipated.

The 7th Regiment had marched with other units forward to within a few miles of the "Chain Bridge" over the Potomac near Washington, DC and, after several successive victories, The Confederate Generals in Virginia were determined to go on the offensive. They wanted to take the fight across the Potomac and invade Washington. The Generals had made a plea to Acting Secretary of War Judah Benjamin to furnish them with the reinforcements and supplies necessary to accomplish this. Benjamin then asked President Jefferson Davis to meet with the Generals in person. At that meeting in early October, Davis told them the government could not furnish what they required. The Generals decided to fall back into a defensive position and abandon their plans for an invasion. A decision which could have changed the war, and history forever.

After Confederate victories at Blackburn's Ford, Lewinsville, Leesburg, and Little Bethel, the troops thought there would be no more fighting in Virginia for the remainder of the winter. Once in winter quarters, the chances of an early release from duty were reduced significantly. In camp, the continued "obstinate denial" of furloughs dominated the talk amongst the 12 month volunteers, although John Francis still held out hope he would be granted one. On a smaller scale, privates were offered furloughs, but only if they re-enlisted. Officers were not authorized furloughs under any conditions. The Generals intentionally held down the number of furloughs offered because of the high rate of sickness in the Regiment and they also feared any further reduction in troop numbers would be detrimental to their ability to wage the war as new recruits were slow in coming to the field.

John Francis also grew increasingly more anxious about happenings at home and his growing debt from the operation of his farm, mill and tan yard, as well as the conduct of his employees and slaves during his absence. He persistently asked Rebecca to watch over the farm and livestock, and to try and prevent any waste of products or supplies.

Even through December his head was alternately filled with thoughts of resignation and appealing his application for a furlough believing it still may be possible. Upon his appeal, John Francis was told that he was an officer serving "the post of honor and danger" and was again denied a furlough.

October 1861

FLINT HILL, NEAR FAIRFAX CH
October 3d 1861
No 35

My own darling wife:

The last letter I wrote to you was on the 30th ultimo whilst on Picket and when I returned to camp I found all the tents struck and the wagons loading to move everything back to this old camp whilst the Regt was ordered forward and Gen Bonham told his brother in law Capt Bland[4] that we would Bivouac in the woods until after the fight so we started about eight or nine o'clock and marched to a pine thicket near one of my Picket stations filed into the thicket and rested on our arms. Nothing disturbed our sleep but cold during the night and the next day about ten o'clock we recd orders that Col Winders SC Regt would relieve us, and in a half hour it came and in it I met two College Classmates Major Woodward and Capt McClure.[5] We marched back to Flint Hill as soon as relieved and here we are still. I begin to think that even our Brigadiers are kept ignorant of the future plans and intended movements. It was a misunderstanding about moving tents in the first place after our return from Lewinsville we were ordered to Bivouac and to throw out advanced Pickets for four or five days and then another Regiment was to relieve us as it did. President Davis[6] arrived at Fairfax a few evenings since and together with Gen Beauregard and other Gen's &c have been riding around the country reconnoitering. Many think that a fight is not far off nearly all of our forces have been brought forward from Manassas. It is reported that the President said to some of Col Williams[7] men a few days ago as they collected on the road side to see him, "to cheer up, you will soon get home to see your sweet hearts." I can't

4 General Bonham and Captain Bland had married sisters from Edgefield, SC. Ann Patience Griffin and Rebecca Griffin, respectively. *History of Edgefield County.*

5 Major Thomas Woodward, 6th South Carolina Volunteers and Captain E.C. McClure of Company F, 6th South Carolina Volunteers. Both were classmates of John Francis Calhoun at South Carolina College in 1851-1852. Chester County, SC Rosters, S.C. Genweb, *Kershaw's Brigade*, p. 576.

6 President Jefferson Davis came to meet with the Generals as requested (Letter of September 28, 1861, note 87) and during their conference informed them that the Confederate Government could not reinforce or resupply the Army in the manner necessary to support an invasion. Thus, the Generals were forced to postpone any offensive into Union territory and return their troops to a defensive position and await any further movement by the enemy.
After several consecutive Confederate victories in Virginia, an invasion at this point could have changed the outcome of the war and history forever. *ORWR*, Vol V, Chapter XIV, pp. 883-887. *Kershaw's Brigade*, p. 78.

7 Colonel James H. Williams , 3rd South Carolina Volunteers. *Kershaw's Brigade*, p. 551.

vouch for the truth. The weather is again pleasant. We have now 107 members in our company, rank and file. I think we have the largest Co in the Regt. I doubt very much that Ed can stand camp life. He has been frequently sick lately. I hear a Band a few hundred yards from us in the woods on the Germantown road. It is the Brigade of Gen W. H. Walker[8] of Georgia consisting of 4 Louisiana Regt and Maj Wheat's Special Battalion, the Tigers who fought so desperately at Manassas. This entire county for miles is one encampment and Bands continually playing the air is filled with music and darling it has a strange influence on me. It fills my every thought of you and I feel our separation when delightful strains of music fall upon my ears, more if anything than at any other time and if it be possible I think then more tenderly of you and love you more than ever. I dreamed of riding with you in our Buggy last night and we drove Netty. I dream often of you. Nothing has been done with the pay rolls yet. I am afraid it will be like the other time. It was three weeks from the time they were handed in to fill out to the time we were paid. Notice everything you learn at the Mills. Would it not be well to lock up everything in the little room that you may not wish used? Where do Mr. & Mrs. A. sleep? I think you ought to select bed clothes &c for them. Notice and caution them about our furniture, crockery &c and the stove and utensils. Tell Clarissa I don't want that stove burnt up or broken. I will examine it should I ever return. Tell her and Mr. & Mrs. A that it is against my express orders for the negroes to be cooking on it after night and they are not to be congregated in the kitchen after night. Ask Cupet if my orders about visitors are carried out. I will get Mr. Andrews to write me what negroes visit there. Tell him I do not allow a crowd around my negro houses or around the place any where. They may use as many potatoes as they wish from the patch in the corn field. Use them first as I want them out of the way so I can turn my hogs &c in the pasture as soon as the corn is hauled in. I did not think about the pasture when I planted there they ought to have been planted elsewhere. Make Clarissa take particular care of the cotton in the garden and pick it as fast as it opens. She must be made to do something else besides cook for Mrs. A. Tell her that Mrs. A can set the table and make up the plates &c and when there is much work to be done she ought to make up her bed too. Tell her. Are we not to receive nothing from the firm for the use of Clarissa and the beds, furniture, cooking utensils, &c? Tell Mr. Andrews to write to me every ten or twelve days. I must close as the drum is beating for Battalion drill. The last letter I have received from you was by W. Darricott, surely one will reach me today. Give my love to all and kiss "sweetness" for me.

Most Devotedly Your
Loving Husband

8 General William H.T. Walker (1816-1864) Born in Augusta, GA. Graduated from West Point and served in the US Army. Resigned in December 1860 to join the Confederate Army as a Colonel. Promoted to Brigadier General in May 1861. Later resigned and returned to the Georgia Militia. Killed at the Battle of Atlanta July 22, 1864. *Find a Grave.*

JOHN F. CALHOUN

Friday morning Oct 4:1861

I was again disappointed in not getting a letter from you, none has been received since the one sent by Wm D. Gen Bonham told us yesterday evening that the President would review his Brigade this evening perhaps, and as he had heard something of it he was anxious for it to come up to his expectations . President D reviewed four Brigades yesterday. No one can get any kind of a furlough excepting a sick one. Some strong appeals have been refused, so don't expect me until we go into winter quarters. I won't apply until I know I will succeed in getting one. Some of the best flannel for drawers &c. that I ever saw was some sent here from SC a home made article, but it was intended for blankets – doubled. If I can get any wool I want you to try and have me some woven for late winter near Dec or Jan as mine will not last through the entire winter. I like the thick stout home made, although this was not intended for flannel. Tell Carie that she must have me two pair of socks knit by Dec as she will have leisure, and you can have two pair knit can't you my darling? I think I know the first pr that you knit – they are the best of all. I want them as fine as possible and long legs. I don't know whether or not it would be better to have them colored, do as you please about that. Tell father when he goes to Augusta to get me two silk handkerchiefs as mine are wearing out and silk will be better any way for the winter. Ed is not in good health and unless he improves I will advise him to return home. He can't stand the hardships that we have to undergo sleeping out on the damp ground and frequently with not enough cover. Give my love to all and tell your mother I have not rec'd her letter yet. It is getting time for me to write to your father. I will do so soon. Kiss my darling little Fannie, and Believe me dearest Fondly ____ own

J. F. C.

FLINT HILL, NEAR FAIRFAX CH
THURSDAY NIGHT OCT 10, 1861
NO 39

My own darling wife:

I wrote to you this morning and write again as I received a letter form you this evening. It was No 22 dated Oct 2d. Our Regiment is going out on Picket and will not return until Monday so I may not have an opportunity of writing again until I return. If you have any negro cloth left after cutting our negroes clothes you ought to sell it. You ought to have 150 yards left and it ought to be worth 45 or 50 cents a yard. I am glad your father has bought me the sow and pigs they are very cheap and if the sow weans the pigs in time I will kill her this winter. I am willing to take one or two more and you might get some from the free negroes and pay them in shoes or cloth. I want to have 18 or 20 pigs. Mr. Rogers sent me word that he would send the two down to me soon, do have them well attended to. I would greatly prefer selling the leather to making it into shoes. Try and get the $25 from Mr. Burt send him word by your uncle William sometime when he goes up and make him pay you. He ought to know they are cash.

Oct 11: I will not have time to answer you letter fully this morning as we are to start off at 8 o'clock. I write to you when out on Picket and mail it when I return then I can write you a long letter. This is to mearly to keep you from being uneasy in case you did not hear from me in three or four days then you would know the reason. Try and improve Fannie's temper. Kiss her for me and give love to all and Believe me Most Devotedly Your loving husband

JOHN F. CALHOUN

FLINT HILL, NEAR FAIRFAX
Oct 15, 1861
No 41

My own darling wife:

I mentioned in my last the receipt of yours of the 4th inst and I promised to write on Wednesday, this is Tuesday. My last of the 13th was long enough was it not darling? You can not complain of the brevity of that letter nor of any of my regular ones. And if you never wish me to write a short one not even a hasty note upon any sudden order to march or anything of that kind, I will not to do so but wait until I can find leisure to write a long letter. The long roll beat this morning about an hour before daylight throughout our entire Brigade and all the Companies formed but orders came about daylight to get breakfast and I suppose that will be the last of it, no one can inform me as to the cause of the alarm. The enemy are said to be in large force near Lewisville but I think they are mearly foraging, or as Capt Brooks just told me one of his men said "no danger of them coming they are just Chestnut hunting." I dreamed of you last night thought that I had resigned and returned home, it was perhaps owing to my having conversed several times yesterday about furloughs and resignations. Two of Cols Cash's Captains, Stackhouse[9] and Evans, son of Judy E. told me yesterday that they had resigned as they had applied for furloughs and had been refused and they had business which they were forced to attend to and could not neglect it. Capt Evans said that Gen Bonham told him that there were a great many resignations but this will not diminish our strength enough to be felt as a private can not get off it is confined entirely to officers and proceeds from no dissatisfaction, mearly men of family and business returning to attend to business and family affairs and most of them intend returning again. One of these men Capt E. told me that one of their privates, a man of character and standing received a letter informing him that his wife was dead, and that his mother-in-law had his children, another letter came informing him that she was about to die, and these letters he took up to Head Quarters and upon them, applied for a furlough, which was refused. He is a member of the Legislature but will be forced to resign his seat as he can't get off to the seat this winter. One of Brooks Lieuts 1st told me he intended to resign to return home to attend to some business. He applied for a furlough; he said fifteen days would satisfy him. I suspect there will be many resignations this winter if this system of refusing all furloughs is persisted in. I will not apply for a furlough for more that a month yet and in that time I hope we may either be in winter quarters or something will in the mean time

9 Captain E.T. Stackhouse of Company I, 8th South Carolina Volunteers and Captain W.H. Evans of Company F, 8th South Carolina Volunteers. *Kershaw's Brigade*, pp. 565, 566.

transpire to quiet the times so that furloughs will be granted, for I must go home before Christmas. My business, I don't doubt is going on very well but still there are some thing that I must attend to myself, the notes and a/c, books &c and there are some things that Mr. Rogers nor any one can understand. And I want all closed up in a business manner, moreover I must attend to making arrangements for another year. I feel that my family has some claims upon me and I am too much in debt to entirely neglect my business. All I ask is a furlough and I shall regret the alternative of not going home or resigning to be submitted. I will not wait and hope. A serious difficulty occurred yesterday evening between Major Seibles and Capt Bland which will result in duel.[10] It occurred during a game of Chess. Capt B gave the lie, Maj S rushed at him and pushed him over, when they rose a crowd began to collect, and Capt B said Maj S it is unpleasant to attract a crowd by a fight. I suppose we will understand each other and I propose we continue the game as if nothing happened, they began picking up the chess men and Capt B said "I suppose of course you will waive your rank and take off your shoulder straps." Maj S said he would not, whereupon Capt B said he was no gentleman. Maj S struck him and after coming out of the tent they were separated and began twice again. Seibles cursed B[l]and in the fight had decidedly the advantage. Once when Lieut Buress and others were holding them Capt B said let the d.d beast loose, and I will cool him and again when Maj S fell or was thrown by B, he B stood and twisted his moustache as coolly and said set up the beast and let me at him again. From the first Capt B tried to get S to agree to give him satisfaction immediately. S said after our six months were out; B at last got him to consent and he turned off said I am now satisfied d.m him. I have brought it out at last but I am sorry that I had to resort to brute force. Bland sent immediately for Brooks, and Brooks told me confidently that Bland at first wanted Ham to act as his second, after reflecting he said no he could not ask him to act for him as he would lay himself liable to be cashered. He will select some one not connected with the Army, Dr. Tom Pickens,[11] Brooks thinks he is on ____ and not in the Army. Capt B is a cool, brave, gallant, high toned man, and if they fight I look for him to kill Siebles. he is popular although he mingles but little with the men and is a stiff haughty-looking man. Maj S is a coarse ruff fellow and unpopular and if he loses his rank or resigns Capt Bradley is the senior Capt and will rise to the rank of Maj. Siebles is very ruff and I have heard insulting in playing cards or chess and interferes when others are playing and he not interested although some say not with-

10 Major Emmett Seibles, 7th South Carolina Volunteers & Colonel Elbert Bland, 7th.
South Carolina Volunteers. During a heated Chess Match, Seibles challenged Bland to a duel. After brief fisticuffs, the parties agreed to postpone the event until after their 12 month enlistment period was up (approximately 6 months). *Kershaw's Brigade*, pp. 79, 80.

11 Dr. Thomas J. Pickens (1831-1917). Graduated from South Carolina Medical College in 1854 and was a physician in Pendleton, SC. Lois K. Nix and Mary Kay Snell, Thomas Boone Pickens, His Ancestors. *Calhoun Family Genealogy*.

standing his roughness he is good hearted. The wagons have just come with the boxes containing our uniforms. We have just heard the glorious news of the naval engagement at New Orleans[12] and hope it will be followed up at Savannah, Charleston &c. I see from the papers that Edward Noble,[13] Esq. is a candidate for Congress and I do hope he will be elected. Ham Brooks received a letter from Edgefield and it stated that they thought there that E Noble would be elected. Ham said that all about "96"[14] they were strong Noble men that when his brother Preston was spoken of for Gov and the Senate that he said that he would name Edward Noble as his favorite as his successor in preference to any man in the Congressional Dist consequently his friends continue to support Noble. Gen Bonham may defeat him as many of the Edgefield people seem to think they belong to him. Tell your cousin Edward that I am sorry that I am not at home to support him. I would vote for him in preference to Bonham, John A.[15] or any one else. It is rumored that the enemy are slowly advancing in large force and I suppose from what I can learn that they are gradually advancing their lines, and it is rumored that they have 150,000, some reports go over that. We can not bring much over one third that number to oppose them but our gallant band of Southrons will stand like a mountain and resist to the death any number they can send against us. It will be one of the greatest battles recorded in modern history; hundreds of Cannons will peal forth their death dealing shots at a time. I doubt that the world ever witnessed or will witness such a battle of Artillery. We will have I suppose 150 or 200 guns if the engagement becomes general. Our Generals will rely greatly upon the Bayonett, and will charge as soon as possible. The yankees can't stand the cold steel. Gen Beauregard has 37 Regiments in his Division and Gen Smith[16] 38 in his. An order has just reached us to pack up, strike tents and be ready to fall back by 2 oclock tonight, it is ten nearly now.

---

12 Battle of the Head of the Passes on October 12, 1861. The small gun boats of the Confederate "mosquito" fleet under the command of Captain George N. Hollins attacked the Union blockade vessels at the head of the passes, Mississippi River Delta. In what was ultimately called a comedy of nautical errors, the Confederates made several raids on the Union blockade vessels forcing them to slip their anchors and proceed downstream. Many vessels grounded in the escape. The Confederates meanwhile, maneuvered back up river, out of gun range and fired at the fleet without much success. The results were the Union had two damaged sloops and one schooner damaged. The Confederates had one Iron-clad damaged and neither side had any casualties. The accomplishments of the mosquito fleet were exaggerated in newspapers in Confederate cities in the east. *ORWR*, Vol VI, Chapter XVI, pp. 751-752.

13 Edward Noble, Esq. A lawyer in Abbeville, SC and 1st cousin once removed of Rebecca Noble Calhoun. He was the son of former S.C. Governor Patrick Noble. *Calhoun Family Genealogy.*

14 Town of, or District of 96 (Ninety Six) in South Carolina.

15 John Alfred Calhoun, 1st cousin once removed of John Francis Calhoun. Was a signer of South Carolina's Ordinance of Secession. Ran for Confederate Congress against General Milledge L. Bonham. *Calhoun Family Genealogy. Find a Grave.*

16 General Edmund Kirby Smith, Graduated from the US Military Academy 1845 and held a commission. Resigned from the US Army in 1861 and served as Chief of Staff to General Joseph E. Johnston. He was severely wounded at Manassas. Served out the War as Commander of the Trans-Mississippi Department and surrendered the last Confederate forces on 26 May 1865. *Kershaw's Brigade*, pp. 63, 68. *Find a Grave.*

We are to return to Bull Run again. I suppose that the fight will certainly come off soon now as we make this movement. I doubt that the enemy will come on for some time yet or at least for a few days, as they will proceed cautiously and perhaps fortify as they come. I must close. If I am spared my darling I will write to you immediately after the battle and I may have time to write before. I can but feel that God will spare me and permit us to meet on earth again. I pray that he will, pray darling not only for my safety, but for the safety of our brave boys and for the success of our arms. Direct to Manassas again. Give my love to all and kiss my darling sweet little Fannie and may God bless you all my own dearly loved wife is the prayer of Your_Ever constant loving true and Devoted

Husband

JOHN F. CALHOUN

Oct 17 – Landed last night on Bull Run. No enemy advancing yet, no nearer than they were ten days ago. I will write tomorrow or next day.

J.F.C.

CAMP NEAR BULL RUN VA
Saturday Oct 19th 1861
No 43

My own darling wife:

I wrote you on yesterday being the third long letter that I have written since you gave me that scolding so you see what effect it had. You can just do what you choose with me. I am completely under your thumb but it is because I love you so devotedly darling. You can't complain of my last three letters can you? I have not received a line from [you] in eight or ten days, the last was dated the 4th but surely one will come today, two will surely come. On yesterday Ham Brooks and I went to Centerville to see the troops and I assure you it is a sight for miles the fields a white with tents, those sands can be seen at one view and wagons, officers, &c moving in every direction. We are making breastworks or forts on all the commanding hills and it will be impossible for any Army to pass there. After looking around Centerville we took a walk to the Battle field of the 18th[17] and saw where the musket and Canon balls raked the trees &c, saw the graves of the Yankees; most of the had earth thrown on them just as they were lying not more than eighteen inches of earth covered them and hogs and visitors had exposed the bodies, the legs, skulls &c were lying about on the ground and decaying flesh was very offensive sometimes. I am surprised that the enemy with the great advantages that they had in both numbers and position did not defeat us; on this side there is a high bluff thirty or forty feet high covered with thick growth and they could move up to within twenty or thirty yards of our troops without being discovered, and fire down on them and then retreat twenty yards and reload, but the cowardly rascals permitted our troops to cross the creek, charge up the steep bluff and whipp three to one. Now we hold all the strong points and ten thousand can hold them against 40 thousand. It is surprising that Gen Beauregard ever permitted the enemy to get such a great advantage in ground when he could have held all the strong points and that he posted our troops on the low banks on the other side of the creek, and at many points the enemy had an open fire on them. Our immediate position was strong. I now sometimes doubt that the enemy will make an attack on us here knowing how strong our position here is. they will perhaps harass our coast and make Kentucky and Missouri the seat of war. They would have attacked us if we had remained at Fairfax and may advance upon us here, it is thought Gen McClellan will be obliged to give battle this winter but it will be suicidal. I am more sanguine than ever since looking at all of our strong points and the thousands and thou-

17 Battlefield of the 18th is a reference to the battle that took place at Blackburn's Ford on July 18,1861.

sands of our brave troops. The Mountains are in plain view on one side and if they advance they can only advance certain ways, and we hold all the passes. Artillery can not be carraid along any road that wagons travel. The mail has just come and as we have not had any for some time it is very large and will take some time to arrange the letters in packages for the different companies. I will cease writing until I get my letters so as to reply in this. The mail brought me four letters two from you No 24 dated 9th and No 25 of the 11th one from Cousin Lucretia[18] and another from Ben Andrews. Darling I will not scold you for not writing a long letter, one was very short but I think nothing of it. I don't expect you to write long letters every time. I am sorry too that I can't come home in Nov. I could not come if I wished as no one under any circumstances can get a furlough but I still think that I must come in Dec as my business demands it. Unless there is an imperative demand I shall not re-volunteer as we will have a large force of Kentuckians and Missourians in the field if we are lucky there. I am glad to hear that Fannie is walking about. I know she must be sweet. As to the name, it is unnecessary for me to say anything for you know my wish. but one middle name do I wish her to bear besides Adelia that is Middleton[19] if she is not to be named after my mother I don't wish her to have any middle name. Now if you wish to give here a middle name under the circumstances do so and I shall not object. She is my only child and as I may yet have some bloody battles yet to go through no one can tell whether or not I will ever return and I want my child to bear my mother's full name but do as you wish my darling for should I fall upon the battle field I will never be the wiser as regards what Fannie is named. I think it strange that Ida does not write to me. I don't intend writing a line until she writes to me. She has not written to Ed since he has been in VA. I wrote you long, long since to let your father and mother have anything that they needed or wanted that we had and mentioned about the sugar. And you ought to have attended to it and why can you not yet do so? Is it not yours? Tell father that you wish to keep half for our own use and that you are willing to divide the other half between your mother and him. Do save half at least for if I am spared I wish to spend next year at home. I don't need any socks now I only wanted you to have them ready by the time I need them. I never recd but four pair. Sometimes we have to send out a mile to get our clothes washed and in half an hour may get and [*sic*] order to move and leave everything, this sometimes occurs not to me as yet, but I wish to provide for it in case it should be my misfortune. Mr. Rogers is kind and does not charge me for many little things so I am willing to let Clarissa cook &c for nothing; he will do what is right. Mr. Andrews wrote me a long letter and he seems to take a great interest in every thing. Tell him the regular price for ___ and bound shoes ought to be

18 Lucretia Calhoun Townes, widow of Dr. Henry Townes of Willington, SC and 1st cousin once removed of John Francis Calhoun. *Calhoun Family Genealogy.*

19 John Francis Calhoun's mother's maiden name was Frances Middleton. John and Rebecca named their daughter Frances Middleton Calhoun, called Fannie. *Calhoun Family Genealogy.*

325 or 50 and kipp skins 75 and 87 ½ the lowest 62 & 70 is the old price. Tell him not to forget to credit my a/c with those four or five hides that I had in tan and that calf skin, Kitties calf. I wish will [*sic*] dressed and kept to make my own shoes and yours. As I will have a large grain crop to sow I intend proposing to let my hands help father for eight or ten days, and then get him to help me sow my grain that is when they finish with the peas & corn, they may help him. Do try and get your father to try and buy me some pigs. I wish 18 or 20 in all with the three at home. I would not object to 25 as I may loose some. Attend to this for me. I am willing to pay even higher than your father thinks they are worth. What about Jim and Bess? Has your father taken Jim over yet? Champ Guillebeau has been discharged and will start home tomorrow. He has never done but very little service always complaining. Sam Harris and Wm Darricott have been sent off again to the Hospital again. I wrote to you some time since requesting you to consult your and my father as to my best plans for the ensuing year. Let me know you views. Shall I plant any cotton and where? In co partnership or not? It is time to arrange my plans. I am partly inclined to plant all grain again and can get ten acres of low ground from father. I once thought of planting cotton, but corn &c may be scarce next year and I can raise my own meat if I plant grain only. Give me your views. Has Mr. Burt paid for the pigs? Send him word to please pay for them. You must not be too modest, if you are he will not pay you soon I assure you. You must get someone to ask him for it. I will write you a few lines in the morning so I must close now so Good by 'til then

BIVOUAC 7th REGT SO.CA V
Oct 23, 1861
No 45

My own darling wife:-

I received your last letter, No 26 dated Oct 14th on the 20th inst or it may have been the 21st and as we are again in the woods I will take this opportunity of replying. I am truly glad to hear that we have at last succeeded in engaging a tanner but in the first place I object to promising any land for his son to work as I have not enough for myself. I am willing for him to have the patch that McKay planted and if it is the intention of father and Mr. Rogers to put them in my house I wish you to tell father that I shall most strenuously object. They must not go in my house for they ought to have driven McKay off long ago. I have written to them both about it and if they had used the proper means they could have had him off. You must speak up it is your right and I am sorry to see that you are so timid. You must have more independence for what is mine is yours and you must not hesitate to have a voice in anything that concerns us. It has just been five months this morning since I last saw you darling. Does it not seem like eight or ten? It has been a dull and trying time and I hope never again to be separated for so long a time again. How delighted I will be when the time comes for me to turn my face homewards and depend upon it if I am living by the fifteenth of Dec but little over six weeks. I will turn my face towards home unless sickness or some unforeseen accident occurs to prevent. I will apply for a furlough, and if I can't get it I must go if I resign my Commission that is one way I can get off. I must attend to some matters and put things "a going" for the next year. I can't get a line from either father or Capt Rogers. Capt Talbert has been away for a month sick and returned last night looking very well indeed. His1st Lieut. told me that the Capt intended applying for a furlough and if refused he would resign as he said that he must go. He wishes to be present the last of Nov. The obstinate refusal to grant any furloughs will prove to some extent a misfortune to the Army as many good officers will resign, whereas they would have been satisfied with a short furlough to return home to arrange their affairs. We are still doing Picket duty when there are thousands and thousands of troops only a few miles in our rear who have never done any Picket duty or work and we have been at it nearly five months. I can't see why Gen Bonham does not have his Brigade rested, there is no sense in his killing up his men for his own glory just because we are in the advance and are the 1st Brigade Army of the Potomac. He wishes the credit of continuing all the time in the lead and perhaps foolishly wishes it said his Brigade did nearly all the work and Picket duty. He will get the honor at the expense of his men. Gen Evans, who mustered us into the service when Maj completely routed the enemy at Leesburg[20]

20 Also known as the Battle of Ball's Bluff (October 21, 1861) A reconnaissance mission based on a

a few days since. He had six Regiments - the enemy 12. We took five or six Cannons, 500 prisoners and killed 100 and many were drownded in trying to cross the Potomac. I give you the statements as given to me, the numbers may not be entirely correct. I can't say it is sure that Gen E defeated and routed the enemy completely. Gen Bonham told me. We heard the firing. Gen E married Miss Gary of Cokesberry a few years since and Gen Bee who was killed at the battle of Manassas on the 21st of July was his first groomsman. I am feeling unwell today. I had charge of a detail from our Reg to assist in building a Bridge under the direction of Maj Baxter of Williams Regt and it was a rainy day. My feet were wet all day, and at night I had headache, sore throat and cold. There was no necessity in the world to have exposed us such a day. There were several working parties of 100 each for our purpose and another and all were dismissed but the Bridge party. I went to see Gen B and asked if we must go out. "Oh yes the Bridge must go on rain or shine but the other working parties may be dismissed until better day." It is to carry Artillery over in case we are attacked and one of his aides told me he doubted it even being used. Certainly he ought not to expose his men unnecessarily and kill them up for nothing. It is now late in the evening and I will close for today and finish tomorrow as it will in all probability be the 25th before I can have an opportunity of mailing this. Good bye until then my own precious wife, my darling Becca.

Thursday morning Oct 24th I have heard positively that Gen Evans completely defeated, demolished the enemy at Leesburg. Gen E had only 4 Regts, the enemy 12. They divided into two columns and tried to surround him but learning this object, he fell back until their columns met - thinking they had him then he opened upon them in front. Va 8th and one Mississippi Reg on the right and one on the left and he cut them in pieces, taking 552 prisoners and six pieces of Artillery. And the boats that they had loaded with the dead and wounded, the retreating rascals rushed in until they sunk some of them and all perished. It is said that a scouting party sent out by Gen Evans the next day took 250 prisoners and if that be true it will make 800 and many were killed and drowned. Gen Magruder has defeated the enemy at little Bethel with great loss on the enemies side. We only heard it yesterday evening but no particulars. It seems the Yankees have made up their minds to be whipped in every engagement no matter how many odds they have against us. Gen Evans had four Regiments in his Brigade although he had only three in the action. the enemy had great odds. I suffered a great deal last night with headache caused by cold. I wish I had those silk handkerchiefs now. You can send them in the box with the boots that I have sent for, the others did not fit after

---

false report resulted in a humiliating Union defeat and cost the life of Colonel Edward D. Baker, a sitting US Senator from Oregon. Confederate Colonel Evans had left Leesburg as reported by the Union scouts, but returned unbeknownst to the enemy by order of General Beauregard. The Union crossed the river into a nest of waiting Confederates and were routed by Colonel Evans with the help of the newly arrived 17th Mississippi. *ORWR*, Vol V, Chapter XIV pp. 348-352.

half soling they were too small. I wrote to Ben Andrews to make me a pair and John Belott and Nathaniel Leroy and McGowan have all sent for Boots. Tucker got me to write for a pair for him some time since and all had better be sent in a box together, at least McGowans, Tuckers and mine and you can get ___ to mark it and send it by Adams Express unless you can find someone coming on. I will write to you again about this matter. I write frequently in great haste and it will be impossible to write about Pat Robinson and everyone in the Company, when I say nothing about them you may know they are all well. They have the same opportunity for writing that I have. Zeke, Gib, Pat T, and Pat R are all well. Wm Darricott and Sam Harris have been sent to the Hospital and I have not heard from them since. The weather has been warm and showery for the last three or four days but it is now clear and cool. We have had but very little cool weather this fall. Cold weather will soon be on us and I dread it. Had you not better have our potatoes banked in the Garden, the corner nearest the house. Give out enough to last the negroes a long time. I don't wish the banks opened until I come home. I will write to father once more and give him full directions. Have as many pumpkins hauled in as possible and have everything well attended to. Tell the negroes I expect if nothing prevents to be at home by the middle of December. I want to find everything going on as I directed. Tell Cupe to attend to all of my orders feeding the hogs, littering the stables ox shoats &c and making ____ spare moments. I will expect a letter from your father in a few days giving me a full account of all my affairs &c &c. There are more who write now in the belief that there will not be any more battles fought here this winter, that at any time heretofore and if we go into winter quarters we will not get out before our time of service is out. We have about 60,000 troops around Manassas & Centerville and 20 or 25,000 on the Occoquan ten or twelve miles below this, enough to resist 200,000 of the enemy. Give my love to all and many kisses to sweet little Fannie. Dearest as the time approaches for me to go home I get more impatient. How anxious I am to see you my darling. Write often love and Believe me dearest Ever your Most loving and Devoted Husband

JOHN F. CALHOUN

Thursday evening Oct 24 the prisoners taken at Leesburg or at least upwards of 300 of them were at Manassas on yesterday. Capt Hodges of our Regt saw them, there are more to come on yet. The enemy lost between ten and fifteen hundred in killed, prisoners &c our loss from 2 to 300 about 50 or 60 killed. Some of our men were drowned in pursuit of the enemy who sunk several boats containing their dead and wounded. I will write again Saturday or Sunday. We will not return to camp until Saturday and I may not have time or may be too tired to write the same day. It is reported that cars sufficient to transport 700 prisoners were ordered to be in readiness at Manassas today or tomorrow, these are the ones taken towards Newport News it is said. Write often Dearest, Ever thine

J.F.C.

November 1861

CAMP NEAR CENTERVILLE VA
NOV 1ST 1861
NO 49

My own loved wife:-

I received two letters from you day before yesterday and I replied briefly on yesterday, promising to write again in a few days and true to my promise as I am always I will no[w] fulfil it. I have been busily employed all day with a detail of ten men from Col Cash's and Kershaw's Regt and ten men from ours, clearing up a campground for General Bonham, he wished it well fixed as we will remain here for a long time in all probability. I dislike very much overseeing white men, my gang today consisted of 30 and they had to clear, pile brush and burn &c and after this discharging the duties assigned to me for the day, I am seated on my-your trunk with my candle in a bottle writing to my own darling wife. There has been a perfect dearth of news for two or three days, none at all scarcely a rumor although Tom Lipscomb[21] told me today that the Generals were all expecting a battle in ten or fifteen days. They think McClellan will be forced by outside pressure to advance. A spy of ours came in a few days since and he says so Lipscomb told me that he mingled with the troops of the enemy and they all say that McClellan is opposed to advancing and says Bull Run, Centerville &c &c is a perfect Sabastipol in strength. They say they are compelled to advance although the[y] are sure of being defeated. I still doubt their coming, but if they do their defeat will prove far more disastrous than Bull Run. Bonham is not a Maj Gen as reported. He intends resigning but will hold on until it is decided whether or not we are to have any fighting here this winter. He now thinks McClellan will advance along the whole line and there will be an engagement of two or three days which will decide the issue between the two sections. That is merely his opinion. McClellan may come, but he will not unless he is forced to do so. Colonel Ben Lane Posey's[22] Regt is in Centerville. I must go to see him before long. The Browns and Dr. Cade are in Col Thomas'[23] Regt near us. We are all

Centerville to Union Mills five or six miles. The telegraph line passes through our camp and a new military road. Generals Beauregard and Stewart passed through this evening with a long escort of cavalry. Gens Johnston

21 Lieutenant Thomas Jefferson Lipscomb (1833-1908) Company B, 3rd South Carolina Volunteers. His brother James was the son- in- law of Governor Francis Pickens and 2nd cousin of Rebecca Noble Calhoun. *Kershaw's Brigade*, p. 90.

22 Colonel Benjamin Lane Posey (1827-1888). Born in Abbeville, SC but moved to Alabama. Commanded Company K, 38th Alabama Volunteers. *Find a Grave*.

23 Unidentified

& Beaury[24] came dashing through a few evening since. Whenever Gen Johnston is along he keeps all in a dashing gait but when Beaury is alone he rides slow. Col Burt[25] of the Mississippi 18th who was wound[ed] in the battle of Leesburg died a few days since. Senator A. G. Brown[26] of Miss. is a Capt in that Regt. He says Napoleons old guard never made a more gallant charge than the Va 8th did in that battle. Gen Evans sent one of the Miss. Regts around to flank the enemy and led the Va 8th to attack them in front and a Regt of the enemy were concealed in a gully with a dense growth of small bushes along the edge and when the Va 8th was in a short distance a soldier put a hat on a bayonet and waved it above the tops of the bushes and shouted "don't shoot us we are the Mississippians" and when within about thirty steps of the gully they poured a deadly fire into them which staggered the entire Regt, but the brave fellows recovered fired and charging the villains, carried them at the point of their bayonets to the banks of the Potomac. Capt Bradley left a few days since for the Hospital, Dr. Hearst accompanying him. Ed joined the Company tonight. I told him that I doubted that he could stand it as his health has been bad. He intended joining when he first came on but Capt Bradley and I both advised him not to do it until he felt sure that he could undergo the hardships of the camp. Cothran advised him to remain as an independent and not to volunteer yet a while. Nov 2d: It rained all night and is still raining and may continue all day from appearances so much so that I fear we will not have any mail today. Winter Quarters are now being talked about and in ten or fifteen days if the enemy does not advance we will begin preparing for winter. The Quarter Master of our Regt has $30,000 in SCa. & Ga money to pay us off and will begin today or Monday. We will be paid for two months and I will send you some my darling. I wish I had a thousand to send you. I owe three months board or at least that for provisions to the Commissary. I will get some Confederate stamps and send you by the next mail if I can get them by that time. I can get them from Manassas I know. What do you have to pay on my letters now? Yours are all marked 5 cents Paid. Let me know what you pay on ___. My darling of course I did not think hard of you for writing short letters. I am entirely satisfied, generally you have done remarkably well and I am truly delighted dearest that you find no room to complain and thinks no husband writes oftener and longer letters to their wives than I do to mine. My darling I have often told you that there were few husbands who loved their wives as I did mine and I still think so. Don't you love? I suppose you and Ida went to Augusta last week.

---

24 General P.G.T. Beauregard was given the nickname "Beaury" by his troops.

25 Colonel Erasmus Burt (1820-1861) Born in Edgefield, SC and was the brother of Armistead Burt. He studied medicine in Alabama but practiced in Mississippi. He raised a regiment of volunteers in Mississippi called "Burt's Rifles." He was shot at the Battle of Ball's Bluff (Leesburg) and later died of his wounds. ORWR, Vol V, Chapter XIV, pp. 349-352. *Find A Grave*.

26 Senator Albert G. Brown (1813-1880) of Mississippi. Mentioned in a letter of June 12, 1861. Born in Chester, SC. Served as Governor of Mississippi from 1844-1848. Was a US Senator from 1854 to 1861 when he resigned to join the Confederacy as a Captain. Served in the Confederate Senate from 1862-1865 and was said to possess "magical powers." *Biographical Directory of the U.S. Congress. Find A Grave*.

I wrote to father to buy me 60 or 80 pounds of bacon for my negroes which will be enough to last until Christmas. Enquire and find out if he has got any and tell him to get that $25 from Mr. Burt and buy bacon with it and I will send you more. I don't wish to kill my young hogs until the last of Dec. Don't forget to buy me more pigs. Ben Andrews can find out who has any that can be bought, tell him to buy me a few more. Ida wrote me that father had sold some of my negro cloth for 60 cents a yard and thought he could sell all at that price. It will bring us in near one hundred dollars and can go toward paying off my store accounts for the last two years at Taggarts[27] & Mars. I made by the sheep skins and wish I could get a few hundred more. Do they keep all the vats full at the Tan yard? They ought to do so. Notice the wheat and see that it is not wasted tell Mr. Crawford to keep an account of every bushel of my wheat that is ground and by whose orders so that I can tell if they have wasted any. Tell father to let the negroes get their allowances of meal from the mill as ten bushels will do them until the last of Dec. You may let them have half allowance of flour if you wish and tell father. Have your bran saved. If I can't get this off in time today I will write again in the morning. Give my love to you father, mother Carie, and Sam and many kisses to Fannie. Zeke, Gib, Pats &c are all well. Love to you Aunty & uncle, Mrs. Cowan & Mr. C. Write soon and write me long and affectionate letters like you last my dearest. Fondly and Devotedly Your Husband

J.F.CALHOUN

SUNDAY MORNING NOVEMBER 3RD 1861

It continued raining incessantly all day yesterday and only ceased during the night last night so I had no opportunity of sending this letter as the mail did not go out. I will write a few more lines this morning my darling, as I always write up to as late a moment as I can. About the last of the week the 6th or 8th I will expect a letter from your father and Carie, although from what you say I will be disappointed if I look for one from your father in ten or twelve days yet it will be a lengthy letter any when it does come. Darling I would not let Clarissa idle as she does. She is not to employ all of her time in cooking for Mrs. Andrews, give her something to do, if nothing else make her rake up leaves &c on the hill behind the Tan Yard for littering the stables &c. Enquire every time you go down and find out what she does and tell her that I have asked you to write me. As I have heard three times of her getting trifling and lazy, tell her that I am determined to pay her and she is working not only for a severe chastising if I return but a separation from Henry. I won't stand her. Give my love to all and many sweet kisses to darling little Fannie. I am so anxious to see you all and hope and pray that we may be permitted to meet before long. I will not apply

27 William H. Taggart, merchant in Calhoun Mills/Willington, SC. *Ancestry.com*.

for a furlough until it is decided that there will be no more fighting. Good bye my own darling, precious wife. Ever your fond and Devoted Husband

JOHN F CALHOUN

CAMP NEAR CENTERVILLE VIRGINIA
MONDAY MORNING NOVEMBER 4, 1861
NO 50

My own beloved wife:-

Being Officer of the Guard today I will have a good opportunity of writing and am now seated in the sunshine near the Guard House writing to the idol of my heart, and Oh, how delighted I would be to embrace that idol, the fates permitting before another year sets in. I will again clasp thee in my arms mine own once more. My darling I fear that this will be less lengthy and uninteresting than my other last letters have been as there is no news afloat now at all. I have never known fewer rumors in Camp than at present and you must know that when the soldiers are not able to start a rumor it must indeed be a dull time. It is said that we will begin making winter quarters soon unless McClellan advances and now that the ground is so thoroughly saturated with water after the continued rain of the last few days. I think it very improbable that he can advance soon and as this weather is warm for the season and unsettled. I think before the ground becomes dry enough to maneuver Artillery it will rain again. Dr. Williams and old Virginian say that he does not think the ground will be in a condition to maneuver Artillery again until spring as we may expect rain frequently from this on and the ground must be firm to manage Artillery. If McClellan fails to advance, it will have all the moral effect of a victory. Our Chaplain, Mr. Carlisle, intends resigning this month, the Major and three Captains from Col Cash's Regt have resigned and two more Lieut's from our Regt. It is a mistake about Gen Bonham's being promoted to the command of a Division. The Richmond papers so stated a few days since. He still intends resigning as soon as it is ascertained that there will be more fighting this winter. Bob Middleton[28] received a letter from Eugenia yesterday and she says that your father, Ida and Mr Rogers were all at her house on their way to Augusta, or at least father and Mr. Rogers going down and I think you and Ida were to remain with her until the others returned. Eugenia's letter was dated the 28th from Woodlawn. I suppose by the time this reaches Mt. Carmel you will have returned home. I am expecting a letter from you this evening darling for I know you never fail writing twice a week. I am behind bad in writing, I think one letter but it is owing to the failure in the mail as you will see from my last, I had it on hand two days this will sometimes occur but when I can mail my letters you may depend upon my writing three times a week but dull times like the present you must not expect long ones and so long as the weather continues pleasant I can very conveniently write but should it become very cold I fear it will be a difficult matter. The Regiment is being paid for two months services today beginning

28 Robert Middleton and his wife Eugenia Calhoun Middleton. He was a younger brother of John Francis' mother Frances. *Calhoun Family Genealogy.*

on the right of the Regt, our Company will come tomorrow and I will send you ten dollars in my next letter and if you need more darling let me know it. I owe twelve or fifteen dollars and three months account to the Commissary besides and I must save enough to last me two or three months as we may not get any more soon. I will need twenty five dollars to go home on and if I get off on furlough I will need some to return on so I will not have a great deal to appropriate to paying debts. I must save some to send you occasionally. It is rumored in Camp today that thirty thousand yankees landed from the fleet at Port Royal SCa but I don't believe a word of it. I am afraid Gov Pickens will not be sufficiently particular in fortifying and guarding the coast. Gov Brown of Ga is one of the most watchful and cunning Governors in the south. He is a match for the Yankees. Our Regt will have to go out on Picket the last of this week. I can't imagine why some of those Regts which have never done any Picketing do not relieve us; it seems we are to be kept at it all the time. A number of our men are being sent back to the Hospitals with Camp fever, Pneumonia &c. We sent four yesterday and two today from our Company. I am as healthy as I ever was in my life. I will not finish until the mail comes. I received yours of the 27th written Sunday evening before you went over to fathers. Carie's of the 28th reached me by the same mail. All of your letters up to date have been received, none miscarried. When we fell from Fairfax, the mail directed to that place was stopped at Manassas. <u>No, no</u> my <u>darling</u> I am not hurt although at first I did think if you were in earnest you were wrong to complain as I generally wrote long letters and it was only when I was pressed for time that I wrote less than <u>three</u> pages but I soon understood you and in turn thought I would tease you. <u>All is right</u> darling only we are still like <u>young</u> lovers and occasionally tease each other. Well we are <u>lovers</u> and will always be like lovers. I will continue <u>wooing</u> and will always be <u>a lover.</u> Now darling won't that be delightful? <u>Sweet dear</u> little Fannie, how anxious I am to see her. I know she must be smart and smart, but Carie says she doesn't seem to care much about you; darling don't let her learn to forget her mother nor cease to love her. Keep her attached to you and learn her to walk well and to talk plainly. I expect she is he pet of the Household isn't she? Who pets her the most? And she calls you "<u>Beck.</u>" Saucy little creature, she will be spoiled. Champ Guillebeau gave me an order on the Capt Bradley for the amount of his note. He has not been paid up and the Capt has authority to draw his pay. Palmer has not yet paid me all, he paid $6 six dollars some time since. You seem anxious my darling to know whether or not I intend volunteering after my twelve months is out. No darling I do not unless there is a <u>pressing</u> <u>necessity</u> and the war is renewed with increased virulence in the spring. You know <u>dearest</u> that it is painful for me to be separated from you and from my character and habits. I am not one who can in any way enjoy such a life. Those who are fond of being from home or who are fond of spree-ing or anything of that kind can <u>doubtless</u> can find more enjoyment such as it is, if there can be any in such a life. I am one of those who love home and the dear ones there more than anything on earth and if I am blessed in reaching home again I assure I will be loth to leave under any consideration. Captain Brooks says he would never remain here all winter if he was not a Captain. And if I can't get a furlough in Dec I still think it is decidedly to my interest and I am not certain but that it will be my duty to resign, and then if the war continues I can go to Charleston and then I can the better direct my affairs at home, occasionally I can visit home. Many think the war will end by spring but no one knows it is very uncertain. I am glad to learn from Carie's letter that your father will make both a good Cotton and corn crop. She said he had out twenty-one thousand when she wrote. He sent me word that he would write when he next went to the Mills. I will look anxiously for it. Tell Carie I will answer her letter in a week or "so" and tell Ida I will expect that long letter that she promised me when she returned from Augusta. Her last was a mere note. Gib, the Pats, Zeke, Ed and all our neighbors and acquaintances are well excepting Sam Harris and Darricott who are still at the Hospital but walking about when last heard from. Give my love to your father, mother, Carie and Sam and many kisses to my dear, sweet little Fannie. Love to your uncles and aunts. Write soon precious to your Most loving and Devoted Husband

JOHN F. CALHOUN

HEAD QUARTERS OF COMPANY "C" PICKET
STATION "NO 4" FRIDAY NOV 8TH 1861
NO 52

My own darling wife:-

I wrote you a short letter of three pages day before yesterday in which I enclosed ten dollars $10 which I hope may reach you in safety. When I write again I will send you ten more and should you need any more my darling let me know it unhesitatingly and I will send you as much as you want I only want money in order that I may be able to add to your comfort and it gives me pleasure when ever I can contribute in any way to your comfort or happiness. As I mentioned in my last the 7th Regt came out on Picket yesterday and one Lieut from Company C was detailed to remain in Camp as officer of the Guard and Cothran requested to be left so I am in Command of the company. We came out from the Bivouac of the Regt this morning and relieved Captain Denny's Comp. Capt Brooks' Head Quarters are in sight. I sent The Rogers with with [*sic*] 14 men to our post and Ed is with him. Last night was quite cool and this morning there was a white frost ice and the ground frozen in some places. A little later in the winter and Picketing will be severe and no doubt many a poor soldier will be frost bitten. From what Gen Bonham told me himself a few nights since I feel confident that he is the cause of our being kept on Picket and not relieved by other Brigades. I told him that the men and officers complained of the injustice of our being kept on Picket - and whilst there were thousands of troops near us who had never done any Picketing, and they certainly ought at least to divide the duties with us. The General said that South Carolina choose the front in this great movement and having selected the position that we must keep it without complaining. He intends returning soon and he wishes to have it said that Gen Bonham's Brigade was in the advance all the time that he had nearly all the work and Picketing to do and he will make capital out of it. And it may aid him in getting some position but his men will have to suffer for it. He exposed his men to add to his own glory but this is common with all ambitious men. When Gen B leaves, no doubt other Brigades will Picket with us and our men will have an easier time. Some few Brigades are doing Picket duty, but we have been all the time doing it and there are many Brigades doing none. The papers on yesterday contained an account of the Federal Fleet of forty two vessels attacking Port Royal on the coast of So Ca[29] and the fight was still going on at the latest accounts. I feel confident of success in nearly every engagement and the[y] will be defeated no doubt at Port Royal. And even if they could succeed in landing

29 The Union fleet had sailed from Norfolk, VA down the coast, captured two Confederate Forts at Cape Hatteras, NC and had now arrived at *Port Royal*, SC. The overwhelming guns from the fleet pounded Forts Beauregard and Walker at Port Royal forcing the Confederates to flee and their gunboats to retreat upriver. This decisive victory now allowed the Union to control the coast as far south as Port Royal. Battle of Port Royal by Michael D. Coker. *ORWR*, Vol VI, Chapter XV, pp. 3-6.

it would be the worse for them. I don't think they can hold out much longer. Scott an old villain has resigned[30] and it is reported that McClellan has been superseded because he refused to advance, that may be so, in any event the result will be the same and it is evident that the Lincoln dignitaries are not agreeing very well together. I am looking for a great "rumpus" among them before long. I dreamed of you last night darling and you could not guess what a singular dream I had, and one that you would not like very well. I dreamed that you were again in a delicate situation &c. Take care you don't know but that dream will be realized in six or eight weeks. What has become of Sallie? Does she intend waiting until Ed comes home in the Spring before she has the matter over? I thought from what you wrote me two months since that the event was near at hand. Darling have you made arrangements about feeding the negroes until the last of Dec? I wish you would do so. I wrote to father to buy me 60 or 80 pounds of bacon and that amount would be an abundance until the last of Dec. Enquire of father whether he has bought any or not and if not tell him get some but beans would be cheaper that is part beef and part bacon. I wish you would would [*sic*] get your father to select some suitable and convenient place for making a pen for my hogs as it will soon be time to put them up. I don't want the pen far from the house as some one may steal the hogs and I wish a floored pen and if you can make any arrangements to have the foods boiled it would be a great savings to do so then you could have turnips &c boiled together. Ask Mr. Rogers to have the boiler fixed if it can be done. I may not be able to leave here before the fifteenth of this Dec and I don't want any of my hogs killed until I come so make arrangements to feed the negroes until even the last of Dec. I will write to father also about having the hog pen built - for I don't wish to wash my corn throwing it in a pen knee deep in mud. I wrote to father to get that money from Mr. Burt and buy bacon with it. Has he got it yet? If not tell him to make him pay. Mr. B gets the advantage of nearly everyone in money matters and I don't want him to be too smart for me. Send him word again and again until he pays for he knows stock of that kind are cash. If you have boiled food for the hogs Clarissa has ample time to boil it as she has little or noting to do. I hope father and bought sheep skins and hides when when [*sic*] they were in Augusta. How did you enjoy your trip to Edgefield? Did Fannie know you when you returned and how did she receive you? My darling I hope you wrote to me from Edgefield, if so I will get it today. Saturday the 9th I will finish my letter this morning as we are to be relieved in a few hours by Capt Talbert's Company, and we will return to the "Bivouac" and the Post Master will bring out the mail in the evening, then darling I will get a letter from you. I know I will and I will send this back by him. I slept comfortably last night after I got to sleep, but it was one oclock before I fell asleep as I sat up until half past twelve to see that all

30 General Winfield Scott resigned as General in Chief of the Union Army on October 31, 1861 and was replaced by General George McClellan on November 1, 1861. *Encyclopedia Virginia. ORWR*, Series III, Volume I, pp. 611-614.

was going on well. This morning is dark and cloudy, and will either rain or snow. I expect we will have much bad weather from this time on, but it will prevent any movement on the part of the enemy, and it would [be] the same as a victory. I dreamed last night that an order came from Gen Bonham to pack up and get ready to return home to South Carolina and Oh, how delight[ed] I was to get back to see my darling. Whilst I am writing some of the boys are cooking biscuit, making coffee, frying meat &c and it would surprise you to see how well they cook. Some of hem killed a large fat unmarked hog and I will enjoy a breakfast of ribs. The yankee residents who fled from this county left cattle, hogs &c. and the soldiers kill them whenever they can get a chance. If I have time I will write a note to father and enclose in this, which I wish you to hand to him as soon as you can. This will be mailed on Sunday morning and I will write again by Tuesday or Wednesdays mail. Tell Ida to write to me, give my love to her and your father, mother, Sam, Carie and last but first in every respect my darling little Fannie, and many kisses to her. Gib and Zeke are well. Pat Robinson also. Pat T is complaining but that is common in camp. Write often and affectionate letters my own darling precious wife to your own Fond and Devoted husband

JOHN F CALHOUN

CAMP NEAR CENTERVILLE VIRGINIA
SUNDAY EVENING NOV 24TH 1861
NO 58

My dearest:-

I will write you a short letter this evening to keep up my regular period of writing not that I have anything of any importance to write, there being no news to write and not having any letter to answer. The last one I received was dated Nov 10th which was written on the day before you went up to see Sallie. I can't imagine what is the cause of this. The Rogers has received three letters from home since I received your last which proves to me that Jim Covin fails to mail my letters promptly. I will enclose a slip which you will please send him, and it will make him a little more particular and I would here suggest that you put the date in one corner of the envelope, and seeing that he will know that it is done to detect any carelessness on his part and he will perhaps attend a little more promptly to his business. I do not blame you darling for I feel sure that you write twice a week regularly as you promised. We had a grand Review today. Three Brigades and three Batteries of Artillery, with the Brigadiers and the Maj General of the Division, Earl Van Dorn,[31] and all was reviewed by the General commanding the Army corps General Beauregard. But such shows are getting to be nothing new. I saw Sam Pickens[32] son of T. J.

[*Missing page(s)*]

The box sent by father has never been heard of - he ought to have sent word how it was directed and whether it was sent by Adam's Express or not. It is snowing tonight and on yesterday it snowed and sleeted both but not much. I hear that the Governor has ordered back the "Shotgun" Battalions. I expect there were more spectacles shinning on the coast a few days after the Port Royal affair than ever before. I expect your father can tell jokes on some of the party. He ought to have had uncle Dock along. Tell him to write me all about his trip. You all must not *[manuscript ends]*

31 General Earl Van Dorn (1820-1863) was born in Mississippi and was a grand-nephew of President Andrew Jackson. He was a graduate of the U.S. Military Academy. He resigned his commission and joined the Confederacy in January of 1861. Was made a Brigadier General in the Mississippi Militia, replacing Jefferson Davis as commander of the Mississippi state forces. Van Dorn was killed in Tennessee in May 1863 by a jealous husband who claimed Van Dorn was carrying on an affair with his wife. *Find A Grave.*

32 Samuel Bonneau Pickens (1839-1891). Named for his uncle, he was one of the Citadel Cadets to fire on the Union vessel "Star of the West" on January 9, 1861 in Charleston Harbor. After graduation, he joined the Confederate Army and rose in rank to become Colonel of the 12th Alabama infantry. He was the 2nd cousin of Rebecca Noble Calhoun. *Calhoun Family Genealogy. Find a Grave. Thomas Boone Pickens, His Ancestors* by Lois K. Nix and Mary Kay Snell

CAMP NEAR CENTREVILLE, VA
SATURDAY EVENING NOV 31, 1861
NO 61

My own darling wife

Two more mails have been brought in and the bright November sun is drawing a curtain over the last day of this month and the same bright luminary that closes the last day of November[33] will in a few more hours usher in cold December and no letters from my darling wife yet. Yes surprising as it may appear yours of the 10th and 17th were the last ones received and the worst of it is that I can't as yet find evidence to convict the Post Masters as The Rogers has received another from home since I last wrote to you making three since I read one, his last was the 23rd. Ed gets his, Gib Tennent received two 22nd and William Darricott received one from Mt. Carmel dated the 23rd and why could not one come for me? Tomorrow will be two weeks since your last was written. I will try neat pretty colored gilt-edged paper and coaxing and petting and wooing and everything that I can possibly think of hoping as a reward that you will at least write to me once a week. But my dearest (I will now try the wooing) don't you think that such constancy, fidelity and devotion merits two letters a week? I know that your dear generous heart cannot withstand the appeal from your absent John in who though far, far away where the bright November sun ere he plunges his fiery chariot into the western seas, throws his golden rays over the blue mountain tops of Virginia still distance fails to obliterate from his faithful heart the image of his blue-eyed one at home. Do dearest write to me at once and in the same loving tone of your absent one. We will go on picket tomorrow and will return on Wednesday the 4th of December and it may be so that I will not be able to write again until I return. If I should not don't be disappointed. When I fail to write to you for three or four days you always know the cause for I prepare you for it in advance. Dr. Gibert wrote to his nephew today and told him to tell me that my partner was asking little or nothing for shoes and leathers and to tell me to come home if possible or he would ruin me. Dr. G said that others were asking high prices and he saw no reason why I should not get a high price as well as anyone else. Now how is this? Do tell your father to write to me and let him know all about it. Tell him to send me Covins prices. Dr. G told his nephew to show me this letter which he did and I am surprised to hear it. I am afraid my affairs is badly managed and if there is no prospect of a fight I don't know but that I will resign and return home. Gen Beauregard positively refuses to grant any furloughs for the present and in fact he refused to accept should there be any chance of a battle here in two or three weeks. I will not apply or if I find that there will be no use in applying you know it would be

33 This letter was dated November 31, 1861, but was probably written on November 30th, the last day in the month, as evidenced by its content.

prudent to wait. So you must not look for me until I write to you that I have obtained a furlough. Gen's Johnston, Beauregard, Smith &c including other smaller Generals and Cols dined with Gen Van Dorn a few days since and Col Cash who was present said they all expected a battle some where on this line during the winter. Col C said that Gen Smith was brilliantly interesting. He is a Major Gen next to Beauregard. He said McClellan was forced to give battle here or "give up." Gen S said that the fleet can affect nothing of any consequence that the taking of Port Royal or any other southern seaports will not avail them anything of permanent importance as they can not carry on a successful southern campaign. We are not to move yet a while, some say until after the battle. Gen Smith says that McClellan is waiting until the ground freezes deeply so that he will not be caught by thaws but I don't believe a word of it if a Maj. Gen does say so. If it is true then McClellan is a great fool to put off coming until we fortified strongly. Once the Generals said we would go into winter quarters and would be furloughed as soon as the severe winter set in so that the roads, weather &c would prevent the advance of the enemy, and now they pretend McClellan is waiting for freezes. "It's all in my eye" still you know that will be a good excuse for not granting furloughs. The news in the papers from Missouri and Kentucky[34] are very encouraging. All is going well. We have just returned from Picket. Last night was very cold indeed. I got up two hours before day this morning. I was so cold. The ice was more than an inch thick. The ground was frozen all day and tonight will be very cold again. The box is on the way from Manassas. When I open it I will write to you so I will close until then. The box has come and all the articles came safe. I was pleased to get my handks but darling you ought not to have deprived yourself of your silk hanks. The boots in the box had Ed's name on them so mine has not yet come. There is a box containing boots for Bellot & LeRoy, Tucker and myself I suppose, but I was under the impression my boots were in this box. The letter came to hand too. Darling such a pair of boots as Ed's would not be too high at $12. They are choice and made in the military style, hope mine will do as well. I have been out for three nights and have been writing at night so excuse my imperfect letter. I will write again in two days. Give my love to all and many kisses to sweetness and my dearest continue to write often and long letters to Your Most loving, Constant and Devoted Husband.

JOHN F. CALHOUN

34 The people of Kentucky and Missouri were split between the Confederacy and the Union at this time. Missouri was admitted as the 12th Confederate state. e ill The secessionist government was driven into exile when the Confederate Army failed to control the State. There were similar circumstances in Kentucky where the Governor declared the state's neutrality, although it operated a provisional Confederate government until the end of the war. *ORWR*, Vol III, Chapter XII, p. 179.

December 1861

BIVOUAC "NO 4" VIRGINIA
Wednesday December 4th 1861
No 63

My own darling wife:-

The mail at last brings me two letters from you dated Nov 22nd & 26th one mailed the 25th the other 26th and you see my darling it has been five or six days between the one on the 17th and the 22nd which was not mailed until the 25th. If it is James Covin's neglect in mailing the letter tell him of it. My darling you can't imagine how delighted I was to get a letter from you and dearest you must not think hard of me for complaining about your not writing, it is my exceeding love for you and anxiety to hear from you that makes me so uneasy when six and eight days passes by without my hearing from you. I am glad all of my letters have reached you safely including the two containing the ten $10 each. My darling you must not save it for me. I don't want it but send it for you and you must use it as you wish. From my salary, I intend saving one hundred dollars for you to buy silver with should we both be spared to see the close of the war and we will hand it down to our children as a family relic with the history of its purchase. I will give you a hundred besides what I have already sent you. I am very sorry indeed to hear of the death of our fine Durham we are so unfortunate with our cows. Do have the calf well attended to and we can make a fine cow out of her. I have written to father again about my fattening hogs. I don't expect darling ever to have anything attended to as I wish so long as I am away. When you go down again tell Mr. Andrews to have the pen floored as I directed and a good trough. I want my hogs as fat as corn can make them. How many hogs are in the pen? Are there not 13 besides the 2 (half) ½ Chester pigs? Surely the half Chesters are too young and small to kill. I want all my hogs well fed particularly my two Essex pigs. I want to make large sows out of them. Caution Cupe about them and tell him and Henry both that I will look to both of them about my fattening hogs, they must watch them closely and not let anyone steal one of them. I judge from your letter that they are asking too high for shoes &c at the Mills so Dr. Gibert must have intended the opposite of what he wrote I will tell him about deceiving me. I don't like it in him at all and tell him so for me. I will try and come home in a month to regulate the prices and fix things up generally. I will apply for a furlough as soon as there is a chance for me to procure one. I may apply in six or eight days but in the mean time you must not stop writing. I may be disappointed when I apply and should I succeed I will telegraph you from Manassas so you will know it in time. Circumstances will of course influence me in applying [*Letter ends*]

CAMP NEAR CENTERVILLE, VA
SUNDAY DECEMBER 8TH 1861
NO 65

My own dearest:-

I have acknowledged the receipt of your last letter of the 30th ultimo and replied to the same but will write again today this being truly a day of rest, which is a rare thing in Camp or at least with our Regiment for nearly every Sabbath for the last two months we were either on, going or returning from Picket, but today after troop and Inspection of arms all the duties are over. This is a bright, pleasant, quiet day, the holy Sabbath and oh my darling how I do wish that I could enjoy it with you. I said it was quiet today so it is in our Brigade, unusually so, but since I commenced writing, I hear the booming of Cannons and the bursting of shells over in Centerville. The Artilleryists (sic) are practicing but I do think it is wrong there being no necessity for it and not being one of the standing orders of the Army, like troop, Dress Parade, Inspection of Arms &c it ought to be dispensed with on the Sabbath. Ham Brooks and I went over to Kershaw's camp and took supper with Captain Perryman last night and I met a College mate, Burnett Rhett,[35] Captain of the "Brooks Guards," he is the son of Senator Rhett. We had turkey hash for supper and you know how fond I am of turkey. The great excitement about all of McClellans available force having crossed the Potomac and advancing has measurably died away. A large force, perhaps from 50 to 75,000, may be on this side, no one doubts that but still they may or may not intend advancing. I can well see why they may have crossed and still not advance. Congress is in session and as Washington is filled with ladies it would be a bad idea to keep such an Army of rowdies there, again wood is selling at $10 per cord in Washington and a few miles on this side it is bountiful and the Federal Army may be going into winter quarters. All the Generals excepting Bonham say a battle is inevitable before long. I don't know how it may be. There is no doubt we are to be moved whenever the fight comes off and if so I may be prevented from writing to you for four or five days whenever that move is made so don't be uneasy should you not get a letter for several days. Captain Evans of Cash's Regt resigned two months since but his resignation was three times refused, and at last he went to see the Secretary of War in person and succeeded in getting it accepted. His was an extreme case. His mother or mother in law had died, his wife had become insane, and he had six or eight children, still his resignation was rejected three times. Darling it looks hard but we are engaged in a great cause and not to "win" will be ruin to us all, and our unborn children will be made slaves. We must conquer at any hazard. I wrote to father and told him not to kill my hogs until the last

35 Andrew Burnet Rhett (1833-1879). An 1852 graduate of South Carolina College. Captain Company A, 2nd South Carolina Volunteers and son of S.C. Senator Robert Barnwell Rhett. *Find a Grave. Kershaw's Brigade*, p. 551.

of the month and to make them as fat as they can be made. I told him to let you know when he killed them so you could go down and attend to the lard &c. Tell him again to let you know when he expects to kill, so that you can be ready, and to send you word the morning he kills. Tell Mr. Andrews to attend to it closely until you get down. Had you not better have our room prepared and get your mother to go down with you and stay until the lard is all dried up &c. If our hogs are well fattened and attended to we will have $150 worth of bacon & lard to sell. I intend giving some of the hams and lard to your mother for her kindness to us. Do make a great deal of sausages and put them up so you can save them until I come home. I like the way Mr. McBride puts them up. Make some of them highly seasoned. Tell father not to kill all at once unless they are thoroughly fattened. What about my cotton seed? Do have them all carefully saved and have all of our hominy corn saved. How much did we make? I wrote to father and told him if he had my wheat ground that I wanted him to have all of my wheat brand saved carefully as I wanted some to feed my mare and colt with and the cows, blooded pigs &c. See that it is done. And when you next to down to the Mills find out how many hogs have I in all; the three sows will soon have pigs I expect. I want them well fed all the time for if I am fortunate I wish to raise enough next year to do me two years [*manuscript ends*]

PICKET STATION NO 2 VA
Friday Morning Dec 20, 1861
No 72

My own darling wife:-

The left wing of our Regt came out on yesterday morning and relieved the right. Capt Bradley in command and ours being the first company, we had to go immediately on post. I was in command of Co C, Cothran remaining in camp on Guard. I came out from the "Bivouac" and found the Head Quarters of the out post in a comfortable house plaistered with five comfortable rooms, so I sent The with twelve men and Dr. Hearst with the same with number to the two out posts where they have been all night. This morning I will send out two Sgts, two Corpls and twenty four men and relieve them. The sun is just rising my darling and you are still in bed with our sweet little Fannie by your side whilst I am seated upstairs by a window writing to you my love. I think of you by day and dream of you by night. Time is rolling rapidly away although it appears slowly to me and in a few more weeks I hope I may be permitted to clasp you to my bosom all mine once more. I don't wish to go until the last of Jan or the first of Feb as we will then be in the midst of the coldest of the winter and I don't wish to stay long after I return to camp. The weather is still pleasant and dry, the nights are a little cold, the ground frozen in the morning but it soon thaws, and the days are very pleasant. I suppose you must be having delightful weather in SoCa are you not? Some of the last few days seems like spring. Capt Hester was unwell when I left the Camp and he had procured some kind of a sick certificate from the Assistant Surgeon and said he intended applying for a sick furlough of a month. He complains of his left knee. He will give all the news of Camp &c. I neglected to enclose John Belott's measure for the Boots in my last letter, but will send it in this. Send it to Mr. Andrews and tell him if the price is $8.00 to charge the next pair to me as he has paid me that amount. The boots are cheap at $8.00 the way everything is selling. The firing which we thought was a fight was only practicing or sham fighting within the enemies lines. I suppose you will get this during Christmas week. Let me know how you spent the week. Has you mother recovered yet? You must "put up" with a short letter this time as it has only been two days since I wrote to you and nothing has transpired since then worth writing. All is quiet in the Army of the Potomac. Let me know how many volunteered from our part of the Dst, if any were drafted and who were they. I am anxious to hear. Ed, Zeke, Gib, Pat R, Wm D. and Sam are all well and with me on Picket. I write you a longer letter on Sunday night the 22nd when I return to Camp. Don't forget Mr. Rogers to get DeWitt to "post up" our Books and draw off the a/cs. Give my love to all and many sweet kisses to darling little Fannie. Write soon dearest to your Fond loving and Devoted Husband

JOHN F. CALHOUN

CAMP NEAR CENTERVILLE, VIRGINIA
December 23d 1861
No 73

My own darling wife:-

I wrote you a letter whilst on Picket and sent it in and when I returned I found that Cothran had failed to mail it so I burned it and will write you another. One of the letters No 72 written from the Picket Post I hope will reach you. I received one letter from you whilst on Picket No 2 and the mail today brought me another No 3 Dec 16. I am so thankful darling for your regularity in writing, you are indeed doing well and I will repay you by also writing often and regularly. It is now placed beyond a doubt that furloughs will be granted, for there was an order issued by Gen Beauregard permitting the Commanders of Regiments to furlough two Captains and five Lieutenants from each Regiment also ten more commissioned Officers and privates from the average sized Companies. The Commanders selecting those whose families or affairs require their presence. Capt Bradley and Cothran have been furloughed and I am to remain in Command of the Company until they return, the[y] have 30 days. Ed is one of the privates furloughed and he will go down to see you and tell you all the news &c in a few days after he gets home. Many of our Lieuts are away and Col Fair could easily have furloughed me for Gen Beauregard has giving him permission to furlough five and he has granted only four. He pretends that he can't leave a company with only one officer, whilst all the officers well know that some of the Companies have been reduced to an Orderly Sergeant and often to one officer. It is true the[y] were off on sick leave but the Army Regulations says distinctly that at no time shall a company be left without a commissioned officer, one must be present. Again Gen B in his order distinctly says that the Col. must select those whose affairs or families require their attention at home, the Col admits that my application was strong and my business urgent still he does not furlough as many as Gen B ordered and among the four was an unmarried Lieut who entered the service in July and my application is rejected. All the officers who have spoken of it say that the Col is wrong, and Brooks one of the Cols warmest friends says that he can't sustain himself and told the Col that I could make it appear that he had misconstrued the order. He says Bland thinks it a hard case and he wanted to get up a petition and he and Bland would get the officers to sign it in my behalf. I told him no. I would remain until the 15th of April before I would buy a furlough. I told Brooks [that] Col Fair had done me injustice and I intended demanding a furlough as a right and not beg it as a favor. I would not permit friends to persuade him to do me an act of justice. I will meet Brooks & Bland and enter a protest appealing from his decision. And as some of the officers who have been home on sick furlough during the summer and at the Hospital nearly ever since may return and stand the same chance with me the next time. I may feel it but justice to myself to resign. Ed will give you all the particulars, some things are unkind and dirty trick in certain officers - which I can't write. I am sorry to hear about my hogs tell father not to kill them until they are fat if they remain until Feb. Tell Cupe that he is a neglectful, trifling scoundrel and I intend paying him for neglecting my hogs. I must finish so as to send by Captain Aiken tomorrow. I will write again day after tomorrow. Love to all& many kisses to Fannie. Ever Your own loving Husband

JOHN F. CALHOUN

CAMP NEAR CENTERVILLE, VA
CHRISTMAS DAY DEC. 25, 1861
NO 74

My own darling wife,

I wrote to you on the 23rd and promised to write again in a day or two and I will write to you dearest today and wish you a "Merry Christmas" although I know it can't be a very "Merry Christmas" without me. Can it love? Today is a little livelier than other days, as some made preparations for a "spree" today and are carrying it out but taking everything into consideration this Regt. is behaving very well. The furloughs are all not in the head as it is said that it was a mistake in the order which contemplated furloughing only those who would re-volunteer. There is much disappointment among those who thought they were so sure of getting off. I entered a protest and appealed from Col. Fair's decision respecting the distribution of the furloughs. Capt Brooks and Bland aided me in the matter. I handed to the Col. to read and asked him if all I stated was entirely correct. He said it was. I told him I did it in no unkind spirit and mentioned in the protest that our Col had entirely misconstrued the order, according to my understanding, although I stated that "I would acquit the Col of any but the purest motives as I know him to be a conscientious and honorable man." The Col admitted that he had furloughed one other Lieut. whose claims to a furlough were not so strong as mine and only assigned as the reason that in furloughing me the company would be left but with one Lt., and this Col had a long talk with me and said that it was a hard case, but he said he did not think the Company ought to be left with the 3rd Lieut. and he asked me if I would be willing for some one to lead the company in an engagement. The Col. wrote off a recommendation and mentioned that the camp would be left in command of a 3rd Lieut., he recommended that a furlough be granted to me and sent it with my protest and appeal. The appeal &c Bland informed me was sustained throughout by Gen. Bonham, but it has to pass Gen Van Dorn and Gen Beauregard. I could only reach the latter through the Adjutant Genl Jordan. I addressed him. An officer below reaches the higher through the Adj Genl, for instance Gen Bonham would address this Adj. Genl. of Beauregard's staff in order to reach him, but Beauregard would address Bonham directly being an inferior Genl. Col. Fair says he sincerely hopes Gen. Beauregard will overlook his decision as he wishes me to get the furlough, but now it will make no difference as no one is to get any still. I am contending for a principle and am interested in its success. All is done in good feeling, although the Col. could and should have granted me the furlough in the first instance. I will send the paper when it is returned, then you will the better understand everything concerned with it. No one believes that Gen. B misconstrued this order granting furloughs. There is something behind the curtain yet. If we are to be kept lying here doing nothing until April I can be of such service to myself at home that I would resign if I thought my resignation would be accepted. I will find out soon what to do. I have thought of you often today my darling and know your thoughts are often of your fond and loving husband upon the tented fields of VA. Oh, how I long to be with you and hope that before long we may yet meet. I suppose by the time this reaches you our hogs will have been killed and I do hope this improved rapidly after you saw them last. Do attend to our meat well and save an abundance of sausages, and if father does not kill all at once tell him to let them remain until they are thoroughly fattened. Tell Cupet I find that he has failed to attend to my fattening hogs as I directed and expected him to do and I will inquire how he is treating my sows and pigs. When my hogs are killed let him know how much they weigh and how many are there in all in that pen. I have never yet heard how many I had. I am glad Mr. Crawford is to be retained as long as we can do so. If Mrs. Andrews leaves tell father to have the locks fixed so that the door can be locked, tell Mr. Rogers also to secure the doors so that one or the other will be sure to have it attended to. Why don't you write me about your father's cotton, how much has he made, how much wheat has he sowed, how much oats does he intend sowing etc. etc. Tell him by all means to sow a large crop of oats. Is he having land cleared? He ought by all means to clean up the branch bottom over up to the slopes of the hills. I won't be satisfied until I hear that he intends taking from fifteen to twenty acres of land on this branch. I would like to see it well prepared and planted in corn and pumpkins next year. I suppose your father intends planting but a small cotton crop as everyone should do. Did you get that article I enclosed in one of my last letters about the next crop? Has Mr. Rogers carried the books up for DeWitt to post up? Continue to remind him of it every time you see him until he does it as I am anxious to hear how much we have booked. I am afraid now Mr. A over calculated. Send me the blanket by Tucker. I was so sure that John E Bellot would go home on furlough that I did not enclose his measure. I send it in this. Have the boots made and sent by Tucker. Don't forget to have them charged to me as he has paid me $8.00 for them. Col. Bacon is said to be very low. Maj. Seibels has returned to duty. Col. Fair is nearly well. Jeff Nixon, Bob and William Middleton were furloughed a few days since to begin on the 26th, but they got off a day or two in advance, as no one in our Regiment will report this fact. They are fortunate as all furloughs granted under the orders of Gen. Beauregard were revoked, so as they are off no one will notice their leaving, but no one else will be allowed to leave. Bob will be delighted to get home. Give my love to your father, mother, Carie and Sam and many kisses to sweetness. Bless her little heart. Did you give her any eggnog? I will write again soon. Zeke, Sam, Pat R, Ed and all of us all well. Write soon dearest to your loving and ever Devoted Husband

JOHN F. CALHOUN

CAMP NEAR CENTERVILLE, VIRGINIA
MONDAY DECEMBER 30TH 1861
NO 75

My own darling wife:-

I received a letter from you today dated the 23rd inst No 5 and as usual my darling I was delighted to hear from you. All of your letters reach me now regularly and I hope that you are getting mine. I sent one hundred and forty $140 dollars by The Rogers to Charlottesville to send you in a check from there which I hope will reach you safely. he started this afternoon and if he gets the check immediately after he gets there it will reach you by the same mail with this, but don't be uneasy should you not get it until the next mail. Let me know as soon as you get this whether or not you received the money or check by the same mail. I will send you ten {$10} dollars in Confederate bills enclosed in this. And it is all for your own use my darling, although I wish you to lend the amount of the check to your father but let it come from you and the amount sent in money you and Fannie must appropriate as you may wish. The Confederate Bills will answer for the specie[1] in paying postage, taxes, buying stamps or anything in the way of dues to the Government. In ten or fifteen days I will draw one hundred $100 more and send to you my love and with that amount I hope you will be able to get on until I return. I now give you all that I have heretofore sent you and it is not my intention to call on you again for it but if at any time you want any more let me know and I will send it to you darling. Has Mr. Burt never paid the $25 yet? Tell father he must get it or if you can manage in any way to get it, do so and keep it. Don't put off annoying him any longer and ask your father about it how to proceed &c. The prospect for getting a furlough at present seems almost hopeless although nearly any of the officers so disposed can get a sick furlough to extend to sixty days, they complain of ill health &c get the Surgeon to recommend a furlough of any reasonable length of time, many go off in this way. About six or eight of the field officers out of twelve have gone off. Col Bacon is said to be very ill. Col Fair is to leave this evening or tomorrow on a 60 day furlough and in every company in the Regt one or more of the officers have been home but ours. Still we will never get any credit for it, "so ways the world." I may be able to get a furlough between this and April. There is much dissatisfaction about the way we have been treated; although we have no idea of an advance and nothing to do and business of the greatest importance to call us home, still the Authorities persist in refusing to grant furloughs. An occasional one is granted and singular to say in every instance they are from Edgefield. 4 officers and four or five non commissioned officers & privates. I don't include sick furloughs. This is the "post of honor and danger" the grand army of

1 Coins.

the Confederacy, but I must say I am tired of it. There are many complaints against our great Beauregard, they seem just too, but I can't make up my mind to join in against him as I entertained such an exalted opinion of him. I am sorry to hear of your mothers continued ill health, hope she has improved. Sweet Fannie must be sweet and interesting, how I long to see her and you too darling. I am glad to hear that your father is clearing up the branch bottom, tell him to take in as much as possible. I will anxiously expect the promised letter from him. The next letter I write will be Jan 1862. I want time to fly rapidly now. I am so anxious to see you. Give my love to all and many kisses to my darling sweet little daughter. The boys are all well, excepting W. D,[2] he is unwell today. I will write again in a day or two, darling. Tell Ida to write to me. Believe me dearest, Ever your fond and Devoted Husband

JOHN F. CALHOUN

2 William Darricott, member of Company C, 7th South Carolina Volunteers and 3rd cousin once removed of John Francis Calhoun. *Calhoun Family Genealogy. Kershaw's Brigade*, p. 559.

[*INCOMPLETE,* DEC. 1861]

...Captain Hester told me again a few days since to write to you and request you to select a pair of the finest pigs from Bess' next litter for him and as soon as they are large enough to wean he will write to his wife to send for them. I told him they were yours and that the price was $25 a pair. Don't forget that Capt H has first choice. He spoke to me three or four months ago about the pigs and has reminded me of it two or three times. You will make money on Bess if you have her well attended to and remember darling it is all to be yours. I owe you $25 for the first pair the same for the last and I intend for you to have it. I will wait until the mail comes in and see if there is a letter form you to reply to, and the remaining two pages must be left for that purpose.

Sure enough my darling the mail brought me a letter from you dated Friday December 6th. It was short but interesting as they always are and I hope you will always write twice a week whether you have much to write or not. You said that you had my letter of Nov 26th No 58. I did not know that any number was delayed you never mentioned it before. Let me know if any miscarry and always let me know the number you receive. I must praise you my darling for being so industrious as to finish five pair of socks and nearly all at night. You have indeed done well. How many pair are for me? I thought you knit some for the Society. I am afraid my boots are lost so when you go down to the Mills tell Mr. Andrews to make me a pair like the ones he made Ed, thick soles, loose fitting and tell him to put in a pair of insoles for fear they may not fit. Tell Mr. A to make the legs large but not as high as Ed's. And not to put the piece in front after the Military style. The legs ought to be larger at the top and taper down. Tell him to try his hand on them and if my others come to hand I can sell one pair. Capt Hester's servant, Lee, a free boy from the CH will return to spend the Christmas in Abbeville and return the first of January some time and I will get him to bring back my boots & blankets. Those who revolunteer will get a furlough and the others will remain until April. I doubt that many will revolunteer here. A rumor is afloat that several squares of the city of Charleston was burned, supposed to be the work of an incendiary.[1] Brown I hear is cleared, he ought to be hung. He married a niece of C.P. Sullivan of Laurens. Fannie must be sweet, how I long to see her. I would like to see her rolling up her sweet blue eyes as you tell me she does sometimes. She must look sweet. Learn her to talk. Does your father intend buying hogs from your uncle John? Col Fair and Aiken just came in and the Col pointed in at me writing and Aiken said I was always writing. I will let them talk and I will write. When you write always let me know what your father is employed at, his hands. Ask him how much corn does he intend

1 On Dec. 11, 1861, a fire of unknown origin along East Bay in Charleston spread rapidly. Gen. R.E. Lee was there at the time, staying in the Mills House Hotel. The fire burned 540 acres and destroyed over 570 homes along with many businesses. *Harper's Weekly*, Dec. 28, 1861

planting next year. He ought to plant nearly all corn. Give my love to all and kiss Fannie. Write a long letter in reply Dearest to Your Fond and Devoted Husband

JOHN F. CALHOUN

PS The box has just come and my boots came safely. Ben Andrews need not make the ones I ordered in this. ONeall Palmer sold the ones sent to Nathaniel LeRoy for me. He sold them for $12. tell Ben A. to let me know how much the pegged ones are worth and the sewed ones too. Good night love

Ever Thine

[*INCOMPLETE,* DEC. 1861]

. . . go into winter quarters in January sometime as many think we will, and there should be no prospect of any more fighting during our term of service and I find that the Authorities still continue to refuse to grant furloughs, but that Resignations will be granted, must I resign or wait until he 15th of April and then come home? I doubt that any resignations will be accepted even after we go into winter quarters but I merely wish to know your wish should I find that mine will at any time be accepted. I think darling that I ought to tough it out without a murmur unless something more should turn up than I now am aware of to cause me to resign. Thousands are in for the war and it may be a long while before they can see home and I can at last get to return to you my love in four months if my life should be spared. Now don't you think my darling it would be better to serve out the time for which I volunteered and then I can the better reconcile it to my feelings to remain at home for a few months. The war may be at an end in that I hope it may. Those who will not now come forth and strike a blow in defence of our homes, do not deserve the name of freeman and. the benefits and enjoyments of a free government. W.T. and A.H. will never get over their shameful conduct. Young and hearty and far better able to leave than thousands and thousands of poor men who have left large families unprovided. And when their own soil was invaded by our enemies with their avowed intentions of inciting insurrection, destroying our property, murdering our wives and children and they refuse to go forth to meet them. Where would we all be if only one half of our men were made of such material? Ruin would soon be on us all. The blush of shame shall never mantle your cheek dearest on my account. No even should I fall upon the battle field I will feel covered with glory in defense of our homes, our firesides, and our alters. And you my darling shall at last feel proud that you gave to the cause a husband whose name you will feel proud to bare and my daughter shall feel not ashamed to call me her father. This feeling should actuate all patriots and none others deserve the name. My boots have not yet come. I will write for another pair. When our hogs are killed give some of the ribs, backbones &c to Mrs. Andrews divide liberally and take a portion and a large portion over with you. I see wheat is selling in Augusta at 175 & 200, flour from 10 to 11 3/4. I hope father will make a good sale. The Rogers says the Captains Mill wheel broke a few days since. Let me know about it. Ed, Gib, Zeke, and Pat R. and Wm D are all well. Give my love to all and many kisses to our darling little Fannie. And Believe me dearest love your Faithful and Devoted Husband

JOHN F. CALHOUN

PS Sam Harris has not returned yet and all the officers of our Company are talking about him and saying he will not return until he was compelled to do so. Wm Darricott says Sam was well and looking as well as ever. He has been off or will be <u>two</u> months on next Friday. He will injure himself and it would mortify his father. I don't know but what it is my duty to let him know it, as Sam is a mere boy still. Tell your father to let him, the Dr. know it or not as he thinks best. The Dr might write and give him some advice as to his duty. Good night dearest

Ever Thine

JOHNNIE

[*INCOMPLETE*, Dec. 1861]

...I have concluded not to send this by Tucker as he might lose it and it will reach you nearly as soon by due course of mail. John E. Belott has sold his boots for $12.00 as they did not fit or at least they fit too tightly for marching he paid me $8.00. Ask Mr. Andrews if that was the price. John wishes another pair made exactly like the others only a little larger, he sends his measure which is full. Have the boots made and sent on by Tucker. The boots are very reasonable in fact such high legged boots ought to be worth $9. The Kipp shoes are too high I think but I cant regulate everything when away. Col Pendleton a Virginian chief of Artillery in the Army of the Potomac proposed, and set on foot a plan to raise a subscription for those of Charleston who were sufferers in the great fire. His plan was to raise the money by each volunteer giving so many days pay, say one, two, three or more, and for the amount to be deducted from their next pay as many would give in that way who would not give the cash, all might not have the cash or change. Our Company gave three days pay. $110 for each private - and it will be $8.00 for me. Thousands and thousands will be contributed. Col. Pendleton was Capt of an Artillery Company under Gen Johnston before the battle of Manassas and every time he fired into the enemy he would exclaim, "Lord have mercy their poor souls." He is an Episcopal minister. The weather for the last five or six days has been very pleasant but today has been cloudy and looks like rain. Cold weather will set in sometime in Jan and I want to be at home during the coldest weather. Tell father to please attend to giving allowance to my negroes, particularly meat so that it will not be wasted, and tell him to see that there is a good lock on the smoke house and that it is in every way secure. Tell him to try and save some until I come home if all are not fat enough to kill before Christmas. Now darling don't be too much elated from the way I write as it is still very uncertain about my coming home. I may again be disappointed or something may take place to prevent my coming at least until the first of Feb. I have no doubt but that I can get a furlough then. Think of me darling when you are enjoying good Christmas dinners. I will think of you, love. I am anxious to hear from the draft in Abbeville. I am anxious for certain ones to be caught Jim Chiles, W. Mars, Aleck & Wm &c &c. Tell the negroes that I will give them all Christmas gifts &c when I come home. It would be useless to give them orders now for everything is too high, tell them to be faithful and I will reward them when I come home. Tell father to engage

Clarissa & John for me for another year. I want <u>both</u>. Give my love to all & kiss Fannie. Most lovingly your own Devoted Husband

John F. Calhoun

[*This letter was likely written sometime between the Great Charleston Fire, December 11 & 12, 1861 and Christmas of that same year.*]

IV.

Letters of January, February, & March of 1862

WINTER QUARTERS! Now that the troops (on both sides) had started setting up winter quarters, fighting along the Potomac subsided somewhat. January's weather was cold and it snowed heavily enough that the 7th Regiment was ordered to suspend building their winter shelters. Most opted to just stay in their tents for the winter. Various orders were given and then countermanded regarding troop movements which added to the confusion in camp until they moved from Centerville to a camp near Manassas in February to finally settle in for winter quarters.

Prospects for furloughs remained dim and John Francis was now resolved to complete his twelve-month enlistment without further application for a furlough. He also refused to feign illness or try to go off on sick leave. All the while, new recruits were very slow to make it to the field.

Camp conversations were mostly about the continuing war and concerns for the affects on families at home. John Francis' letters became longer and longer. In spite of the ongoing combat, his thoughts were more and more centered on his own economic situation. He instructed that sales transactions at the mill and tan yard be handled in cash, avoiding the extension of further crediting while operating in these uncertain monetary times. He advised his family to keep what cotton they had on hand, hoping the coastal Blockade would be lifted and prices would rise. John Francis also suggested that the family stop growing additional cotton and plant more foodstuffs such as corn, potatoes, peas, wheat, and all kinds of grains. He believed the prices for those commodities would certainly rise as the war continued affirming that the troops had to be fed and that horses, mules and other livestock all had to be fed and cared for as well.

In late February the 7th Regiment received the dismal news of Union victories at Roanoke Island, North Carolina, and Fort Donelson in Tennessee. John Francis reasoned the defeats were caused by the Confederacy beginning to ignore the hand of Providence and that they had stopped asking (praying) for assistance from the Almighty.

The troops were assembled for another movement in late March. Rumors were they were to either march to Richmond and be disbanded or make a move against the enemy. Most of the Confederate force was falling back to the Rappahannock by mid March and then to the Rapidan rivers as General Stonewall Jackson faced the enemy at Winchester (Kernstown).

January 1862

CAMP NEAR CENTERVILLE, VA
TUESDAY NIGHT JAN 7TH, 1862
NO 80

My own darling wife:-

I wrote to you on the fifth instant by Captain Bradley and enclosed a fifty $50 dollar confederate bill which I hope will reach your safely and I hope the $15 dollars in bills and the check of one hundred and forty $140 dollars which I gave Theo Rogers when he started to Charlottesville to send you have all come safely to hand before this. Now my darling you must not deny yourself and sweet little Fannie anything and after supplying yourself and reserving ten of fifteen for future use, lend the remainder to your father and tell him to hold on to all of his cotton. I think he ought to buy another mule and if he needs any more money I will be able to send him 75 or 80 dollars in one month or six weeks. My expenses were much higher for the last month as we sent up to the mountains for turkeys, chickens, butter, eggs, lard, etc and we intend sending up again soon.[2] I expected a letter from you today but did not get one. Tomorrow's mail will surely bring one for me and father or Ida ought to write to me. How does Ida employ her time? She rarely ever writes to either Ed or myself. The ground has been covered with snow for several days and the weather is extremely cold, but we don't feel it near as much as we would at home having become gradually accustomed to cold. Were I to come home now I don't think I would complain much of cold weather. The late bad weather prevented the troops for going on with the building of winter quarters and this morning Gen Bonham sent around an order to go to work preparing their winter quarters at our present encampment. We nearly all intend spending the winter in their tents. I intend trying it in my tent. We have been pulled and hauled about in every imaginable way since we have been in VA and it seems that we have more that our due proportion of work and hardship to do. Gen Beauregard issued an order this morning which from its tone seems to anticipate "the long hoped for exigency" but I believe our Generals occasionally issue such orders to keep the troops on the alert and to keep them quiet, they get restless unless kept busy. I am officer of the day tomorrow assisted by a third Lieut. I dined out on yesterday with Lieut. Harrison of Bland's Co. We had a delightful dinner. Darling don't neglect to have your garden well manured & spaded and begin in time and have a fine

2 John Francis' brother Edwin gives a corroborating account of this shopping expedition in his book *Reminiscences of a Confederate Soldier*, p. 7

garden for us. I hope to enjoy it with you next summer. Have my colts well attended to and all my hogs &c. Have the crib locked and the corn & fodder fed economically. Tell father to have the bottom below the tan yard well manured. Tell him to sell my wheat when he can sell at what I wrote him to ask. Give my love to all and many kisses to sweet darling little Fannie and write often dearest to Your Fond and devoted Husband

JOHN F. CALHOUN

CAMP NEAR CENTERVILLE, VIRGINNIA
Thursday morning January 9th 1862
No 81

My own darling wife:

I received your short though welcome and affectionate letter written on the 31st ultimo and the same mail brought me one from Ida to which I replied last night and mailed this morning. I say yours was short but don't understand me as complaining loved one, no indeed, for you have written regularly for a long, long time, and your letters have generally been long. I don't expect all to be lengthy, mine are sometimes short, and as I must sometime crave your indulgence I am willing to grant a like indulgence. I am very sorry indeed to hear of the death of Louis Rogers. I heard sometime ago that he was ill. What was the matter with him? Ida wrote me a great deal about sweet little Fannie. She wrote me about her capers she cut when you took the doll that Ida gave her. Bless her darling little heart. I do wish I could have seen her. You let me know what kind of toys &c I must bring her when I come home. I must bring her something. Last night I dreamed of buying candy to take her and in selecting small sticks so that she could hold them easily in her hands and I dreamed of selecting fancy sticks to please her. Darling you must dress Fannie handsomely. When I return I want to find her dressed finely. I have sent you the money and will send you more so there will be no excuse. I want to find her her [*sic*] with an abundance of nice dresses, stocking &c a complete wardrobe now don't forget. I intend inspecting the little ladies wardrobe. Mr. and Mrs. Andrews must have got entirely above themselves. Mrs. A is no doubt a perfect wild cat, she seems to be a quiet, easy person but you can no more judge of what a woman is from what she appears than you can judge of the character an infant will have when it is grown. Get all your jars &c from her and before she left. I hope you examined all of your bed clothes &c to see if all were there. You were over liberal both in the charge per month and the time charged for. Were I superintending the business at the Mills in person I would as soon have Ben Andrews for the price as nearly any one I know. I can get on with him but it would not do to trust him by himself, but he is not alone in that. My darling you want to know what I think of you going down to the Mills to live I wrote you twice or three times that I disapproved of your doing so. I still think it imprudent, but in the event of your going down I gave directions about many things that I wanted attended to. I am glad to hear that our hogs are not killed or at least were not when you wrote last. I do hope they will be well fattened when they are killed and do, my darling, attend carefully to everything. What sow is it that is in the pen that you speak of as being so fat? I did not know that one of the sows were in the pen neither have I heard how many hogs I had fattening in all. Let me know also the weight. Darling save me two heads, jowls and backbones until he middle of Feb as I may be able to get a furlough by that time if at all. An order has just been sent in to our Regt to have all the horses shod and for the men to suspend building their Winter Quarters. I never heard of as many orders given and countermanded as have been lately to our Brigade. I am tired out with such management, if it does come from Gen Beauregard although we don't put any confidence in scarcely any order we hear now. The Rogers will return in four or five days. We have not recd a line from him since he left on the 30th of Dec. He went off on the sick list. Cothran and I are the only two who have never been off either on furlough or the sick list, one other excepted, but who here lost a good deal of time from indisposition whilst in Camp and all the Captains in the Regt excepting two Capt Denny & Brooks, the former is old and has lost a great deal of time but has never been off on sick or well furlough. Capt Bradley headed the list for the war in our Company but only 7 men in all have joined. Many declare they won't join unless the Lieuts do. Those who are instrumental in getting it up told me if we would join the most of the Company would. I am surprised to find the Capt so unpopular for he is a kind, good old man & I like him although he is influenced by Dr H who is very unpopular. I did not know until the last month that our boys thought so highly of me. Without paying myself any compliment. I am proud to believe that there is no officer more liked in the Company than I am. I find this out from the men themselves and they go even fa[r]ther than I have, but you know it would not do for this to get out as coming from me for one officer to claim to be the favorite in his company, but I feel that I can write to my wife what many of my men have told me, but at the same time I write it under this injunction of confidence, so by no means let no one know it, not even Ida. When our Company returns then the men will be free to express themselves and they will do so, then the popularity of all will be freely canvassed and I am willing to risk my popularity with the members of our Company. Darling ask father where does he intend sowing my oats and how much will he sow for me. I want a large crop sowed. How many bushels were thrashed out from my oats? What about our wheat &c has any been sold, and how much and at what price? It ought to be sold soon if a good price can be procured. I wrote to father or at least I told Ida to tell him to ask you how much you wanted saved. I would save at least ten bushels so that we will have enough to last us until the last of July or August. You know best, as you are accustomed to attending to such matters. You may sell Nettie at any [time] you may have an opportunity and at any price you may choose to take although I think $250 little enough, $225 any way. If she is not sold by March I intend sending her down to Edgefield and will raise another fine colt from her. William Darricott has been complaining for some time and has just told me that he intended getting a sick furlough and going home. John E. Belott will go off to the Hospital to-day or tomorrow. It rained last night and is much warmer today. I sent Ida twenty 20 postage stamps this morning. Do you need any more, if so let me know and I can get any amount at Manassas? Do the Post Masters at Mt. C & the Mills keep them? Don't forget to tell Capt D M Rogers to have our Books posted up & a/c drawn off. I am anxious to know how we stand. I wish you would engage some ground peas. I want to plant some this year. How much Hominey corn have we? Take good care of it. Secure an abundance of Garden seed in time. Tell your father to write to me and when you write darling answer all of my questions. My next will be short as this one is so long. Give my love to all and many kisses to our daughter. Sam H, Zeke, Gib Pat R &c are well. Write soon dearest to you Ever Fond loving and Devoted Husband

JOHN F. CALHOUN

CAMP NEAR CENTERVILLE, VIRGINIA
TUESDAY JANUARY 14TH 1862
NO 83

My own darling wife:

I did not go on picket as I was feeling too unwell and it is well that I did not as I have been in bed nearly all the time since they started. I have been taking medicine for three days. "Sampson pills"[3] some that The Rogers brought on with him, but as usual they prove worthless with me they nauseate me but fail to produce proper action. I have just taken Seidlitz.[4] I have a severe case of jaundice and some have been so long recovering from them that the surgeons gave them sick furloughs from 30 to 60 days. Col Fair's was 60. I will get one just as soon as I can travel but it will be eight or ten days yet before I can get off as I am quite sick three-fourths of the time headache, sick stomach and pain the the small of my back. I have ate little or nothing for three days. I vomit every once and a while and then for an hour or two I feel much better which is the case now. I am seated in my bed writing to my own darling wife sick as I am so dearest you must excuse this letter. I received one from day before yesterday dated the 4th inst which you mention that our darling little Fannie is sick. I hope the little darling is well by this time. So you are going home to live. Well my darling I know that you will attend to everything as well as possible. I am glad our hogs are so fine and hope you will save some spare ribs for me don't put on but little salt so they will be fresh. Have the two sows put up as soon as their pigs are large enough to wean as I want to save as much bacon as possible, the pigs ought to be well fed when they are separated from the sows. Do have them well attended to and as Bess has but one pig you ought to put it in a pen and slop it or keep it in the yard as I wish her Bess to begin with another set. Darling don't forget to prepare the garden in time. Have the manure hauled and some of the beds spaded up. Tell Cup to attend to my pigs carefully and tell father to allow him time. See to my colt &c. I am glad you did not send the old ham. I am greatly obliged to your mother but tell her I hope to enjoy one of those old hams with her in Feb; save one for me and don't kill all the turkeys. I don't know what has become of Tucker. He has not come yet. I am getting sick at my stomach so must close. Give my love to all and kiss Fannie for her father. I will write as soon as I am able. Write often darling to your Loving and Devoted Husband

JOHN F. CALHOUN

---

3 Pills developed by a Dr. Sampson of New York. Made of powdered cocoa, powdered iron and morphia salt, they were taken to induce nausea and vomiting. *Canadian Pharmaceutical Journal*, Vol 12, p. 15.

4 Seidlitz Powders was an effervescing salt containing sodium bicarbonate, rochelle salt, and tartaric acid. It was used as a laxative and digestive regulator from the mid 19th century. pharmaceuticaljournal.com, December 2001.

CAMP NEAR CENTERVILLE, VA
WEDNESDAY NIGHT JAN 22: 1862
NO 87

My own darling wife:-

I replied to your two last letters of the 10th and 12th on the day before yesterday and I will write again tonight although there is nothing of interest to write. I wrote to your father today and to Cupet - the latter I will enclose in this, read it over once or twice to him and then destroy it. You can keep it a while to read to him so that he will be the better able to remember all of my orders. And tell him he ought to be very faithful and prompt in all his duties as I place so much confidence in him. See that he attends to all of my orders and encourage him. If we have enough peas to plant and to feed the negroes on I would advise you to have the others threshed out and sold. 10 or 12 bushels will be enough to plant for the negroes. Get father to attend to it. We ought to sell everything of the kind and if we are saving we might have 100 bushels of corn to sell. If father has not sold all of my wheat tell him to send it down to Augusta any time in Feb and to send all of my peas after saving say 12 bushels. He can either grind the wheat or send the wheat down if it is ground, save all of the brand [*sic*; bran] for your cows & pigs it will be fine for Nettie and the colt. What has become of all the brand of the wheat? If Nettie is not sold soon I don't care whether you sell her or not. Ask $250 for her from this and if she is not sold in a few weeks I intend holding her at $300 for horses will be enormously high next year. And mares for raising colts I think will be in demand. Another one of our horses died last night. Tell father he may have Jim to keep if he wishes. I am nearly entirely recovered from Jaundice. General Bonham told Lieut. Burriss last night that he thought we would be disbanded by the first of April. I do hope it may be so. Another Brigadier has been promoted over Gen Bonham. Gen Ewell[5] is now our Major General. Gen B is the first Brigadier of the Provisional Army. Darling I can't see how to write tonight the lines are indestinct. I am expecting a letter from you tomorrow. Do you need any more stamps darling? Let me know if you do I can get any quantity of them. My darling when you are at the Mills you can while away a great part of your time in writing to me. Write at your leisure and whenever you

5 General Richard S Ewell (1817-1872). Born in Georgetown (Washington, DC) but raised near Manassas, VA. Graduated from the U.S. Military Academy in 1840 and served in the US Army. Resigned in May 1861 to join the Virginia Provisional Army. as a Colonel. Nicknamed "Old Bald Head," he was commissioned Confederate Brigadier General in June 1861. After the Battle of 1st Manassas, Ewell proposed to President Davis that in order for the Confederates to win the war, the slaves must be freed and join the ranks of the Army. Ewell even volunteered to lead the blacks in battle. President Davis simply replied, "That is impossible." *Find a Grave. Encyclopedia Virginia*. Edward H. Bonekemper, *Myth of the Lost Cause*, Chapter 9, Conclusion.

think of anything you can get your letter and write it when you think of it. How much does Mr. Crawford grind a week? How much toll on hand &c? Love to Sam and a kiss to Fannie. Lovingly and Devotedly your Husband

J.F.C.

CAMP NEAR CENTERVILLE VIRGINIA
Friday morning January 24th 1862
No 88

My own darling wife:-

I continue writing every two days four times as week or at least I have been writing that often for the last two weeks, but you must not expect me to continue writing that often in future as we will have to move camp in a day or two and then Picket in a few days afterwards, so it may sometimes occur that I will only write twice a week but be assured darling that I will only cease writing three times a week by some duties preventing. I am expecting a letter from you today the last one I received was dated the 12th. Ed got a letter from Sallie day before yesterday she was at Aunt Lou's and Aunt Lou wrote some in the letter. Tell her she has never noticed my last letter and I never intend writing another line until she replies. I am not feeling so well today, swimming in my head and sick stomach. I may have been imprudent in eating boxes of provisions, Hams, Sausages, spare ribs & butter were sent on to Capt B, Dr. H and Cothran and we will have an abundance to last several weeks. You need not save me anything but the sausages which you put up for me. Tell Mr. Crawford[6] to send me the amount ground this month, of both corn and wheat. I want to see how we [are] doing in the way of grinding. Have you put the two sows up? Be governed by circumstances it may be too late by the time they fatten to insure their keeping well. Don't forget to let me know how many pigs we have in all and let me know whether or not all of my wheat has been sold, and the price. How much did father get for our negro cloth? Who bought it. Darling be sure and have my peas thrashed out now very soon, and after saving 12 or 14 bushels sell the others. Father is very slow about such things, and you tell him what I want done and if he doesn't attend to it just keep all the negroes someday and have the peas thrashed and then you can make some arrangements about sending them to Augusta. I will get father or Mr. Rogers to send them. Darling don't sell Nettie for less than $250 cash or interest from date of note for I am more convinced every day as to the correctness of my conclusions about the high prices that mules and horses will bring even next fall. Maj Seibles told me yesterday that the day before on his way to Manassas he saw three die out of one team. The wagons are nearly all the time going rain or shine, it requires so much firewood. And then they sometimes go 30 or 40 miles for corn & hay, their hauling Commissaries Stores &c and the roads are in an awful condition. Sometimes the teams are without anything to eat a day and night. Thousands & thousands are compelled to die this winter. The great and continued demand for horses in the Army alone will force them up to a very high price. Darling, read over my last

6 Accountant at Calhoun Mills

three or four letters carefully as they contain all that I wish done and reply to them as I do to yours. Take the letter before you and read it slowly and reply to it as you go and in that way you will be sure to answer all of my questions. Do you reply in that way darling? How many stamps have you left? Ask Ida if she doesn't intend writing to me. It seems a task for her to write to me only a few hurried lines and then on some business for father. The mail has come in and no letters for me. Only one letter came for our Company yesterday and one today. The Rogers has not recd one in five days, he does not know what to think of it. He generally gets one every two days. I will get one tomorrow I feel sure. Find out what the boots sent on to John Belott, LeRoy[7] &c are charged at as I have sold LeRoy's and I want to know the price. Does your father need any more money? There is no news here. Give my love to all and many sweet kisses to sweetness and be sure and always write me about her and mention all of her sweet and smart tricks. Howdy to the negroes. Write often and long letters dearest to your Fond and Devoted Husband

JOHN F. CALHOUN

---

7 Members of Company C ,7th South Carolina Volunteers. *Kershaw's Brigade,* p. 559.

NEW CAMP ON BULL RUN NEAR
MANASSAS VA January 28, 1862

My own precious love:-

This morning was cold, cloudy and rainy still we packed up bag and baggage and moved to the new Camp which is a bout 2 ½ miles from the old one, in the direction of and in about 2 ½ miles of Manassas, it will be much more convenient in many respects than the old Camp. Wood is more inconvenient. The mail today brought me your letter of the 20th and I will lay it before me and reply to it at once. I am glad to hear that you have succeeded in keeping the measles from the Mills thus far, but were I at home to assist you in attending to the sick ones, I don't think I would try to prevent our little one from having the measles. I am glad father has recovered from the measles. Ida is with you. She ought to spend a good deal of her time with you. Ed got a long letter from her today and she begins by saying she had just rec'd a "long nice letter from brother John" but still she replies to my letter by writing to Ed. Tell her I don't understand that kind of a correspondence. I am glad your father has accepted the loan of the money, and tell him that I will be able to lend him one hundred or one hundred and fifty more by the middle or last of Feb and he must not hesitate if he has any need for it at all as I will not need it. I have sent on $250 for father and if he sells Nettie I will lend him that and then I will have the proceeds from the sale of my wheat, peas &c which either of them may have if they wish, as I have written to Capt D M to send a lot of leather to market and sell it some time in Feb, as I want $200 to pay taxes and certain a/c and when I return I will send another lot down and pay off all my accounts &c. I wish your and my father to be enabled to hold on to their cotton and by lending theirs they will be able to do so. Father will pay me interest. As you have been staying all year with your father you may lend him your money free of interest. All I have sent you is your own and I intend giving you $150 more with which you can furnish your house &c. Darling if you are not afraid to stay at the Mills and can always have Sam and Carie, Ida, Rosa, or Mat Cowan to stay with you, I am willing for you to do so but I don't wish to advise you to do it. That is right. Notice our meat. I am glad it is not spoiling. I suppose Nettie is sold from what Ida wrote but I think 225 is not enough Horses are enormously high on the coast and if I was at home I could get 250 or 300. I expect I will be satisfied if she is sold for the cash. Tell Cupe he must not use the Hominey corn and put it aside as he comes to it. Save all of your wheat brand when our wheat is ground and give the shoats to the negroes & give them some of the seconds and save some for yourself. The remainder ought to be sold. Tell father to send the wheat down or grind it up just as he may choose, and tell him to be sure and send as many of my peas off as I can spare. Capt Hester has returned and little Tim Taggart with him. Give my love to all and tell Ida to reply to the letters I wrote father if she won't reply to the one I wrote her. Kiss Sweetness for me and howdy to all the negroes. I will write again in two days. Ever your loving Husband

JOHN F. CALHOUN

P.S. I send a few stamps for Rosa, give them to her. Sam Harris has gone off to the Hospital again, he is no account. Zeke went off last week. Ed, Gib, Pat Robinson and Wm D are all well. Peter Gillebeau returned from the Hospital today as fat as he can be. He has spent the most of his time at the Hospital and did his best to get a discharge. Many will be spotted after the war. There are many others of the same kind even in our Company. Tell father not to forget the Molasses for my negroes. Good-night love – Forever Thine.

CAMP NEAR MANASSAS VIRGINIA
Thursday January 30th 1862
No 91

My own darling wife:-

I wrote to you day before yesterday and promised to write again in two or three days, and as this is a rainy disagreeable day, I will devote a portion of it to you dearest. There is very little of interest to write, nothing of any importance having transpired in the Army of the Potomac. I believe this entire line has gone into winter quarters, and are lying on their oars waiting for McClellan to advance, but there is no prospect of anything of the kind before May or June if then, so we will have two more long, cold, dreary, winter months to worry through before we turn our faces homewards with the joyous anticipation of once more clasping the loved ones there. Time is passing rapidly by, and it is the impression here that we will be disbanded by the first of April. Gen Bonham thinks we will be disbanded by the 25th of March, twenty days before our term expires. Won't it be delightful to meet once more darling? Oh, how anxious I am to be with you. I wonder love if it can be possible for you to be as anxious to see me! I can scarcely realize the fact that we have a daughter running about prattling. From the way Ida writes Fannie must be a beauty – and as sweet as she is pretty, with heart breaking eyes. Ida says Fannie seems to be aware of her beauty and is really affected young as she is. Come darling are you really spoiling the little creature? Ida says Fannie is prettier than Kate[8] – but she thinks K will improve and become as pretty. Learn Fannie to talk and take pains with her and try and raise her up with a good disposition. Don't let her be fretted, still make her obey. Captain Talbert came in this morning. I have not seen him yet. From Ida's letter I learn that none of my wheat has been sold. I am glad of it as there is plenty of time although it may be prudent to send it off early in February, and if we can spare eighty - 80 bushels it will bring us at least $160. We made 128 bushels and none was ground for the negroes until late in August, and if half allowance was given them for two months at 1 ½ bushels per week it would only be twelve 12 – bushels leaving 116 bu then, if twenty bushels were planted it leaves 96 and 16 will then be left for our use and we will have 80 to sell. I don't know how much father sowed out of my wheat, find out and let me know, perhaps Cupet can tell you. You must have all the brand taken up to the house and locked up and it will be excellent food for your cows, the pigs and the colt. Cupe must cut up oats and fodder and dampen it, then pour wheat brand and ground corn over it. The colt must have as much as it can eat. Tell father he ought to sell all of the Seconds excepting what you may

8 Katharine "Kate" Calhoun, the oldest daughter of Edwin and Sallie Calhoun.

wish for our own use and the negroes. Make Cupet collect all of the wheat from around the smut mill for the poultry and pigs, tell Mr Crawford to save it for you and tell the ox driver not to use it for it does the oxen very little good as they swallow the whole grains. Don't fail to send off as many peas as we can possibly spare as we can get $1.25 per bushel – and we ought to take in as much money as possible. Will we not have some corn to sell? We ought to have 100 bushels to sell, by being economical which we could be and still feed everything well. Ask your father how much corn is in the Crib now, and how much ought to do us by feeding the mules on wheat & oats as soon as they come in. As soon as Mr. Scott adds up the Accounts, find out how much was booked in the Shoe Shop, Mill and Tan Yard. Tell him I am glad to hear that he his having a few more vats put in and I think we ought to put in about five or six, and if he thinks so to urge it upon the Captain and I will get father to assist me. And he can employ father's negro men at night to work on the vats, he must ask father however. Tell Mr. Scott that the more leather we send off to Charleston & Augusta and sell for Cash, the better for us, and try to have as much sent off as possible. Bess' pig ought to be taken away now. Have it done and if your father does not wish it, let father have it if he wishes. Let me know if your father wishes any more money, and if so, how much? He must not hesitate if he needs any to let me know it, and the amount, and at what time he wishes it. I wish to know in advance so I can make my arrangements accordingly. One hundred and sixty dollars are due me now or at least will be tomorrow, but sometimes the Paymaster hasn't the money to pay up to date, so we have to wait sometimes on them. An officer can claim his pay monthly and can draw it in Richmond up to the day and can do so here most of the time. I can draw the $160 by the time I hear from you. I can spare 150 I expect, 140 any way. All I can do without. I intend lending your and my father so as to enable them to hold on to their cotton and if two thirds of our leather is sent off to market I can pay up my debts, and lend them enough to do them without them selling any cotton. If the Blockade is not raised by May and the Campaign opens with spirit I don't know but that it would be prudent to sell then at 8 ½ or 9 cents, as it would be impossible to raise the Blockade after that and get the old crop in market before the new Crop of 1862 would be coming in and then the prices fall, two crops can't enter the market together without depreciating the price. I would hold on to my cotton now with the hope of the raising of the Blockade, recognition of the Southern Confederacy, or something of the kind before May - but should the Campaign open in May it will continue through the Summer. Your father ought to watch these things and be governed accordingly. Don't you want fifteen or twenty dollars more darling? Do you not need some stamps? Zeke retuned to Camp this morning entirely recovered. He did well in returning so promptly. Darling let me know if Mr. Burt has paid for the pigs or not, if not I will enclose a note for you to send him. That is your money and I owe you $25 for the one Dr. Y got. How much toll wheat & corn is there in the Mill, how much sold weekly and the price? All of our old customers still patronizing us? Any new customers &c. Ask Mr C and write me. Tell Ida I will expect a long letter from her like the once she wrote Ed and tell her to answer the one I wrote father. Give my love to all and kiss my sweet, darling little Fannie. Do write often love and long letters.

Most Devotedly your Husband

JOHN F. CALHOUN

February 1862

CAMP NEAR MANASSAS, VIRGINIA
SUNDAY FEB 2ND 1862
NO 92

My own Darling Wife:-

I wrote to you on the 28th or 29th inst and I did intend writing last night but had nothing of interest to write and was feeling somewhat fatigued building my chimney, fixing my tent, &c. The mail will be in this afternoon and I feel almost sure that I will get a letter from you. The last one I received from you was written on the 20th inst and was received on the 28th. We have at last gone into winter quarters in a large pine thicket two or two and a half miles from Manassas. Most of the men are living in tents with chimneys for them, some have put up huts. I am in a wall tent about ten feet square. Ed is the only one with me. All of the wagons have been employed moving the Reg't over and one thing and another so that we have been scarce of wood and have been burning green pine and you may imagine how hard it must be to kindle and kick up a fire with old dead pine limbs as kindling stiff. If it were not [for] picketing we could make out very well until the expiration of the term. The camp duties are light, the guard duties boring nearly nominal nothing to do but to wait patiently until April and oh how anxious I am for the time to come for me to hasten home to meet my "dearie." My heart is in the great cause in which we are engaged and I am inclined to reenlist but darling I can't do it for a few months. I must spend a few months with my young wife to whom I am so devotedly attached. So you may rest satisfied that if my life lasts I will return to your love as soon as I can and as fast as steam can carry me. A member of our company returned from the hospital at Charlottesville the morning and brought a few sheets of paper like this on I am writing on. I send it merely to let you see a picture of the University of Virginia. Most of the buildings have been converted into hospitals. Ed received a letter from Sallie yesterday in which she mentioned that the baby was sick and she was afraid she was taking the measles. If she does take the measles now it will not be as severe as she is so young. I am glad that father recovered so soon as I feared that he would have a severe attack. Theo Rogers rec'd a letter from his wife on yesterday which was mailed on the 27th. It came through somewhat quicker than usual. I ought to have received one by this same mail but I know it is the fault of the Post Master. The right wing of our regiment went on Picket today and I hear a change has been made so that the right wing of our regiment shall relieve the right wing of the other if so we will not go out until the 11th. Cash's right will relieve our right on the 4th then comes Williams and then the left wing comes in. Today is the first clear day we have had in some time. It snowed and sleeted night before last and when it is doing neither it is raining. We have had an awful spell for the last three or four weeks nearly all of this time raining, snowing, or sleeting. Some of the men, Edgefield men - are going ahead fixing up today, building their chimneys & one I am sorry to say married your Aunt. Say nothing about it as it might offend them with me. I will wait until the mail comes in and then finish my letter tonight hoping to receive one from my darling wife to reply to.

CAMP NEAR MANASSAS, VIRGINIA
TUESDAY MORNING FEB 4, 1862
NO 93

My Own Darling Wife:-

I wrote to you on the 2nd instant thinking that I would get a letter from you on yesterday and would reply to it today, but I was greatly provoked upon learning that the Post Master did not go to the office on yesterday so my letter did not go until this morning. I feel sure of getting two letters from you today. The last one I received was written on the 20th of last month and reached me on the 27th, yesterday one week ago. Night before last it commenced snowing and continued but with slight intermission all throughout the day and last night it rained and sleeted, the ground is covered three or four inches in snow but the day not very cold. We have awful weather and if we could get wood enough and had no picketing to do we could make out very well, but the time is not long now, by the time you get this it will not be more than six weeks, I don't think. It is reported now that in six weeks from this time we are to be disbanded. Gen Johnston sent around a day or two ago to know when our time of service expired. It seems the authorities are beginning to make arrangements for supplying our places. I have no idea that we will be kept until the 15th of April. General Beauregard's report[9] of the battle of Manassas has just been published, which I will send you. From it you will see that it was the intention of Gen B to make an attack upon the enemy in front and on Centerville but the orders miscarried. From Gen B's report you will see we were exposed to a heavy fire from the enemies' batteries all day, and he considers we did good service in maintaining our ground under their fire, and held in check, and completely paralyzed two of the enemy's brigades. Read it, it is an able report and speaks for itself. The mail has just come in and brought your letter of the 24th, No 12 which was not mailed until the 27th, why was this? I ought to have received two letters today but may get the others tomorrow. Your letter is so short that I will have but little to write. You ought to write me longer letters darling you are breaking down again as to your failing to write long letters thinking that I may get a furlough. I have told you often darling that such things were very uncertain and it is now nearly reduced to a certainty that no furloughs will be granted so it will be impossible for me to come home until our term of service expires so write often and long letters. I am very glad indeed that Dr. Parker did not take Nettie. Nothing now less than $250 will buy her and I am not anxious to sell her for that. Zeke asked

9 General Beauregard's report on the Battle of Manassas, July 21, 1861. *ORWR*, Vol II, Chapter IX, pp. 484-504.

me last night to let him have her at $250 if Dr. P did not take her. She will pay to raise colts from. I am sorry about the measles on Sophia's and Judy's[10] account. Have them all well attended to. Letters take a long time to go from here to home eight and ten days—it ought not to take longer than five at the outside. I am in hopes that your next you will reply to all my questions about our affairs. Do, do take my letters before you and read them as you reply, take time. I know why you fail to answer all of my questions. It is because I write too often, you sometimes get two and three by the same mail and you have too much to write. Zeke has just come in and is quite well. Pat R, Gib and all. I am hearty. As I am expecting a longer letter from you in a day or two I will close. Why doesn't your father write to me? Give my love to all and many sweet kisses to darling little Fannie. Write me more about her. Tell Carie to write to me and my dearest do write to me often and write long letters and answer all of my questions. Fondly and devotedly your

Own Loving Husband

JOHN F. CALHOUN

PS

At night. I will send Gen B's report some other time and will enclose the note to Mr. Burt in my next. I have just copied off Gen Johnston's address to the twelve months volunteers. Read it and preserve it and show it to Ida and tell her to copy it and read it to father. It is patriotic, grand, powerful and soul stirring equal to Napoleon's great address to his army. We are looked upon as the veterans of the war and are now holding McClellan's Grand Army at bay. He dares not advance upon our tried soldiery who defeated the greatest General of the age on the blood stained plains of Manassas, if we leave he will be sure to come. Now must we leave? It is hard to leave our Southern Banner as long as a shred remains aloft to flutter in the breeze. We are making history as we go and our actions will be read hundreds of years to come. What shall I do? I have no idea the war will last more than six months if that long, and if this line is kept unbroken there will be no more fighting here. I am anxious to spend the next few months at home if I can honorably do so. No action is being taken yet. Furloughs will be granted to those who re-volunteer.[11] Read this address remembering that it is to soldiers under arms, striking for independence, their homes, their firesides and their alters. Our revolutionary fa-

---

10 Believed to be Negro women at Calhoun Mills.

11 A policy for reenlistment was developed whereby furloughs were promised to the "12 month volunteers" if they reenlisted. General Joseph E. Johnston wrote Secretary of War Benjamin stating that if too many furloughs were given, he would not have troops enough to maintain his position in the event of a Union attack. The 12 month volunteers constituted 2/3 of General Johnston's army, therefore the majority of furloughs were never granted to them. *ORWR*, Vol V, Chapter XIV, pp. 1016-1018 (policy); Vol V, Chapter XIV, pp. 1036-1037 (letter); Vol V, Chapter XIV, pp. 1058-1059.

thers fought seven years, half-fed, poorly clad, and in the dead of winter they were often bare footed, and could be tracked by the blood on the snow and ice from their bleeding feet; and are we unworthy of the rich legacy they handed down to us - shall we falter when we are "almost there"? The Promised Land is nearly in sight, a bold and determined front and all will be won, the day will be ours and in coming years our children can say with pride, our father was one of the heroes of our second revolution, and belonged to that veteran band who resisted the Grand Army at Manassas, and who stood the rigors of the winter's campaign and refused when his term of service expired to turn his back upon the foe until they had been driven from our sunny land preferring the home of a freeman or the grave of a patriot. Write to me at once dearest your views. I want my children to be proud to call me "father." Forever your own fond Husband

CAMP NEAR MANASSAS VIRGINIA
Thursday February 6th 1862
No 94

My Dearest:-

Your very welcome letter of the 27th ultimo "No 13" reached me on yesterday and I will reply immediately. My darling I am sorry you were disappointed by not getting a furlough when I had jaundice and for my not applying, it was because I could not consent to do so when I knew that I was not sick enough to deserve one.[12] As regards others applying for sick furloughs upon shallow pretenses you know darling that should not swerve me from my duty, it is nothing to me how many "play the possum" it should not induce me to do so. My anxiety to see you was so great that I was inclined to apply but all things taken into consideration I acted wisely. I am looking ahead and wish to so deport myself that when I leave the service I can show a perfectly clean sheet. Again, should I not return home until the expiration of my term of service I can then return with a clearer conscience without reenlisting, so darling notwithstanding you think now that I ought to have applied for a furlough, take my word for it you will be entirely satisfied hereafter and will see then that I acted wisely and you will be proud that your husband stood up unflinchingly to his duty with the loss of only a few days from sickness. Now darling don't say if I thought as much of you as you do of me or at least if I were as "anxious to see you as you are to see me," I would have applied for a furlough. You know who loves the most. I have often and ever thought the same thing darling and I am glad you love me so much that the same thought is forced upon your mind. Dearest I have no doubt but that we both love devotedly, but I must claim the credit in a great degree of having tutored you to be affectionate. You know love that you were cold-hearted at first and it was some time before I could bring you out, but by kindness, tenderness and petting I have drawn you out and my sweet precious little wife is as affectionate and devoted as any ones wife, yes more so than nine tenths of wives. Darling you explained about your last letter not being mailed for several days knowing that if you did not that you would get a "good scolding before long." Now darling you are "putting on." You pretend that you are afraid of a scolding from me. Come love, to make sport of me away here in old "Virginny." As you will not have Sam to stay at the Mills with you, I think you are right in not staying there altogether; it would be very well to go down and stay one or two days at a time in good weather suitable for gardening. Try and have a good garden it is an easy matter. Plant an abundance of peas, tomatoes, oysters [*sic*, salsify] and okra. Do your best darling. I am glad to hear that Fannie is improving so fast. I know she must be sweet. And she is calling her

12 John Francis Calhoun's sense of patriotic duty to the cause of South Carolina and the Confederacy was much greater than his desire to obtain a short furlough to go home, or to resign.

"bubba" already. Of course I expect the next to be a boy and I fully calculate on seeing him in ten months after I return, no accident occurring. Darling you pretend that you don't want another child you know we want a house full. Fannie must have a little "bubba" to play with as she seems to have set her heart upon it and you know it won't do to disappoint her. We must humor her. I received a long and interesting letter from Ida on yesterday giving me a full description of my affairs on the farm. Father sowed 22 acres of wheat for me and manured it with five loads of cotton seed which will prevent him from giving the load I requested. The wheat is well manured and ought to make fine wheat. Ida says father had my oats thrashed out and it turned out 77 ½ bushels after saving enough to feed the colt. He intends sowing 25 bushels for me and he will buy the remaining 52 bushels. I don't suppose my negroes did not have more than a half allowance given to them for two months and that would not amount to more than 6 or 7 bushels - then 22 sowed would leave 100. And with what you have used, and will reserve for our use until new wheat comes in, 15 bushels I expect will do, then we will have 85 bushels - which at the price wheat & flour is selling ought to bring $2.00 a bu. $170. And the oats I don't know what they are selling at, 87 ½ or 90 cents so my oats and wheat will bring me in two hundred dollars after making enough bacon , corn and everything of the kind for my own use and $200 besides will do very well under all the circumstances. My cloth he sent up to William Mars to sell for 62 ½ a yard. When the wheat is ground don't forget to have all of your brand taken care of and give out the shorts to the negroes, tell father to give the negroes some and sell all that he can. I think most of the seconds ought to be sold, all of it will be too much to save and if sold will bring a good amount, tell father about it and get him to sell all that we can spare. I wish to feed all my stock well but by being at the same time economical. I think I ought to be able to save 75 or 100 bushels if I made what I hear I did. Corn will be worth one dollar a bushel at the crib and if the war continues by May or June I would not be surprised if it brought $1.25 or even more. Upper leather is selling in Richmond for one dollar a pound, Harness 68 and 75. sole, 60 or 70 near about double the old price. McKay said one of our vats full of a choice lot of leather at the old price was worth $300 it is now nearly double, but suppose they are only worth that amount now. Twelve vats would be worth $3600, that is a very moderate calculation - then every vat ought to turn out leather on an average of once in every four months, some takes five months others, three or two, but it will average four, then at $3600 for all the vats for four months, and three times that for a year, amounts to $10,800-ten thousand eight hundred dollars. I am sure if I were at home I can make the tan yard make that, then the shoe shop and Mill will make something. Henry and Tucker ought to book five dollars apiece a day - which is $260 dollars a month and $3120 a year, but even say $2500 making allowance for loss time &c. Such a fine opportunity to make money. It is true I dislike selling to our neighbors at such high prices but what am I to do. I can get high prices, and cash, by sending it off. Darling don't you think we ought to get a spinning wheel so that we can have yarn spun. Sophia & Judy will have one or two months to spin in the summer. What price are they selling corn and wheat flour at the Mills for? As soon as Mr. Scott gets through posting the books let me know how much we booked in all. When did Capt R send off any leather to sell? And how much. Ask Mr. Scott when do they intend sending off a lot? You might send down all the lard you can spare when the flour is sent off and sell it. Darling write long letters and often. Why doesn't you father write? Give my love to all and many kisses to Fannie. Ida says Mr. B has not paid for the pigs. I will enclose a note for you to send him there is no use waiting. I told you he would never pay unless he was compelled.

Tenderly and Devotedly your Husband

JOHN F. CALHOUN

CAMP NEAR MANASSAS, VIRGINIA
THURSDAY NIGHT FEB 7TH 1862
NO 95

My own darling wife:

I wrote to you last night but write again tonight to prevent your being uneasy about my re volunteering, thinking that the tone of my letter last night may have led you to the conclusion that I intended to re-enlist and I must confess that my first impulse was to re-enlist and I still should regret to leave here when my term of service expires. From present indications I am strongly inclined to the opinion that the majority of our Regiment will not re-enlist. Should even thirty or forty of our company re-enlist we would be furloughed and when we return, as that would not be the required number for a company unless we could recruit we might be thrown with say forty or fifty from another Company and as that Company would be the strongest they might elect officers from their own Company to the exclusion of those from our Company and in this way many will be prevented from re-enlisting here. In the entire Regiment there are not more than 120 or 30 married men and they, or many of them, think that unmarried men who have but little business at home should be the ones to re-enlist and give them an opportunity of retuning home. Again many are anxious to know what is to become of the volunteers on the Coast after the winter campaign. It is well known that the Federals will not be able to remain on the Coast during the summer months and when they are withdrawn it is thought that the majority of the troops on the Coast will be disbanded, then that would be very unjust to insist upon our staying in the field and fighting through the whole war after enduring the rigors of a winters campaign and serving out one entire year. Again it is contended that if all the twelve months men were to leave this time it would be disgraceful, but it not expected that they will leave, it is know[n] that they will not as there are thousands who have nothing particularly to tie them at home and Gen Johnston of course means the 12 months men as a body and not to the hundreds of individual instances as he is not aware of the necessities of all, only shows them their duty as a body, and therefore there would be no reflection upon those individually whose affairs and necessities at home require their presence. Under the circumstances the great majority of the married men intend serving out their time and returning home, that is from present indications. They say they are still in for the war but wish to return home before reenlisting and then if possible they wish to enter the service nearer their homes & families. I will keep you posted up as to the movements of the volunteers in reenlisting &c. I hear there is an order to go out on Picket this morning if so I will not be able to write again until I return Tuesday 11th. I forgot to say that I am writing now in the morning Sat 8th. I enclose the note to Mr. Burt, send it to him by the first opportunity and if you cant get a chance to send it by hand, send by mail. Give my love to all and kiss Fannie. I must close. Excuse haste

Fondly thine own loving
Husband
JOHN F. CALHOUN

CAMP NEAR MANASSAS VIRGINIA
TUESDAY NIGHT FEBRUARY 11TH 1862
NO 96

My own darling wife

I wrote you a very hurried, imperfect letter the night before we started on Picket and whilst out I received a long and interesting letter from you dated Jan 31st No 14. And upon my return I found No 15 Feb 3 awaiting me and I will reply to both of them tonight. My darling I am so thankful to you for writing me such long and interesting letters. You are improving fast. Just see what a competent instructor can do. I made you a sweet gentle affectionate wife and brought you up from two pages to four and five, and that two of the most loving and affectionate character. Darling it is because I am so kind, loving, doating, that makes you so isn't it darling? Oh, you are a dear precious wife. In my last I wrote you about reenlisting and upon my return from Picket this evening I learned that one hundred and twenty of our Regiment had reenlisted and will start home on furlough in a day or two. Only that number can be furloughed from a Regt at a time, and when they return I expect many more will reenlist. Williams, Cash's and Kershaw's men all reenlisting. I mean from all of the Regts the men were volunteering rapidly as many as the Gen commanding is willing to furlough, but one strange thing no officer can get a furlough by reenlisting, consequently but few will reenlist. I am determined not to do so. If an officer offers to resign so as to take the ranks and re-enlist, they can not do it for their resignation will not be accepted. Capt Rhett of Kershaw's Regt has organized a Company and procured furloughs for nearly all of his men and his application for a furlough as yet has never been noticed. Some of the officers in our Regt have tested the matter and in Captain Bland's company. 40 - nearly everyone now present in Camp revolunteered and not one of the officers have been furloughed. Now who is fool enough to submit to anything of that kind? What officer will re-enlist without any prospect of getting home when all the non-commissioned officers and privates can get off and they are required to stay? No one excepting single men who have no ties at home or those who only thirst for a little glory. I am decided now and if I live you may be sure of seeing me after the 15th of April. I was moved by Gen Johnston's soul-stirring address, it stirred up all the patriotic fires in my bosom, moved my very soul and it was all I could do to keep from re-enlisting but it seems it was only intended for the privates, and I feel that I can now return home in honor, with a clean sheet and a clear conscience so my minds at rest upon that point. No furloughs will be granted so the Authorities now say but you know I have written you often of them saying this and then granting them immediately after which kept me from applying. Now I never know when those high in office are saying what they intend they change so often. If Mr. Burt does not pay you for those pigs soon, say by the last of this month the latest send him the note I enclosed. He is very slippery. I will take your advice about Ed's horse it was only on your account I wanted to buy a fine buggy horse. I will try and get George for you when I return. I am glad you do not intend having the two old sows killed as we ought perhaps to keep them to raise from. Do caution Cupe about attending to the pigs tell him to feed them high, and ask Mr. Crawford to notice them and feed them occasionally. Are you having the wheat from the Smut Mill saved? You would be acting wisely if you would read my letters attentively and follow my advice about such things. I suppose you are out of stamps so I will send you some. I am too tired to write much tonight having been sleeping out for three nights under little sheds or huts made out of rails resting with one end on a pole the other on the ground and a few leaves and brush thrown over them. I walked through the snow this evening over a muddy sloppy road near six miles so you can well imagine how I ought to feel. I will write day after tomorrow and will finish replying to your letters. Do have a fine garden. Take Cupe when you need him so there shall be no excuse upon that point. Ed is at the Hospital, had dysentery. Zeke, Pat R, Gib &c are well. Love to all and many kisses to sweetness.

Forever thine own loving and Devoted Husband

JOHN F. CALHOUN

CAMP NEAR MANASSAS VIRGINIA
Wednesday morning February 19th 1862
No 100

My own darling wife:-

As you will see by the number of this letter I have written one hundred letters to you since the first of August last. Now my dearest, have I not written often? I write regularly three times a week whether I have anything of interest to write or not. The mail on yesterday brought me your letter of the 10th inst from which I learn you are having as disagreeable weather in South Carolina as we are having in Virginia. It is continually raining, sleeting, or snowing. What a treat clear weather would be even if it was cold. You say my letter of the 30th ultimo did not do you much good as I did not say anything about coming home on furlough. My darling, you know I am exceedingly anxious to see you and would do anything in my power to get a furlough and I have promised you again & again that I would watch my chance and apply as soon as I thought there was any hope of succeeding in my application, but darling I was satisfied that any application by me would be disapproved and not wishing to be refused I would not apply. I can yet come home before my term of service expires by re-enlisting, but would you wish me to do that? I have given you my reasons for not re-enlisting yet a while at least. I don't know what six weeks may bring forth and by serving out my time faithfully I can return home better satisfied and without reproach for it would surely not be expected of me to re-volunteer without going home. Leave it to me darling and you will hereafter be compelled to admit the wisdom of my course. I must now tell you that there will be little prospect of my coming home until the 15th of April unless disbanded before that time as many still think. I hope there will be but few to disband. From the time you receive this to even the 15th of April will be but six weeks and let us bear it patiently and oh how delightfully we will feel to embrace once more. I hope the time will fly rapidly and bring us together as soon as possible. Don't forget the dream you had about me, a part of which you would not write. When you hang our meat give orders to keep a continual smoke and you had better have some green wood hauled I think. You can easily count all the pieces and every time you go down count them again and in that way you can easily tell if any are taken. If you do that you might safely leave the key with Clarissa and tell her that no one is to have it but her and that I will hold her responsible if any is taken. Your other fattening hog ought to be killed. You have made the bones, &c hold out very well indeed and if the head and jowls should last until the first of March it will be doing well. Tell father to get me a barrel of molasses as soon as he can. So your father does not wish any more money. As to my debts darling, I am not at all uneasy now. I can for the first time see my way out. All the money I lend father I will expect interest. I merely lend it to him as the interest he pays will offset the interest I have to pay and it will at the same time be an accommodation to father as he will need money to buy his supplies, pay taxes &c. He will need nearly $1000 to buy supplies, pay taxes &c and all that I can lend him will enable him to hold on to that much of his cotton. When I return home I can pay off my debts, at least all my a/c &c. As I am away and in the Army no one expects all of my debts to be paid up now, whilst your & my father may feel that all those small a/c should be paid. You must dress my sweet little Fannie and you must not neglect your own dear self. I always want my wife nicely dressed so don't forget and when I return I want you to look like a bride. I know I will feel like being married again when I am led trembling into the bridal chambers. Won't you feel so too darling? Darling you are trying to persuade me that Fannie is not pretty. I know what you do so for. She is pretty and you wish to see me surprised when I meet my beautiful little daughter. You need not try to persuade me that Fannie is not pretty. I will believe anything else you tell me but that. We don't get any other kinds than pretty children. You must not forget my message to William and Aleck. I am in earnest and moreover I want to know if they ever intend striking a single blow for their country. Just such men as they are causing those who first took up arms in defence of their country to continue in the field and do all the fighting; and they must remain in quiet at home surrounded by their families and the comforts of home whilst we are sleeping on the cold ground in rainy, sleeting, snowy weather, and the poor sentinel on this outpost on Picket stands out in the rain, sleet and snow, freezing nights, watching and guarding our frontier whilst many are at home sleeping in warm comfortable beds. Can such men as Jim Childs, Wm Mars, and others that I can mention be respected at home? All who have husbands in the field and all who have sons should hold them in derision, in contempt. The ladies ought to let them know what they think of their conduct. The Rogers made a proposition to Childs and Mars like the one I made to Wm T and Aleck H in my last. We want to hear from them, and if they don't intend giving three months to the service of their Country, let them say so at once. They might as well be yankees for all the good they are doing the country. There are hundreds and thousands of young men scattered over the Southern Confederacy who are doing nothing in this great struggle. I can not respect them even if they are near relations. Don't forget to have the boots and shoes made and sent on. Lieut. Cothran wishes me to have him a pair of sewed boots made like mine. I will enclose the measure. If they are not finished in time to send by Dr. Hearst, tell father to get Captain D M R to send them by John McKelvey who is not at home and will return about the middle of March. Tell Tucker to try his hand on the boots, &c as a great many of the Soldiers will examine them. If there are any ready made boots or shoes on hand you might send them as it would be an accommodation to our men to pay even more than we ask at the shop. Hawthorne sent a box of boots here to sell and they are asking $12 & $15 and none are hinds. I enclose a slip from one of the Richmond papers showing you how high leather is selling there. Hand it to father or Capt. R. Let me know anytime any leather is sent to market and how much. Ask Mr. Scott how much has he sent off to market this year and the price recd. If none has been sent ask him what in the world is done with all of it. Tell him I wish to know mearly that I can form some idea of how he is getting on as the Captain never wrote to me. Tell Mr Scott to send me a list of the prices he is selling leather at and don't forget to ask him how much we booked last year and ask him how much does he think he is averaging this year per month. How many new vats are there? How much corn have we on hand in the crib? Can't we economize so as to sell 100 bushels? Caution Cupe and tell him to save me all he can. Why doesn't your father write to me? Give my love to all and kiss Fannie for her "pa." Write often and long letters my own dearest to Your Loving and Devoted Husband

JOHN F. CALHOUN

CAMP NEAR MANASSAS, VIRGINIA
February 26th 1862

My own darling wife:-

The mail will soon be in and I feel almost sure it will bring me a letter from you dearest, the last one being of the 14th inst. Since writing to you last the papers bring gloomy news from the west, the fall of Fort Donalson and the surrender of 12 or 14000 of our Army and it is said Nashville had also fallen. Tis surely to be attributed to bad management in our Generals, cowardice or treachery for why in the world did 14000 brave, determined, resolute men lay down their arms? They ought to have cut their way through the enemies' lines somewhere and they could have done so if they had made a gallant determined charge. Less than 14000 defeated, routed, and drove the Grand Army from the bloody plains of Manassas to their entrenchments beyond the Potomac and we defeated this Grand Army in an open field fight, our troops were comparatively untrained, undisciplined and we had but little Artillery. Our forces were strongly fortified at Ft Donalson and had heavy batteries, still 14000 men with arms in their hands laid them down. General Evans in his glorious victory at Leesburg in Oct last killed and captured more of the enemy than his entire force amounted to, now suppose that our men at Ft D had each killed or wounded their man or captured him, it would have reduced the number of the enemy 20,000 and it would have resulted in a grand victory upon our part. Our authorities have known for six or eight months that the enemy were constructing Gun boats and that we could not compete with them on water, then why did they not set to work building them, if not why did they order the river obstructed? Nashville could have been saved. I do think with all cases by obstructing the river it would at least give time to fortify it and to have all Government stores moved and troops could have been brought into the field &c &c. Then why did our Generals not do it? Are they crazy? I have never felt as gloomy and desponding since the war began as I have since the two last defeats, not that I doubt our ultimate success, but it will protract the war and gain more hard fighting for the brave troops on the Potomac, who were the first to respond to their countries call for volunteers and the first to defeat the Grand Army sent out to subjugate us. We on this line have stood our ground like men determined to be free, have kept the enemy in check, the nearest point to their lines in a few miles of their Capitol where they were said to have 150,000 troops, still they dared not advance, they dreaded meeting the brave troops who routed and sent their Grand Army disgraced to their entrenchments. I am inclined to the opinion that the best matured of the Confederate Army is here on the Potomac from all the states certainly the enemy seems to think so. The result of the last two disasters, Roanoke Island and Fort Donalson[13] will be to cause our Generals

13 Battle of Roanoke Island, NC on February 7 & 8, 1862 resulted in a Confederate defeat. Union

Commanding the Army of the Potomac to fall back thirty or forty miles so as to prevent our flanks being turned. Kentucky will be lost to us at least for a time and all our lines will have to be drawn in and the war brought nearer to our doors. Of course the enemy can take any of our cities upon the water where they can go with their Gun boats and we must expect a large portion of our country to be overrun but they can't conquer us. When the enemy have to leave their boats and meet us on the land on open field then they will have hard fighting and may look for defeat, but to tell you the truth the great cause of all of our troubles and recent defeats may be attributable to our not calling upon "the giver of all good" for help. Before the battle of Manassas every Regiment that I know of had a Chaplain and throughout the Southern Confederacy prayer meetings were frequently held and from this ____ fervent prayer ascendant to the throne for assistance but how changed now. Since the battle of Manassas the Authorities or powers that be have nearly ignored the Divine assistance. For a long time the Newspapers, both Political and Religious were filled with subscriptions to papers to be sent to the volunteers for Bibles & tracts, prayer meetings and evidence of interposition of the Almighty in our behalf, the finger of Providence being visible &c &c. Since repeated successes almost miraculous we turn away, don't need nor do we call upon God for aid. Congress almost ignored the Almighty they seemed to think that as God was enlisted on our side he could not withdraw his help; it dismissed his agents or at least their salaries were so reduced that they felt compelled to leaving, the poor pitiful salary was not enough to support their families so they left the Service. Religious papers and tracts come less often, and we hear less of prayer meetings and the soldiers on their part are growing more irreligious and we are justly being chastened for it and I hope it may teach us wisdom, our dependence upon this Almighty. It will arouse us I hope, and prove a lesson to us all – for nearly all are guilty of a growing want of zeal and a proper acknowledgement of our dependence upon Almighty God. So it will I hope and believe be well. The mail brought me no letters from my darling, but I hope to get one tomorrow unless the mail is to blame, for I feel sure you write regularly. I will not complain darling for I know there is great irregularity in the mails, and [when] we fail to receive letters when we expect them we must attribute it to the mail. I feel almost certain of getting a letter from you tomorrow. Adjutant Aiken has just returned from home and he informed me a few moments ago that he took tea in Richmond with a brother-in-law of one of his brothers Col Gorgas - the Chief of the Ordinance Department in Richmond And he said that we lost only 21 cannons at Fort Donalson, and

gunboats combined with the Army of General Ambrose Burnside bombarded a group of small Confederate Forts guarding the entrances to Roanoke Island through Pamlico and Albermarle sounds. That combination cut off any possibility of Confederate escape and the Rebels surrendered to avoid further bloodshed. ORWR, Vol IX, CHAPTER XX, pp. 74,183-191, 430. Fort Donelson, Tennessee, was captured by General U.S. Grant on February 16, 1862, delivering the Confederates another defeat. This victory opened up the Tennessee river for Union vessel traffic to the south. *ORWR*, Vol VII, Chapter XVII, pp. 159-160.

at a council of war Generals Floyd and Pillow insisted upon fighting it out to the last but General Buckner[14] and a majority of the war council deemed it prudent to surrender, whereupon Gen Floyd said, "Gen Buckner you are next in command after Gen. Pillow and myself, and you may remain to surrender but we will not," so he and Pillow, with about 5000 retreated to Nashville. It is said so Col G told Aiken that everything excepting commassaries stores was saved at Nashville the machinery for making percussion caps, guns &c all taken away elsewhere Atlanta &c. Col G said Gen A. S. Johnston intended making a desperate stand at some point but he did not know at what point and Gen Beauregard, the General of the ages intending defending Columbus Tenn to the death and one of Gen Beauregard's Staff sent on to Savannah on some Ordinance business, said that Gen Lee said he intended and thought he could defend the city against the Yankees. I hope none of the Generals may be deceived but even if they are we can't expect to always be successful, reverses must come; and should all of our towns and cities be taken we will still be far from being subdued. A brave determined people who are determined to be free will be free with a reliance upon the Almighty. We must not be disheartened but stand firm. And we must all be in for the war somewhere. Even if I come home I must not can not remain long out of the service. I can't let our brave troops breast the storm and contest every inch of soil whilst I am taking my ease at home. No, no, we must only expect a short sojourn home. I will write again soon. It is raining again. Give my love to all and many kisses to my sweet little daughter. Write often and long letters Dearest toYour Constant Faithful and Devoted Husband

JOHN F. CALHOUN

14 John B. Floyd and Gideon J. Pillow were the Confederate commanders at Fort Donelson, but in the heat of battle relinquished their command to General Simon B. Buckner who, recognizing a lost cause, promptly surrendered to General Ulysses S. Grant. *ORWR*, Vol VII, Chapter XVII, pp. 159-160.

CAMP NEAR MANASSAS VIRGINIA
FRIDAY NIGHT FEBRUARY 28TH 1862
NO 104

My own darling wife:-

I was disappointed both yesterday and today in not receiving a letter from you, the last being the one that I have twice noticed in previous letters. I allude to yours of the "14th" inst. Of course darling I was greatly disappointed still I will not complain having been so often assured that you will write regularly twice a week and I feel satisfied that you do so and I will attribute the failure to the mail. I failed to tell you of the severe wind we had here last Monday. I scarcely ever have been in so severe a wind and it continued all day and nearly all night, and blew down nearly all the Tents in the Regiment. And the wind continued with such violence that they could not be put up until the next morning. I grew very cold and I had to crawl in under the tent and spread out my blankets in the dark as well as I could. To-day has been very windy and cold, and it is so windy tonight the tent flapping about &c that I can't write as I wish. This is one of the coldest nights that we have had. Our Regiment is out on Picket now but having been unwell, and as we take it turn about leaving one, I remained and it is well I did, for night before last it rained all night and the same night I was very unwell all night , slept badly and had fever the next morning. All day yesterday I was also very unwell and had fever but to-day I am much better. No news here excepting as I wrote you in my last it is reported that we are to move back to the Rappahannock river and establish a new line. It is said this is to prevent the enemy from flanking us. The Ft Donalson affair made our Generals change the line or at least is said they intend doing so. You as they are in the Northern part of Tennessee and are in NC we must fall back to be in striking distance of Richmond in case the two armies attempt to effect a junction it is for some object of that kind. The new line is the one Gen Beauregard was first in favor of establishing but Pres D overruled him and selected this. Some are looking for A.S. Johnston to gain a great victory over the Yankees if he can get them if he can get them [*sic*] from their Gun boats and they must leave the boats or give up the war. Gen J was a Col in the old US Army and outranked Gen Beauregard or our Gen J E Johnston either, and was an officer of far more reputation than either. As I wrote to father about planting nearly all corn, I would still advise with this exception. I would advise him to plant all corn for the enemy have had nearly one third, I will say one fourth, of Virginia all along and if we fall back it will give them a large portion again, all the finest stock and grain country in the south, clover hay &c. This will be lost to us at least for a long while perhaps a large portion of Ten. at least all agricultural pursuits will be greatly interfered with and heretofore we have been in the habit of getting large quantities of grain from the North West, now where in the world is it to come from? Much more will be needed in the South than ever before for the thousands and thousands of Army horses must be well fed all the time no pasturing them and the waste is enormous. A war on a large scale any where in the world affects the price of breadstuff even with us, look at the Crimean war and such an enormous amount of soldiers engaged in a war as the present I can't tell where in modern times it ever took place. Next summer on both sides there may be one and a half millions engaged one way and another, and now these and the horses required must be fed and near one million are taken from agricultural pursuits even say half a million, just look anyone can see at a glance that all kinds of grains & providers must necessarily be high. How are we to get fodder, hay &c? I will be surprised if corn did not run up to $200 a bushel but I would not be at all surprised if it goes much higher. If only two or three acres of cotton should be planted to the hand throughout the south corn would be worth $150 a bushel at the lowest, but you can't make old cotton planters leave off their cotton they all hope that nearly everybody will plant mostly grain and they will go in for cotton thinking they will get the more, but now it is almost a settled point as to the recognition of the Confederacy by England and again I now am prepared for believing the war [Page 2] will last six, eight, twelve or 24 months and where will the cotton be? I would urge upon your father to plant very little cotton, the less the better. He will be the better off by doing so, even if he did not plant more than two or three acres to the hand, if he should plant altogether corn so much the better. Read this portion to him about the section of country in the hands of the enemy &c. I will write again soon. Give my love to all and many kisses to Fannie. I suppose your father has given out writing to me. You told me at the time not to look for a letter from him for a long time. I am anxious to hear from him. Write often dearest to your

Fond and Devoted Husband

JOHN F. CALHOUN

March 1862

CAMP NEAR MANASSAS VIRGINIA
Sunday March 2nd 1862
No 105

My own darling wife:-

The mail on yesterday brought me two letters from you Nos 19 & 20 of the ____ and 22nd inst which proves that there was some irregularity in the mails. I was indeed delighted at the receipt of two such long and interesting letters. And I will reply to them at once although I am not at all in the humor for writing this morning. I don't know why, for I am feeling well but there are times as you know by experience when you feel very unlike writing and at such times you can't write so well as when you are in the mood for writing. I am not surprised that the Esqr opposed Zeke's buying Nettie. And I told Zeke so at the time and did not want him to give me his note until he heard from home, but no, he wanted the bargain closed. I am more and more convinced every day that horses and mules will be enormously high for some time to come. Some think they may go to $300 or more. Mules, and of course horses will go much higher. I am perfectly satisfied to keep Nettie and raise colts from her. Col Bacon is expected back in a few days and I will see him about sending her down although as yet I have not said anything to Zeke about his fathers opposing his trade. I can raise another colt and then no doubt sell her for $250. perhaps more. Capt D. M. R. ought to have sent off two or three large lots of leather by this time. I am afraid he is doing too much crediting and in such times there ought to be nothing but a cash system, in fact it is the case nearly everywhere here now. Capt Bradley says that Dorn[15] himself can(')t get credit: no one can tell what a mans condition may be after the war. And as all we make in the way of grain, leather &c can be sold for cash I am in favor of sending off four fifths and I intend writing to father again and insist upon his sending off the leather and selling it. Ask him when you see him or the Captain either, how much have they sent off and tell them that I am very much opposed to crediting and hope they will stop it in a great measure. So you think I am getting close wanting you to sell your lard, no darling, I only suggested this as a suitable time if you intended selling any. Of course my darling keep all if you think you will need it. I am sorry to hear our Mill makes such poor flour, and I hope father and Captain R will get a new cloth at any price for soon none can be had at all.

15 William Burkhalter Dorn (1800-1878) from Abbeville. He was a merchant, farmer, miner and for a time one of the wealthiest men in South Carolina. In 1852, after 15 years of exploration, he discovered the 2nd largest gold vein in the State on the property of his neighbor Dr. John Wardlaw Hearst. By the end of the war, however, most of Dorn's wealth was gone. Bobby F. Edmunds, *The Making of McCormick County*, pp. 199-200.

I will send to Richmond and enquire the price there. We will have near 20 bushels of peas for sale and I see from the papers they are selling for 130 & 140 in Augusta. Do have a great many peas planted and tell Cupe to select some spot of three four or five acres and tell father I wish some peas sowed or planted in rows. Pea vine, hay, and forage of every description will be worth a good deal next year. I am sorry you can not get any cards.[16] I will try and get a pair on my way home. Look ahead and make arrangements about your negro cloth, for summer and winter. Tell Cupe to try his hand on economizing in the use of corn. And still I wish nothing stinted feed well and attend carefully to my colt and hogs. Fannie must indeed be a rapid girl and from what you say about her she must be improving very fast. How did she ask you for the tooth brush, how did you know what she wanted? I received Fannies note, tell her I will reply to it soon. I am glad you father intends writing to me. I will look out for it in less than ten days. You think I must have plenty of money. I have, never [been] without it. I can draw any time. The Government is due me $240 but I don't intend drawing until I come home unless some of you at home need it. I want to save $300 to bring home with me for you love. Why doesn't Ida write again? Tell her she is long about it. I suppose we excaped the measles. It is snowing and sleeting to-day. Awful weather. My darling I am at a loss to know what can be the dream you had which upon asking me a certain question and receiving a different answer from the one you expected made you cry. And you intend asking it do you? I am willing and I will be able to give a different answer to what you dreamed I did. I feel almost sure that I can guess what it is and I can unhesitatingly reply I have not, too constant, too true to you love and were I to remain from you until the end of the war it would be the same. I would still be innocent. Now don't you think I know what it is, and you have my reply. I am sorry to learn that you are having so much bad weather, but hope it will soon clear off and remain so for some time. Col Fair returned to camp last night. He stopped a week in Richmond, and he said that Curry Congressman from Ala,[17] said we would soon have Six hundred thousand men in the field, that is the only way to end the war soon. Col Fair says the volunteers on the coast have a delightful time compared with ours, they can get furloughs occasionally, and when they get sick they can get to go home to be care[d] for which is a blessing. Tell father not to have my wheat ground until he gets a new bolting cloth even if he does not get it until the first of May as I am satisfied that grain will continue to advance until the new crop comes in. And the nearer in our lines are drawn the higher

16 Reference is to fabric carding machines, known as cards. This was a mechanical process to clean and mix fibers of cotton and/or wool. This could also be done by hand with smaller cards.

17 J.L.M. Curry (1825-1903). Born in Georgia but raised in Alabama. He served in the Alabama Legislature and U.S. House of Representatives. In 1860 Curry traveled to Maryland to try and convince state leaders to secede. He resigned and entered the Confederate Congress. Curry also served as a Lt. Colonel in the Confederate Army under General Joseph E. Johnston. *Encyclopedia of Alabama.*

will [*sic*] grain will be. Tell father if he can't get the bolting cloth, to let me know the quantity we need and I will go on to Richmond and get it. Now don't forget. I will write again in a few days. Give my love to all and kiss my darling little daughter. All are well. Most Devotedly your

Husband
JOHN F. CALHOUN

CULPEPPER C[OURT] H[OUSE], VA

March 12, 1862

No 108

My own darling wife,

Our entire Army has fallen back to the Rappahannock.[18] On our way last Sunday night I was so tired and having been unwell for this last few days with Dysentery I concluded to get on the freight train the first chance. So I soon found an opportunity and got one, and the next day caught up with the wagons which had been started Saturday morning. Capt. Bradley went with the wagons as he had been unwell for some time so he and W Darricott who was with him, both got on the train and we came on here. But the hotels were so crowded we could not get in, but met with a gentleman Mr. Williams who lives a short distance from the village and he kindly invited us out to his house where we have been for two nights and one day. He and Mrs. W are excellent people and live well. There are hundreds like ourselves who came on ahead of their regiment and have no idea where to go to look for them. We will start out today and go back to the Rappahannock and hunt for our Regiment or the Brigade, but maybe two or three days finding it as this whole Army is scattered, and one Brigade does not know where to find the other. The cars all being employed in moving commissary stores, baggage, etc. there has been no mail to point for several days and this may not go for a day or two yet. And as we may not get back to our Regt. for two days and there it may be some time before we can have an opportunity of sending letters off, you must not be weary if you don't get a letter from me for a week or more after you get this. It will be ten or fifteen days before the Army gets organized again as it was. And I judge it will take several days for Gen Johnston to examine the country and establish the line and assign position to the different brigades. Then we will only have about two weeks to stay, even if we remain until the 15th inst. I will write you a long letter as soon as I get back to camp. In the meantime continue to write and direct as before. The letters will all be stopped at Richmond or some other point until everything gets straight and then they will be sent on to us. Give my love to all and many kisses to Fannie. Fondly and Devotedly

Your Husband
JOHN F. CALHOUN

P. S. Tell Cupet to give the hogs fresh tar on their corn two or three times

18 All the troops under General Joseph E. Johnston were withdrawn from Manassas and vicinity on March 9th as Union forces advanced on their positions in a move toward Richmond. *ORWR,* Vol V, Chapter XIV, pp. 526-527.

a week. I can get cotton cards here, Mr. W thinks for $1.00 a pair. I will get two or three pair and bring on with me.

CAMP NEAR CULPEPPER VIRGINIA
MONDAY NIGHT MARCH 17, 1862
NO 109 OR 110

My Own Dearest Wife:-

I wrote to you on the 12th inst from near Culpepper when I went on ahead of the Regiment and that morning I went back and joined the Regiment at the Rappahannock and there was little opportunity of writing whilst there. All the brigades were ordered out a day or two after I returned ready for a march with the baggage wagons in front and all private wagons in front of them. Wagons belonging to officers or owned by any of the volunteers were the private wagons alluded to. We all expected to be moved but it was only done for the purpose of inspecting the baggage to see if any were overloaded and if any Regt had too many wagons. We again had orders to get ready to move off on Saturday morning by 8 o'clock but just about the time we got ready an order came for us to hold ourselves in readiness to move against the enemy at a moments notice as it was rumored that a large force was this side of Manassas. Gen Stewart [*sic*] with his cavalry guarded the rear of our army as we were falling back and he sent in word to Gen Johnston that he had a skirmish with the enemy so we remained without tents in the rain all day and at night. Cothran and I slept on a pile of leaves and straw that had been rained on all day. Sunday afternoon we moved off and encamped three miles the other side of Culpepper. The next day we came this side and on yesterday we marched 15 miles to this point which is 5 miles from Orange CH and 15 from Gordonsville where it is said we are to march to in a day or two. Tomorrow I expect. We march on the rail road track all the way and you many judge how tired we were walking on the cross ties and even over trestle works. Col Kershaw is now our Brigade General having been commissioned only a few days since. The mail has just come in and I received yours of the 3rd inst No 23 written 16 days since. There are large bays of letters sent back to Gordonsville as the PM's on the way did not have time to distribute the mail as we passed. It is said the PM's at Culpepper said there were upwards of 40 bushels for the army and tomorrow the division quartermaster will get it distributed to the brigades PM's, they to the regimental and I feel sure there will be at least three letters for me. My darling you must not think hard of me for only writing once a week for the last two weeks as it is impossible to write moving as we are. And as the cars are all employed moving army stores etc there is sometimes no mail for three or four days. Even up to Culpepper, a much larger village than Abbeville, I was told they had not had a mail for several days so I can not write as often as usual nor will I receive your letters regularly but I will write as often as possible dearest and when we reach Gordonsville. An order has just come for us to move and we are to go no farther we are only to move a mile or two and begin fortifying. I will not have time to write you fully this time but as soon as I have time I will write again. I am glad to hear that your mother is improving and hope she will now get well. So you are in good sprits because I wrote you that it was my determination to come home if I was spared immediately upon the expiration of my term of service. I have not nor will not change my mind. It is reported that Gen McClellan is at Centerville and intends following on as soon as he builds the rail road bridge that we have destroyed. I don't know how much truth there is in this report. Give my love to all and write soon and direct as before as the mail is always stopped. I will find out in a few days which office we will get our letters from and then will write to you. Don't write for five days and in that time you will get another letter from me and I will let you know where to direct. Kiss Fannie for me and believe me darling your own fond and loving husband

JOHN F. CALHOUN

PS

I forgot to mention that I began this letter on the 17th but could not finish it and this is the 19th. I have written in great haste so excuse all defects. Love, Ever yours.

CAMP NEAR RAPIDAN RIVER VIRGINIA
FRIDAY MARCH 21ST 1862
NO 111

My own darling wife:-

We moved a few miles yesterday to this point, and it was raining all the time. It is probable we will remain here until we are taken to Richmond to be disbanded, but when that will be I am unable to say, in any event by the 13th as our term of service expires at that time. I did intend giving you a full description of our march from Manassas, the great destruction of Baggage, &c at that place &c but as I am feeling tired and somewhat unwell. I will defer it until another time or as I hope soon to be "home again," and then can relate all of my experiences of Camp life. I may postpone every unimportant incident until I return. We are living without tents. Capt B and The Rogers have not been with us but two or three days since we left Bull Run on the 9th they are off sick. Cothran and I made us a tent by ripping mattress tick, and by using blankets and we are fixed up tolerably comfortably, we can't stand up but it keeps the rain off which is all we want, having blankets enough. The mail yesterday evening brought me another letter from you darling dated Mar 8th "No 24." We have been exceedingly fortunate in not have a single letter lost since I have been in Virginia, or at least all of yours have reached me at least all since you began numbering, and as you have not complained of any of mine miscarrying, I suppose all have reached you safely. My precious, your last letter was a long and most affectionate one. And oh, darling you cant imagine how it delights me to get such letters from you. Yes dearest we are devoted to each other, and let us hope that two such loving hearts will soon be united. I will be delighted to get back again after Eleven months absence and my sweet little prattling daughter how anxious I am to see her. She must be improving fast in talking. You must learn her some smart tricks by the time I come home. If you are needing anything darling let me know it in your next and I will get it for you in Richmond, now don't forget it and you must not hesitate for when I come home and find that you and Fannie are needing anything I will scold you. I think you ought to have two good spinning wheels made, as I intend on bringing on two or three pair of No 10 cotton cards and two pair of wool cards. I wish we had a loom too, as the war may continue one or two years, at least that seems to be the impression. I say this year only in any event as I only intend planting grain we ought to make our own cloth so I would advise you to have a loom made. I am glad you are going ahead with your garden, and I hope you will try and have a good garden, and a variety of vegetables, don't forget pepper and try and get some Egg plants. Tell father to have me a good melon patch prepared and have the choicest seed planted, and a plenty of the nutmeg melons planted. I am very fond of them. Tell father not to forget to plant me a large potato patch, two or three acres if he can have time to plant them, and can find enough good land; tell him he may possibly be able to get manure enough to manure at least one acre. Can't you have a few ground peas planted? Don't forget to tell Cupe about giving fresh tar to my hogs. And tell father to select a mark for me, as all of my last years hogs were marked in his mark. Have the wheat from the grist Mill saved, don't neglect it, and you had better have the cow which you[r] father intends giving you driven down the first opportunity and I will get one from fathers. Have a turkey fattened for me. I am glad to hear our pork saved so well, be careful and saving with it. Have my colt well attended to and stock of all kinds fat and thriving. My darling I am anxious about you and Fannie as you will be sure to have the measles and do be very particular and don't put off sending for the Dr, he must attend you and Fannie. I hope you may not have them until I come home. I am glad to hear that your mother is improving and hope she may soon be well again. Your father is wise in planting but little cotton, and the less he plants the better for him, grains and all kinds of "roughness" such as fodder, hay, pea vines &c will be in great demand. He ought to plant a large crop of potatoes and ground peas will be worth several dollars a bushel. [Page 2] I wish we could plant an acre, do try and procure seed and plant a large patch of them. Tell father they sell for 12 ½ cents a pint here, which is at the rate of $8 per bushel and tell him all such things will be very high the last of this year and next year. And I am anxious to plant an acre if I can. You get the seed and I will write to him about it, but deliver my messages any way. And tell him if he would plant less cotton and five or six acres of ground peas it would pay him three or four times what cotton will and he can get the cash for them. Send me the measure of Fannie's foot as I want to get her a pair or two of shoes. Let me know what else is she "proud of" so I can bring some presents to her. You will not get this until about the first of April and you will not have time to write to me but twice after you get this, don't write after the 6th or 8th of April as it takes from six to eight days for letters to come from Mt. Carmel here and I may not get any letters written after the 6th. I will write twice a week hereafter if we are not kept moving as we have been for the last ten or twelve days. I have but little opportunity for writing now. Don't forget to attend to all that I have written this letter. William McKelvey died at the So Ca Hospital in Charlottesville a few days since. I will write to his father in a day or two. All the Twelve months volunteers who have not reenlisted seem determined to go home. They think that as there are a plenty still left at home it was the Presidents duty to have had them in the field so the blame is with him. Love to all and many kisses to Fannie. Fondly and Most Devotedly

Your Husband

JOHN F. CALHOUN

CAMP BONHAM NEAR RAPIDAN RIVER VA
WEDNESDAY MARCH 26, 1862
NO 114

My own darling wife:-

I am in receipt of yours of the 14th inst No 26 and am truly sorry my dearest to hear that you are unwell. I fear you are taking the measles and our darling little Fannie will have them too. You must be very careful love if you do have the measles and I trust you and Fannie will only have a light case. I have been receiving a letter nearly every two days for a week or more. You see it was ten days or more from the receipt of my last letter from you whilst at Manassas to the receipt of the next so several was due and I am expecting another from you today. How anxious I am to see our little Fannie, from the way you write she must be smart and sweet and she must be improving fast. The idea of her walking along with her dress up and her wanting to sew, bless her darling little heart. I can scarcely realize the fact that I have a daughter so large. How I love the little being and I am impatient to see her and last but not least Fannie's ma-ma holds a place in my heart that nothing else can fill and no one excepting as devoted a husband as I am can tell my great anxiety to embrace my own loved wife. I know that I have one of the best wives in the world and I am aware that she is devoted to me. As the time draws near for us to be disbanded the days seem longer and hang more heavily and how long the last ten days will be and then the time going home, the cars will not travel fast enough. I know but my darling I will be thankful to return and we both ought to be thankful if a kind providence permits us to meet again after the trying scenes through which I have _____. Thousands have died and been killed and how thankful I will be to get home once more. I expect we will be kept the full time, perhaps we may be disbanded in Richmond on the 15th although some still think we will be retuned home by that time. We will know in a few days as Kershaws Regiment will be disbanded on the 8th. Gen Johnston seems to be perfectly independent about the twelve months men re-enlisting, he says he does not care whether they re-enlist or not as he has a soldier ready to take the gun of every twelve month man as soon as they can lay them down. I am glad to hear it. All the Authorities and public near about Richmond are in high spirits we are getting a great amount of Arms &c and an ___ ___ Army in the field, and they will have in a few days from this time between fifteen and twenty Iron clad Gun Boats ready on the Mississippi, many equal some superior to the Virginia that destroyed one of the largest of the Federal Men of War. Depend upon it, you will soon hear stirring news from the West in less than one month. When Beauregard strikes, look for victory, a glorious victory. Our entire Army almost idolize that little General and he stands today far ahead of any Gen on this continent, the whole Army love him and their confidence in him is so great that they think his troops can know no defeat and they will follow him the cannons mouth. We are continually wishing Gen Beauregard was here[19] although I expect our Gen Johnston is next to him, he is a great strategist ____ and cunning, keeps everything secret and can break down and defeat his adversary, by advancing and retreating, and thwarting their plans. He and Gen McClellan don't intend giving each battle soon, they have under their immediate command the two Grand Armies of their respective governments and either way the should go would be ruinous to the defeated party. They are playing a game of Chess with t[w]o large Grand Armies. I heard since writing you last that all the cotton-cards were sold, none to be had. I have written to Richmond for some and intend trying all the way home. I see from the Presbyterian of the 15th that corn and meal is selling for $150 and scarce at that. Wheat from $160 to $200, flour from $12 to $13 ½ per barrel, oats 1 & 110, peas $140 to $150 &c. All this will show you how all kinds of grain will sell and next year, if the war continues and moderate crops are made, every kind of grain will be much higher. I see bacon is selling from 28 to 35 cents so do make enquiries every time you go down to the Mills about our hogs and tell Cupe to feed them high, not to spare the corn but don't waste. Ask Mr. Crawford to feed them occasionally and notice them. Tell Cupe to give them the fresh tar as I wrote him to do, he must not fail to do so and take care that they are not stolen he must [Page 2] guard against that in some way. And the smoke house ought to be watched closely. Have it entirely secure and tell Cupe that some one must be in the Kitchen every hour throughout the night. And on Sundays the meat is for my negroes and if they let it be stolen they must do without. I want them well fed as much as they can eat. Do give them an abundance but tell them to save me all they can and attend closely to everything and I will be liberal in giving them when I return. Tell Henry to do his best and make me all he can and he shall have a good opportunity of making a good deal for himself. Encourage him too. And tell all that I hope soon to be at home and want to hear a good account of them all. Don't forget the Ground peas, plant me a large patch ½ acre or an acre if you can. And try and buy me a bushel or more to plant in the corn when I come home. Don't fail. You see I have been correct heretofore in nearly everything that I have written you about, horses, grain and everything of the kind. Tell your father to plant as little cotton as possible and if he will plant largely of potatoes and ground peas he will "hit it," even if he could plant several acres of each. He might prepare the land and plant st[r]ips in May or June. I know what I am talking about and the next year will prove it. All kinds of stock ought to be well cared for, and tell your father he

19 General Beauregard was having "policy" differences with President Davis and Secretary Benjamin, and in January of 1862 he was reassigned to Columbus KY under the command of General Albert Sidney Johnston. General Joseph E. Johnston (no relation) wrote to Secretary Benjamin of his regret for that transfer stating that, at the present time, Confederate policy regarding reenlistment and furloughs was having a "disorganizing effect" on the troops, in particular, the 12 month volunteer troops under his command in Virginia. He felt that transferring Beauregard at this time would increase that effect. *ORWR*, Vol V, Chapter XIV, pp. 1048, 1051.

ought to buy up some shoats, 9 is not enough and he ought to try and raise some to sell. Tell him if he will "buy up" some I will lend him the money when I return home. I will bring about $300 with me $250 or 75 anyway. Fatten a turkey for me. I received you fathers letter enclosed in yours, tell him I am greatly obliged to him. We are still at the same place, no news, all is quiet. I hear some of the officers and men saying this war is making business women of our wives, they are economizing and attending to business like men and learning to be very ingenious in making everything at home. A great many even in our Regiment - have pants, coats, vests, and military overcoats woven and made at home, that does great credit to woman's ingenuity, the cloth looks like northern made, and all woven on the common loom, I suppose. I hope you and your mother will not be behind she can keep up with anyone else I know. Love to all and many kisses to Fannie. Direct to Richmond until the 5th. Do attend to all my letter contains. And Believe me Dearest, ever thine own Devoted Husband

JOHN F. CALHOUN

CAMP NEAR RAPIDAN RIVER, VA
Thursday night March 27, 1862
No 115

My own dearest wife:-

I received a letter from you on yesterday to which I replied briefly in my letter which I mailed this morning intending to reply more at length in the next, but I will not be able to do so now as we have just received orders to prepare one days rations and to draw three more days rations from the Commissary & be ready to move off by 5 o'clock in the morning, but no one knows the point to which we will be moved. An order was read at Dress parade this evening which said that the troops must hold themselves in light marching order and ammunition examined and they must be prepared to move at a moments notice. And the order said that the movement would be against the enemy. The other order came in after dark. I feel almost sure that we are to be moved to Fredericksburg or to the valley of Shenandoah in North western Virginia, the latter most probably as Gen Jackson, "Stonewall Jackson" sent to Gen Johnston for aid as his little band were hard pressed by the enemy. He has ten thousand under his command and is beyond the first rage of mountains sixty or seventy miles from any aid. His force is divided and with five thousand he fought a desperate [battle] with the enemy near Winchester[20] contending against a force supposed to be from 18 to 20,000. Night came on and he retired two miles from this field. Our loss in killed and wounded said to be near 500, enemies near 1500. Banks, I think, commands the Yankee force. Gen Shields had his arm shot off. Gen Jackson sent a white flag according to custom to ask permission to bury his dead and Gen Shields replied "that he neither asked nor granted any favors." It is said that Gen J is only drawing the enemy down to Staunton where reinforcements will meet him. Troops have been sent to him already. It is said that the Yankee Regiments were cut to pieces, and they withdrew their Regts. from the field after they had fought a while and led in fresh ones. All of this or at least the most of it we heard from a modest reliable man from Capt Talbert's Com who has been at Mt. Jackson a small village in the North West detailed in one of the Hospitals as Surgeon or Assistant Dr. Lewis. He said 150 of the wounded were brought into Mt J before he left. Gen Jackson is one of our best Generals, brave and dauntless a perfect ____ and from what I hear he is a modest, humble, Christian. He won the appellation "Stone Wall" at the Battle of Manassas on

20 Also known as the Battle of Kernstown, VA. Union forces under General Nathaniel P. Banks and Confederates under General Thomas "Stonewall" Jackson clashed on March 23, 1862. The battle resulted in a tactical victory for the Union and Jackson's only defeat of the war. However, it was also considered a strategic victory for the Confederates because Jackson's army was still able to stop the Union from bringing troops from the Shenandoah campaign to the east to reinforce the Virginia peninsula campaign. As a consequence, this prevented a Northern movement on the Confederate capital of Richmond. *Encyclopedia Virginia. ORWR*, Vol XII, Chapter XXIV, pp. 379-384.

the 21st July. Bee, Bartow or some Genls in encouraging their troops whilst leading them to the attack pointed to another part of the field and said, "look at Jackson standing in fight like a stone wall." My dearest it may be some time before I can find an opportunity of writing again if we are thrown into "the deadly breach." I will try and do my whole duty, our cause is just and a sacred cause. I am fighting for my home, my fireside, my alter, for my loved wife and child and although I am soon to start to the Battlefield perhaps if I know myself I am calm and determined victory or death must be our motto although I will earnestly invoke the protection of God and in the thickest of the fight I will ask his protection and I can but hope, trust, and believe he will spare me. Somehow I have always believed God would spare me to you love and for some useful object I hope. We may not get into a battle for I know it is hard to entrap a yankee and I am inclined to think they will fall back when they learn heavy reinforcements are being sent to Gen J and again we may not go up there, no one knows although that is my notion. I am afraid the mail will be very irregular in going now for a while. Don't write any after the 5th or 6th and Direct to Richmond. I will write as soon as I can, it may be ten days before I could get a chance to mail my letter. Tell your father as bacon and molasses will be very scarce he ought to plant Chinese sugar cane. It will pay this year even to sell. If he will plant four or five acres and give me half I will make it up by buying the Boilers if they can be had, for I want some for boiling food for hogs, cows &c and we could get Robinson to make the Mill. Molasses or syrup will be worth 75 or 1 a gallon. Tell father to try and make his own syrup and if your father does not wish to go into it tell father to plant five or six acres and as he has a boiler of 120 gal I will buy another, two will do and go partners with him Sam, Zeke, Ed & Pat R are all well, Zeke still at the Hospital. Give my love to all and give many kisses to my dearest little daughter and may God bless & protect my wife & child and permit us to meet once more.

Forever your Devoted Husband,

JOHN F. CALHOUN

EPILOGUE

JOHN FRANCIS CALHOUN completed his twelve month volunteer enlistment on April 15, 1862 without taking a furlough or sick leave. Ironically, the next day the Confederate Congress passed a Conscription Law requiring that all males from 18 to 45 must serve in the military. A week later, on April 21, 1862, that same Congress passed the Exemption Act (or Vital Occupations Act) which exempted men engaged in a wide range of occupations from military service. As the owner/operator of a tan yard, John Francis qualified for such an exemption. Nevertheless, he was mustered back into service on July 18, 1862 as a Private in Company C 1st Regiment South Carolina Partisan Rangers. Also during 1862, John Francis and his tan yard partner entered into a contract with the Confederate Army Quartermaster to supply large amounts of leather for the use and benefit of the Army.

Because of the exemption, and the onset of medical problems, John was discharged in October of that year. In 1863, he was called again as a conscript, which he initially declined citing his exemptions, both occupational and medical. His Southern patriotism, however, called him to return to the aid of his country. He re-volunteered in September with the belief that his partner could and would mange the tan yard and leather contract. That didn't happen and in November of 1863 John Francis filed a petition to the Secretary of War asking to be permanently released from service in order to manage the tan yard and complete the contract that his partner had failed to do. He was released by Special Order 241 and returned home to operate the tan yard. Muster rolls through the end of 1864 report John Francis either "absent without leave" or "detailed."

Having survived the mental and physical calamities of the war, John Francis was now at home, but he suffered from severe sciatica and ailments described as "hemorrhages of the lungs." In spite of all that, he had to face one more major Southern struggle . . . Reconstruction. Now operating with a small labor force, his cotton weights and farm produce were not enough to offset his debts. By 1870 he was no longer associated with the Mill. Debts from mill operations, declining sales, increased taxes, property mortgages, and farm costs slowly began to overwhelm John Francis and his family, which by 1878 included eight children.

William Pickens Noble (The Esquire), Rebecca's uncle, died in 1876 and named her father Andrew as executor of his will. Andrew died in 1880 naming John Francis as his executor. Unfortunately, Andrew died before completely settling his brother William's estate. John Francis was then forced to administer both wills. Years of costly legal entanglements followed and added to the already rising debt of John Francis and Rebecca Calhoun.

John Francis moved his wife and eight children to Due West, SC in 1882 where he took employment with the Due West Female Academy, a teachers college. He traveled throughout South Carolina arranging teaching jobs for graduates. John Francis' new employment notwithstanding, Rebecca decided in 1884 that in order to help sustain the family's financial situation she must sell the Noble family property in Willington that her father had deeded her. The family, adding a ninth child in 1890, remained in Due West from 1882 until 1891. During that time John Francis served as a town councilman from 1888 to 1890 and three of his daughters, Susie, Carie, and Ida, attended the Due West Female Academy. Daughter Susie took a teaching position with a new school in Pendleton, SC in 1889.

Records of the Calhoun property are not clear. John Francis' father Edward died intestate in 1862 and there is a record of his possessions that were sold at auction. Brother Edwin moved into Edward's house in Willington after the war and lived there until 1908. It is assumed most records were lost in the Abbeville Court House fire of 1872.

In July of 1891, John Francis, Rebecca, and the four youngest children left Due West and moved to Calhoun Station, SC where a new college was being built. That was Clemson College, named for Thomas Green Clemson, the son-in-law of Hon. John C. Calhoun. Clemson had died in 1888, after surviving both his wife and two children. He bequeathed the estate he had inherited from his late father-in-law's family to the State of South Carolina in order to build an Agricultural College. In 1891 John Francis and Rebecca were hired by the Trustees of the new college. He was to be the Dining Hall bursar, and she was the dormitory matron. John Francis' other duty was to serve as "keeper of the relic room" or curator, at the Fort Hill home of both Clemson and John C. Calhoun. This was a position stipulated by Mr. Clemson's will. John Francis was to maintain the artifacts and keep the house open for the inspection of visitors. Early records show they made a combined salary of just over $900 per year, and were furnished room and board in the Fort Hill house.

Clemson College opened in 1893 admitting some 400 students, one of which was my grandfather, Patrick Noble Calhoun. He was a member of the first class to graduate from the college in 1896. After the school opened, John Francis' declining health forced him to resign his position with the dining hall but he remained curator of Fort Hill until his death in November of 1897. Rebecca continued to live in Fort Hill, with daughters Ida and Floride, until her death in 1918. Oldest daughter Fannie, frequently mentioned in the letters, married in February of 1897 and removed to Atlanta, GA. Daughter Ida never married, but stayed in Fort Hill, and took on her father's position as curator. She moved out in 1927 when the house was named a State Landmark. Youngest daughter Floride married Charlmers McDermid of Charleston, SC in 1921 and moved there. My grandfather Patrick married in 1908 and moved to Georgia. Widowed daughter Rebekah returned to live with her sister Ida in a cottage near Fort Hill. They would be the last Calhoun's to live in the Fort Hill house, which, in addition to its State Landmark status, is now a National Historic Landmark House-Museum.

John Francis, Rebecca, and several of their children are buried in St. Paul's Episcopal Churchyard in Pendleton, SC.

Bibliography

Biographical Dictionary of the United States Congress.

Calhoun Family Genealogy compiled by Andrew P. Calhoun, Jr.

Encyclopedia of Alabama, 2016.

Encyclopedia Virginia.

Find a Grave: An expansive family history database of records and images of the world's cemeteries, created by Jim Tipton, 1995.

Kershaw's Brigade by D. Augustus Dickert, 1899.

The Laws of the Confederate States.

The Making of McCormick County by Bobby F. Edmunds, 1999.

New Georgia Encyclopedia.

Public Acts of the Provisional Congress of the Confederate States.

Reminiscences of a Confederate Soldier by Eunice Calhoun Sease as told by her father, Edwin Calhoun, circa 1910.

Thomas Boone Pickens, His Ancestors by Lois K. Nix and Mary Kay Snell, 1989.

The War of the Rebellion: A Compilation of the Official Records of the Union and Confederate Armies. (ORWR).

Genealogy

Relationship: James Patrick Calhoun to Andrew Pickens Calhoun Jr.

Andrew Pickens Calhoun Jr. is the 5th great grandson of James Patrick Calhoun

James Patrick Calhoun	Catherine Montgomery
b: 1688 Crosh House, County Tyrone, Ireland d. 1741 Lancaster, Pennsylvania, USA	b: 1684 Londonderry, Ulster, Northern Ireland d. 1741 Lancaster, Pennsylvania, USA

Patrick Calhoun
b: 11 Jun 1727
Donegal, Ireland
d. 15 Jan 1796
Abbeville, Abeville, South Carolina

Patrick Calhoun
b: 03 Feb 1784
Abbeville, South Carolina
d. Oct 1840
Abbeville, South Carolina, USA

Edward Calhoun
b: 1809
Abbeville, South Carolina, USA
d. 1862
Abbeville, South Carolina, USA

John Francis Calhoun
b: 29 Aug 1831
Calhoun Township, South Carolina, USA
d. 13 Nov 1897
Fort Hill, Clemson, South Carolina, USA

Patrick Noble Calhoun
b: 12 Apr 1878
Willington, McCormick, South Carolina
d. 08 Oct 1947
Savannah, Chatham, Georgia, USA

Andrew Pickens Calhoun
b: 09 Nov 1925
Columbus, Muscogee, Georgia, USA
d. 28 Sep 2004
Savannah, Chatham, Georgia, USA

Andrew Pickens Calhoun Jr
b: 23 Feb 1953
Savannah, Chatham, Georgia, USA
d.

About the Author

ANDREW PICKENS CALHOUN, JR.—Andy—is a resident, and native, of Savannah, Georgia retired from Colonial Terminals, Inc. in the Port of Savannah after 26 years as Director of Maintenance. Prior to Colonial, he served with two other Savannah industries for a career spanning 40 years in the Port of Savannah.

During that time, Andy was a member and Past President of the Propeller Club, Port of Savannah, Past President of the Atlantic Intracoastal Waterway Association, and past member of the Board of the Savannah Maritime Association. He is also a graduate of Leadership Savannah and Leadership Clemson (SC). He is an active member of the Saint Andrew's Society of Savannah, Sons of the Revolution in the State of Georgia, and Sons of Confederate Veterans. Andy has a keen interest in Calhoun/Colquhoun genealogy and history as well as the history of South Carolina.

Andy began working on Calhoun genealogy in the early days of computers and before the Internet, visiting libraries and cemeteries along the "Savannah River Scenic Highway" between Savannah and Clemson. Today, he has over 60,000 names in his genealogy database of Calhoun, Pickens, Noble and other associated families. Andy is the 3rd great-grand nephew of Hon John C. Calhoun and the 4th great grandson of General Andrew Pickens, a Calhoun relative, South Carolina statesman and Revolutionary War hero.

After surviving the war for Southern Independence and the brutal reconstruction that followed, Andy's great-grandparents, John Francis and Rebecca Noble Calhoun, came to Clemson College in 1891 as two of the school's first employees. While living in the Fort Hill home of John C. Calhoun and Thomas Clemson, Andy's grandfather Patrick was one of Clemson College's first students in 1893 and was a member of Clemson's first graduating class in 1896. His father safely returned from combat in World War II to graduate in 1950. Andy attended Clemson in the early 1970's and is a third generation "Son of Clemson." He maintains his association with the University today, serving on the Alumni Association's Historic Properties Advisory Board.

Andy is married, and his wife Milree (Mackey) is his best friend, soulmate and fellow genealogist. Between the two, they have 5 children and 9 grandchildren.

Index

D

E

F

G

H

J

K

L

M

S

T

V

W

Southern without Apology.

CPSIA information can be obtained
at www.ICGtesting.com
Printed in the USA
BVHW052306301121
622870BV00007B/522/J

9 781947 660014